£ 5—

8

7.12

7.14

Ben Marshall: The shooting of partridges over dogs had already begun to go out of fashion in favour of driving and walking in line. In this self-portrait the artist shows himself holding his ramrod correctly, between forefinger and thumb.

English Country Life
1780–1830

E. W. BOVILL

LONDON
OXFORD UNIVERSITY PRESS
NEW YORK   TORONTO
1962

Oxford University Press, Amen House, E.C.4

GLASGOW NEW YORK TORONTO MELBOURNE WELLINGTON
BOMBAY CALCUTTA MADRAS KARACHI LAHORE DACCA
CAPE TOWN SALISBURY NAIROBI IBADAN ACCRA
KUALA LUMPUR HONG KONG

PRINTED IN GREAT BRITAIN

TO
ROSEMARY

Preface

THERE was no more formative period in the history of English country life than the last quarter of the eighteenth century and the first of the nineteenth. Many of the inventions and innovations of those fruitful years were felt far beyond our shores. In agriculture and transport, for example, every civilized country modelled itself on the new methods and discoveries of English farmers and British engineers. The domestic influences of these changes were profound. They gave the landscape its present form, and country life a pattern which altered little for a hundred years, and which still governs the way of life of many a countryman.

The period has been much studied by social historians, but chiefly in the wider context of the Industrial Revolution to which country life, in retrospect, was necessarily subordinate. My purpose in this book has been to present studies of certain aspects of country life which appear to me to merit closer attention than they have so far received.

No picture of rural England at that time could be complete without some account of the revolution that then took place in agricultural practice; no less important was the effect of contemporary legislation on rural economy. But these are subjects which have been closely studied and on which there is a wealth of literature. I have therefore excluded them and their like, so far as possible, from the following pages.

Nevertheless, I have been left with a wider field than could be covered adequately in a single volume. I have therefore confined this book to a narrow range of subjects, the choice of which has admittedly been arbitrary, and dictated not a little by personal taste and prejudice. But my aim has been to build up a mosaic of fragmental studies sufficiently related to give in broad outline a picture of English country life between 1780 and 1830.

I have acknowledged the sources of the illustrations elsewhere, together with the names of all known owners of the original pictures. I am very grateful to Ninian Brodie of Brodie, Mr. S. V. Christie-Miller, Sir Richard Graham Bart, C.B.E.,

Mr. Hugh F. B. Tregaskis, Mr. V. Philip Sabin, Mr. N. C. Selway, to Messrs. Thomas Agnew & Sons Ltd., Fredk. B. Daniell & Son, and Sotheby & Co., to The National Trust for Scotland, the Trustees of both the British Museum and the Victoria and Albert Museum, the staff of the Courtauld Institute of Art, and to the Proprietors of *The Illustrated London News* for their kind permission to reproduce pictures in their possession, or for other help over illustrations.

Little Laver Hall   E. W. BOVILL
Harlow
June, 1962

Contents

Illustrations

I

Enclosure and the Landscape

IN the early nineteenth century the English countryside was not
entirely rural; industry was still dispersed throughout the market towns and villages. Local administration was wholly in the
hands of Justices of the Peace, country squires who were seldom
asked, and rarely expected, to bow to superior authority in the
capital. Even the course of politics was directed and controlled
more from stately country mansions than from Westminster and
its purlieus. By the middle of the century all had changed. Industry had become centred in the towns that had grown up
around the coalfields of the Midlands and the North; power and
influence were concentrated in London; county councils were
still some way off but middle-class Dissenters had won seats on
the magisterial bench; the destinies of the nation had passed into
the hands of a vast urban electorate; men of account were more
often town- than country-bred.

Such were the fruits of the Industrial Revolution, the force of
which has not yet spent itself. The flow of population, power
and wealth is still towards the ever-growing urban areas,
which, spilling over into the surrounding countryside, are
eating more and more deeply into rural England, and imposing
on a bewildered countryside their urban ideas and the townsman's concepts of what is good for man. Yet today, with so little
of England seemingly beyond the developer's grasp, there are
few counties which do not include scores of villages on which the
hand of change has barely set its mark. No matter where we
live, none of us has many miles to go to see what an early
nineteenth-century village looked like (or, for that matter, a
seventeenth-century one too). Many a village street and village
green look much as they did a century and a half ago.

The cottage gardens have changed as little as the cottages.

'You see', wrote William Cobbett in 1822, 'in almost every part of England, that most interesting of all objects, that which is such an honour to England, and that which distinguishes it from all the rest of the world, namely, *those neatly kept and productive little gardens round the labourers' houses*, which are seldom unornamented with more or less of flowers.' And the flowers, so lovingly recorded by Mary Mitford a few years later, were the same. In the spring 'their gay bunches of polyanthuses and crocuses, their wallflowers, sending sweet odours through the narrow casement'; in summer hollyhocks, roses, and honeysuckle; in autumn dahlias, chrysanthemums, and china-asters; and all through the year 'the casements full of geraniums'.

In outward appearance, then, villages were much as we see them today — an assembly of stone or brick or half-timbered cottages, usually thatched, clustering, with church and rectory, round perhaps a village green and pond, and often pressing hard against the park of the hall or manor house. But throughout the greater part of England, especially wherever corn was grown, the surrounding countryside had only begun to assume its present form. The familiar pattern of fields and hedges and hedgerow trees was only beginning to take shape.

Until late in the eighteenth century, in all such parts of England, close to the village lay the traditional open field, perhaps a mile or more long and half as wide, divided into scores of unhedged strips, severally owned by large and small holders, and cultivated under an archaic and profitless system to which all were compelled to conform. Beyond and around this bleak and hedgeless field, without shelter or windbreaks for cattle or crops, lay seemingly limitless wastes of scrubby woodland, moor, or marsh, loosely termed the common, on which the villagers had grazing and other rights.

For the most part the common fields were in a deplorable condition. An immutable system of cultivation had exhausted the fertility of most of them; no winter crops could be grown because from harvest till spring they were subject to common rights of pasture; a slovenly cultivator could poison his neighbours' land with weeds; the balks that divided strip from strip harboured twitch, thistles, and other noxious weeds. The wastes were in no better shape. Often unstinted, there was no limit to the number of beasts that might be grazed on many of them. Where there were restrictions they were often ignored by large holders at the expense of the poor. In 1802 someone wrote to *The Farmer's Magazine* about the shocking condition of the animals turned out to graze on these commons: 'In bad seasons, when the weather is uncommonly wet or cold, and the grass late and scanty, many of them die for want of food. . . . It is painful to observe the very wretched appearance of the animals, who have no other dependence but upon the pasture of these commons, and who, in most instances, bear a greater resemblance to living skeletons, than any thing else.'

So long as the open-field system survived, progress was impossible. It prohibited individual enterprise by forbidding change of any kind. The bringing of more land under the plough by breaking the wastes was equally impossible because of the legal and customary rights of the villagers over them, rights which were as essential to the village economy as the open field.

Here and there, but very rarely, common sense and collective effort had broken down the system. Interests had been pooled, holdings had been consolidated and fenced, and commoners had sold their rights to make possible the breaking and enclosure of the wastes, as had happened, centuries before, in Suffolk and Essex, Kent and Sussex. But, as all who know the English countryman will realize, it was seldom that the unanimity so essential to these voluntary arrangements could be achieved. In many a village an intransigent minority of one blocked the road to progress. Nor was it easy to make such voluntary arrangements binding on everyone. In all these circumstances recourse usually had to be made to a private Act of Parliament, a very costly process which, when added to the actual cost of enclosure, was sometimes prohibitively expensive.

Before the end of the century pressure of population had created a problem of how to feed hungry mouths, a problem which the French wars quickly rendered acute. The compelling need to increase food production, to grow a quarter of wheat where a bushel had once sufficed, at last persuaded England to listen to the teachings of Arthur Young and other thinking agriculturists that communal tillage and common wastes must be abolished. The need for private Acts continued, but Parliament made them less expensive and war prices for farm produce made them worth while. Thus, at the turn of the century, enclosure had become the fashion and the English countryside was assuming its present pattern, with the hedge as its predominant feature except where dry-stone walls better served the purpose.

England had not, of course, been wholly hedgeless. As we have seen, the south-east had long been enclosed and the beauty of the hedgerows of Kent had not escaped the notice of the many foreigners passing up the Thames to London. But throughout the rest of the country there had been isolated farms, demesne lands, and sometimes open fields, surrounded by hedges.

But what we may call the pre-enclosure hedge had had a character of its own. It was always crooked, due to the difficulty of ploughing a straight furrow with slow-plodding oxen. It was also composed of such a variety of trees and shrubs — maple, elder, holly, sloe, whitethorn, hazel and, surprisingly dominant in some districts, crab-apple — that it appeared to have been formed, and probably was, more by natural growth than deliberate planting.

As soon as a parish was enclosed, with its common field and wastes apportioned in solid holdings, each owner was under the necessity of protecting his interests by fencing his allotment, no matter its size. This he might do with stone or posts-and-rails, but the cheapest and much the most usual practice was to dig a ditch and plant a hedge of quick, or whitethorn, on the bank of spoil, though occasionally sloe or blackthorn was preferred. Quick was not only the most readily available material, but the easiest to establish and quickest to grow. Moreover, it made a very good fence, especially when, late in the eighteenth century, the art of laying it was acquired. As the boundaries of the new holdings were usually straight, so were the new hedges. They were often planted by men who made it their trade, and pride was taken in the way it was done. 'The fields on the left', wrote Cobbett on a ride from Royston to Huntingdon in 1822, 'seem to have been enclosed by act of parliament; and they certainly are the most beautiful *fields* that I ever saw. . . . Divided by quickset hedges, exceedingly well planted and raised.' Like his contemporary Mary Mitford, who spoke of 'old irregular hedges', we can still often tell a pre-enclosure hedge from a later one by its crookedness and the varied material composing it.

Enclosure by a private Act was very costly. Moreover, to the heavy legal and Parliamentary fees, and the cost of the attendance of witnesses at both Houses of Parliament, had to be added the heavy cost of fencing. The following extract from the Felsted Enclosure Award of 1822 shows how burdensome in time and labour the physical enclosure of the land could be:

The several new fences hereby directed to be made by the several proprietors in their respective allotments shall consist of ditches 4½ feet wide at the top and 3 feet deep and of banks adjoining such ditches and formed of earth taken from the same; and that the banks of such fences shall be planted with white thorn layer in a proper manner and that half-hurdles or thorns shall be set on the summit of such banks and shall there remain, or if taken away or spoiled, shall be from time to time renewed during the space of 7 years next ensuing.

What with Parliamentary and legal fees, and the actual fencing of the allotment, the final cost of enclosure sometimes amounted to as much as £10 an acre, a crippling figure to all but the rich. This heavy cost often had, as we shall see, disastrous social consequences.

The costliness of enclosure had a marked effect on the landscape. Landowners, both great and small, at first contented themselves with placing a ring fence round their holdings, delaying subdivision into fields until such time as they could afford it. Naturally, after so much initial expense, much care was taken to protect these new hedges. Under some enclosure awards sheep were excluded from new enclosures for up to ten years. The tenants of one Yorkshire squire, Sir James Graham of Netherby, were forbidden under a clause in their leases to keep sheep on account of the damage they did to hedges. In Lincolnshire, under an Enclosure Act of 1767, a man could be fined up to £20 for wilfully damaging a fence, and condemned to transportation for seven years for a third offence.

So long as England remained at war with France war prices largely took care of the cost of enclosure. When peace came, followed by the inevitable slump, either enclosure had to cease, which no thinking man could seriously contemplate, or ways had to be found to recover its heavy capital cost. To many landowners the planting of timber which, during the Napoleonic wars, commanded high prices, seemed to offer the easiest way of doing this, and no better place for it than the hedgerows. 'We remember', recalled Surtees some years later, 'when the wise ones used to counsel a man to stick trees in his fences at every yard, and used to calculate to a fraction what they would be worth at the end of the world.' Thus did the English countryside acquire the hedgerow timber to which it owes so much of its beauty.

Some landowners naturally planted the two most valuable trees, oak and ash, but there was a marked, and at first sight a very surprising, preference for elm. This was partly because of certain objections to oak and ash. Oak was too slow-growing and, in many soils, too uncertain for general use. Ash, as Cobbett truly said, 'will grow *any where* . . . in hedge-rows, in the plantations, every where the ash is fine'. It is, moreover, fast-growing. 'Ash', he continued, 'is timber, fit for the wheelwright at the age of twenty years or less.' But from the farming point of view it is the worst possible tree for a hedgerow. The grossest feeder of all our trees, no farm crops will grow within reach of its hungry roots; no cattle will graze where its leaves lie.

Elm is free from all these faults. In southern England and most of the Midlands it will grow anywhere; it produces saleable timber quickly; good grass will grow right up to the butt of the tree. Moreover, a century and a half ago elm commanded very high prices, especially as ship timber. The Navy Board required four kinds of timber for the hulls of the King's ships — oak, elm, beech, and Scotch fir, in that order of importance. The remarkable durability of elm under water made it of exceptional value below the waterline where it was used for planking; and when oak became scarce it was also used for keels for which the great size it often attained made it suitable. At the turn of the century the demand for elm increased, and for a time it became even scarcer than oak, and inferior American elm had to be imported to take its place.[1]

---

[1] The supply had always been irregular and often precarious because in England the elm is usually found as a lone tree rather than a woodland tree which could be conveniently felled on a large scale.

Meanwhile, the demand for elm in the everyday life of the nation tended to increase. Drain-pipes were still made of elm, even by the water undertakings supplying London.[1] And it cannot be doubted that the making of canals, which began in the closing years of the eighteenth century and continued until 1830, greatly increased the demand, for lock-gates and various other underwater purposes. These were the circumstances in which the common elm became the principal tree of the English hedgerow.[2]

There is no commoner sight in southern England and many parts of the Midlands than hedgerows studded with splendid elms, all of the same age, mostly dating from the early years of the nineteenth century. These trees are survivors of more than a hundred years of unremitting war against hedgerow timber, and are no measure of the vast scale on which the planting of hedges with trees was practised at the beginning of the century. When Mary Mitford, writing of the countryside in those days, mentioned a hedgerow, which she constantly did, she nearly always described it as 'thickly timbered', 'richly set with hedge-row timber', or 'thickly set with saplings'. William Howitt, writing a few years later, described Surrey as 'covered with parks, woods, and fields, the very hedgerows of which are dense continuous lines of trees'.

With England growing more and more enclosed, with hedges being assiduously planted from one end of the country to the other, some of the more far-seeing agriculturists began to urge the need to take warning from those southern and south-eastern counties which had been enclosed centuries earlier. 'The first circumstance that strikes an observant stranger, accustomed to the regularity of modern inclosure,' wrote someone in *The Farmer's Magazine* in 1800, 'is, the great inequality in the sizes of fields, in the anciently inclosed districts of England, the crookedness of the hedges, and the strangely irregular shapes of the

---

[1] At the beginning of the century the New River Company still had about 400 miles of wooden mains in London, and near Fleet Street they had a horse mill for boring wooden pipes. The Company did not substitute cast-iron mains for wooden ones until between 1812 and 1819. (Mr. S. D. Askell, Clerk of the Metropolitan Water Board, in a letter to the author.)

[2] The shrouding, shredding, or shroving of elms, and many other trees, was common practice. John Byng, writing in 1782, approved of the Romsey district because 'the trees are not ruin'd (as in most parts of England) by being shroved into the shape of a broom'. Ten years later he was astonished to find them shroving conifers in Staffordshire.

inclosures. But the object which I have particularly in view, in these strictures, and which merits the severest reprehension, is, that almost everywhere the hedges have been permitted to run wild, overspreading an irregular breadth of surface with a belt of useless and cumbrous brush-wood, while they scarcely half fence the fields, which they disfigure greatly, and the value of which they lessen very materially.

'In very extensive, old, and inclosed districts, I am fully convinced these crooked belts of brush-wood, improperly styled hedges, occupy a breadth of not less than eighteen or twenty feet, on every side of all the fields, one with another. Allowing considerably less than this supposition . . . and supposing the old inclosed fields to consist of ten acres each, on the average, which I believe is rather above than below the truth, this loss of productive surface will amount to about half an acre in each field, or five acres in the hundred, upon the whole extent of such inclosed districts. When in pasture, these belts produce little or nothing to the cattle in the fields, besides tearing off a great deal of valuable wool from the sheep, and when the fields are in hay, or under aration, they preclude the employment of the scythe and plough, from a much larger proportion of the land than has been stated above.' Years had yet to pass before there was any public concern about the effect of the hedgerow on farming economy apart from its harbouring game which damaged crops.

Landlords attached so much importance to hedgerows as covert for all kinds of game that tenants might be forbidden to trim their hedgerows more than once in seven years. Sometimes they were not allowed to touch them at all. It is not therefore surprising to read of tenant farmers complaining of having to pay rent for land which not only could not be used but which harboured hares and rabbits to the detriment of the crops. We also hear of tenants buying hedgerow timber from their land-lords in order to be quit of the injury the trees did to their crops and drains. Nevertheless, it was not till the middle of the century that an assault was made on England's hedgerow timber, and more than another half century before much was done about it.

The face of rural England was changing in other ways. The commons and heaths of today are but insignificant remnants of the vast wastes which were enclosed in the eighteenth and early nineteenth centuries, the dire social consequences of which we will consider later. With the wastes went much of the country's woodlands, in which it had never been rich and which it had always neglected. The depletion during the war years of standing timber, already much reduced by the iron-smelting industry, probably encouraged the enclosure and clearing of woodlands. The process seems to have been piecemeal rather than general, though Sherwood Forest is an example of large-scale enclosure at this time. It was anyway common enough to excite a strong protest from William Howitt in the 'thirties. He condemned the enclosure of forest primarily on sentimental and aesthetic grounds, but, he wrote, 'taking them on their own ground, these forest lands are not mere unproductive wastes. They supply our dockyards with an abundance of valuable timber; in them lie farms, and cottage homes, with their orchards, gardens, and little enclosures. They maintain a large population, and they pasture a vast quantity of cattle, sheep, hogs, and horses.' Enclosure was also encouraging the felling of woodlands by creating an unprecedented demand for young timber for post-and-rail fences.

Much more serious were the heavy inroads into the timber supply by private felling, the traditional recourse of the financially embarrassed landowner. A succession of bad harvests in the latter part of the eighteenth century had encouraged private felling which the new turnpike roads, capable of carrying heavy timber waggons, had made more often practicable. In the journals of his annual tours of England between 1781 and 1794 John Byng, who was passionately fond of trees and woodlands, repeatedly records the felling of hardwoods on private estates, and his chagrin at no replanting or, almost worse, replanting with conifers.

At Ricote Park, Lord Abingdon's, nearly all the fine timber was newly felled and 'the noble trees near the house are prostrate'. At Shireoaks the Hewitts had 'lately fell'd a fine avenue. For here, as elsewhere, they levell all timber'; at Haddon all the good timber was felled; at Coleshill there were 'some mutilated avenues; but all the timber is gone'. At Woburn, in 1789, Byng was 'shock'd and surprised to see that the axe had been most busy'; when he went back five years later the Duke had just ordered the felling of 1,000 trees in a single avenue. At Powys

'all the famous timber has been fell'd, and some paltry fir
plantations have been substituted'. Near Oswestry he passed
'Mr. Fly's grounds at Aston, who like most gentlemen of this,
and other counties, fell their oak; and think they make amends
by planting some larches, and Scotch-firs, proper ornaments for
a desert'. A few years later Sir John Morshead, the Lord
Warden of the Stanneries and a notorious gambler, was felling
his timber at Trenant Park, in Cornwall, in an effort to pay his
debts.

In 1816 the landowners, hit by the slump which had followed
the peace, began felling the timber that had survived the war.
There was still a good deal left, for the Navy's lack of ship
timber had not been due to the exhaustion of home supplies
but to gross incompetence in the Admiralty. While Nelson was
complaining that 'my crazy fleet are getting in a very indifferent
state' for want of timber in the dock-yards, and Collingwood
was protesting that he had 'been sailing for the last six months
with only a copper sheet between us and eternity', the East
India Company were getting all the ship timber they required,
which was a very considerable amount. Many large but
impecunious landowners had some mature timber left, but
when this did not suffice they felled the immature. Nor was this
evil practice confined to England. Peter Hawker, shooting near
Glasgow, recorded that 'the lairds of this country take especial
good care to turn their timber into money before it is large
enough to bear a man's weight'.[1] The Grants of Rothiemurchus
were felling timber as hard as the Lucys of Charlecote and as the
impoverished Duke of Marlborough would have done at Blenheim but for the restraining hand of the Court of Chancery. In
real life there was many a squire who, like Mrs. Gaskell's
Hamley of Hamley, had to cut down trees to pay for the education of his sons.

The high price of timber happily led to the planting of hardwoods and conifers on a considerable scale, but the planting of
coppice woods, for felling on a regular ten to seventeen years'
rotation, was also general. These coppices were mostly of ash,

---

[1] The widely held belief that the great Caledonian Forest was destroyed by a
terrible fire that swept the Highlands is of course untrue. The decaying stumps of
fir still found in almost every peat hag are usually relics of the axe. The great
forests of the Highlands were felled both for cash and to provide more sheep
ground. But standing timber was also sometimes devastated by severe gales.

chestnut, and hazel, the two former for hop poles and the latter for sheep hurdles, but all three were put to many other uses. Coppice wood, in the form of faggots, was in great demand for bread-ovens and malting, and what was unsuitable for these purposes found a ready sale as domestic fuel. Cobbett, a keen forester, mentions an ash coppice near Godalming 'which had been planted in regular rows, at about four feet distances, which had been once cut, and which was now in a state of six years' growth. . . . This coppice, at ten years' growth, will be worth twenty pounds the acre; and, at the next cutting, when the stems will send out so many more shoots, it will be worth thirty pounds the acre.'

Cobbett, who on his rides was frequently forced to make detours round impenetrable woodlands, tells us that this particular ash coppice had 'a way through it, made for fox-hunters'. In southern England it was unusual for woods to have rides, but not so in the Midlands. John Byng, writing in 1792, makes the following comment on some woodlands in Rutland: 'In the adjacent woods, Sr. W. L. has been permitted to cut Ridings! That he should not do in the woods, as it much assists the poacher; chills the timber; and gives a very unfair advantage over the fox, who is to be view'd and halloo'd at every turning; but I suppose it is *right*, being the high fashion.' It may be that in the Shires the cutting of rides had become common in the interests of foxhunting.

Early in the nineteenth century they planted woods which sometimes combined forest trees with underwood — what is now called coppice-with-standards. Cobbett thought that in such plantations the underwood might prove more valuable than the trees. Writing in 1825 he mentions a man planting forty acres of ash coppice 'and, at the same time, he *sowed the ground with acorns*. The acorns have become oak trees, and have begun and made great progress in diminishing the value of the ash, which have now to contend against the shade and the roots of the oak. For present profit, and, indeed, for permanent profit, it would be judicious to grub up the oak; but the owner has determined otherwise. He cannot endure the idea of destroying an oak-wood.'

There are few parts of England, outside the rich grazing farms of the Midlands where not an inch could be spared from grass, in which we do not see woods dating from this period, many of them having started as pure coppice although, through enforced neglect in recent years, they have lost their original character.[1] Our debt to those who planted them remains considerable.

[1] The building of railways, which made cheap coal generally available, was a blow to coppices. But in many parts of England coppices dependent on the sale of faggots for fuel remained profitable up till about the First World War when most bakers and maltsters began to give them up.

II

Cobbett's England

ALTHOUGH the open-field system closed the door to progressive agriculture and increased production, which the Napoleonic wars made a compelling need, it gave every countryman the immense advantage of a stake in the land. Nearly all cottagers had at least a strip or two in the common fields, and the rest at least enjoyed legal or customary rights in the wastes where they could graze cows, horses, sheep, geese,[1] and goats. Thus was the labourer able to produce both cheap food for himself and a surplus to send to market. The system also gave him an opportunity to rise in the world by saving and investing in more stock or more land in the common field. It also left him free to dispose of his labour as he thought fit, as best suited his interests, on his own holding or, for wages, on that of a larger farmer.

The loss of these advantages was the price which, all too often, the poor had to pay for enclosure. As Arthur Young, the chief author of enclosure, admitted, 'by nineteen out of twenty Enclosure Bills the poor are injured and most grossly'. A small farmer with an allotment of say ten acres might well find himself unable both to pay his share of the heavy legal expenses of enclosure, with the cost of hedging and ditching added, and retain enough working capital to carry on. He had to sell out to a bigger man. A very poor man's allotment might be no more than an acre with perhaps a small cash payment as compensation for the loss of his rights in the common waste where he had been in the habit of grazing a cow which supplied his children with milk. He probably could not afford to take up and fence his solitary acre, and in any case it would not support his cow. He therefore had to sell both his cow and his land.

[1] 'I have seen', wrote Cobbett, 'not less than ten thousand geese in one tract of common, in about six miles, going from Chobham towards Farnham in Surrey . . . raised entirely by care and by the common!'

Thomas Bewick recorded his distress at the change that over-
came a favourite Northumberland common or fell: 'On this
common — the poor man's heritage for ages past, where he
kept a few sheep, or a Kyloe cow, perhaps a flock of geese, and
mostly a stock of bee-hives — it was with infinite pleasure that I
long beheld the beautiful wild scenery which was there
exhibited, and it is with the opposite feelings of regret that I
now find all swept away. Here and there on this common were
to be seen the cottage, or rather hovel, of some labouring man,
built at his own expense, and mostly with his own hands; and to
this he always added a garth and a garden, upon which great
pains and labour were bestowed to make both productive. . . .
These various concerns excited the attention and industry of the
hardy occupants, which enabled them to prosper, and made
them despise being ever numbered with the parish poor.'

Thus, between the years 1760 and 1840, when the enclosure
of the country was virtually complete, did the cottagers and
petty yeomen of England lose their independence and find
themselves wholly at the mercy of employers from whom they
could not always wring a living wage, and liable to be laid off
in bad weather and slack times. Being landless, they were no
longer able to save for sickness and old age.

Sometimes, again as the result of enclosure, they could not get
regular employment. Many large landowners preferred to let
their land in big rather than small units — to have, say, four
large tenants instead of twenty small ones. This made for more
economical working and higher rents, and was sound common
sense. But it threw many a labourer out of work and deprived
him of his cottage which became redundant and was pulled
down. In the Midlands, where cattle were more profitable than
corn, unemployment was often rendered acute by the laying of
all arable down to grass. Thus we hear of a parish of 2,300 acres
losing 60 families of small farmers and agricultural labourers.
At Foston, in Leicestershire, 34 dwellings were reduced to three,
and at Wistow, only two miles away and the same size, all that
was left after the process of enclosure had spent itself was the
hall house.

Many a small farmer who was able to take up his allotment
lived to regret having done so. The convenience of having his
arable in one piece, instead of scattered over the common

fields, was often more than offset by the loss of his right on the common waste. He required as many horses to plough his land as before but there was no common left to turn them out on. If he had sheep in the common flock tended by the common shepherd he now found himself having either to give up his sheep or engage a shepherd of his own for which his allotment on the common, if he got one, could not pay. For the same reason he usually had also to give up his cows. Without sheep or cattle to manure his arable, diminishing crops ensured his ultimate bankruptcy.

The plight of the new landless peasantry might for many have proved supportable had not enclosure so often synchronized with the loss of cottage industries which the new machinery and the new factories were fast destroying. Until the early years of the nineteenth century not only were there many more mills and factories in small country towns and villages, but the custom was for big and small manufacturers to have much of their work done in cottage homes, whence they collected the finished goods with trains of pack-horses. The blanket industry of Witney, the woollen industry of Norwich, the glove-makers of Worcester, the stocking-makers of Nottingham, and countless other trades throughout England provided work in surrounding villages for the wives and families of agricultural workers and small yeoman farmers. The new machines were making it cheaper to have the work done in the factories, and the small country factories were moving into the industrial towns where coal and transport were cheap. Until the turn of the century there were few villages in England where the rural population did not derive a regular income from the work of their hands in their own homes or in some small mill or factory. This and the produce of their land and their livestock had afforded the villagers an enviable freedom from complete dependence on wages. The new machines took from them their cottage industries, and enclosure took their land and common rights. Thus did they become wholly dependent on the wages which, in the face of growing unemployment, they could not always earn. The consequence of the widespread distress was a great exodus of small farmers to America, and of cottage folk to the new industrial towns.

Our concern in these pages is with those who remained

behind, at the mercy of the big farmers who had never before enjoyed the advantage of having labourers wholly dependent on what they cared to pay them. It was an advantage which few hesitated to exploit except where, as in the Midlands and the North, industry competed for labour and compelled all to pay a living wage.

Here and there in the dreary wastes of agricultural misery there were oases of prosperity, mostly around the few remaining country towns in which a manufactory still lingered. In Saffron Walden, for example, the local silk industry provided such lucrative employment for young women that, according to a local paper in 1823, they were able 'to dress in the greatest extravagance, so much so that on a Sunday those who formerly moved in the most humble social sphere and appeared in woollens and stuffs have lately been so disguised as to be mistaken for persons of distinction. A ludicrous deception of the kind, we are informed, occurred a few Sundays since at a parish church in the vicinity of Saffron Walden, where two young women entered dressed most elegantly in silks of their own production, to which were added fashionable bonnets, plumed with nodding feathers; the clergyman politely directed the strangers to be shewn into a pew suitable to their appearance, and at the conclusion of the service inquired of the clerk whether he knew these elegantly dressed ladies, when behold, it was discovered, that they were two girls from the Walden silk manufactory.'

Such local industries were fast disappearing and, for the most part, the agricultural labourer was at the mercy of the farmer. But his cup of bitterness was not yet full, nor his degradation complete.

In 1795 the magistrates of Speenhamland in Berkshire had met with the object of fixing and enforcing a living wage for farm workers in order to avert the imminent danger of widespread famine in the county. Unfortunately they were persuaded to adopt another remedy. This was what we now call the dole. They decided that the difference between the wages a man earned and what it cost him to live — determined by the price of the loaf — should be found out of the parish rates. As the Report of the Poor Law Commissioners of 1834 stated, under this system 'the worthless were sure of *something*, while the prudent, the industrious, and the sober, with all their care and pains, obtained *only something*; and even that scanty pittance was doled out to them by the overseer'. Wages were so low that a man could not live without supplementing his earnings from the parish. But if he possessed anything, a few pounds saved over the years, not only was he refused help, but no one would employ him. Farmers looked to the parish to help pay their wage bill and therefore preferred to employ paupers. A thrifty hard-working waggoner, who had two cows and a few pounds and found himself out of a job through no fault of his own, declared, 'Whilst I have these things I shall get no work; I must part with them all; I must be reduced to a state of beggary before any one will employ me.'

Over the next few years the precedent established at Speenhamland was followed by nearly every county in England, the exceptions being confined to the North. Thus was removed any incentive the farmer may have had to pay a living wage or keep his men regularly employed. Speenhamland had reduced the farm workers of the country to paupers. It destroyed what self-respect their loss of independence had left them, and deprived them of the means and ambition to rise in life. Another social evil that flowed from Speenhamland was the premium it placed on bastardy. The parish shouldered the burden of the putative father of a bastard and paid its mother more than for a legitimate child. The more bastards a woman had the more eligible she was as a wife.

Speenhamland aggravated the evil consequences of the mismanagement of enclosure which lay at the root of most of the troubles of the countryside. 'Our poor population,' wrote Howitt, 'stripped of their old common rights, have been thrown upon the parish; their little flock of sheep, their few cows, their geese, their pigs, all gone; and no collateral help left them to eke out their small savings; and in the case of loss of work, or sickness, no resource but parish degradation.'

Fortunately William Howitt, unlike Cobbett who delighted in recording all that was bad in country life and turned a blind eye to much that was good,[1] has left us some pleasant

[1] In 1820 one of Thomas Creevey's correspondents described Cobbett as 'a foulmouthed, malignant dog; but', he added, 'there is so much point in his criticisms that one cannot help admitting there is generally *some* truth in his remarks'.

pictures which show that the labourers, hard though their lot, were not wholly condemned to a life of unrelieved misery and gloom. They, like their sisters, started life as farm servants, not labourers, and on most farms they still lodged and boarded with their employer. Sitting at his table they had their fill of his ample fare which must often have been in agreeable contrast to what they had been brought up to. 'The old oak table', wrote Howitt, 'is spread in the homely house-place, for the farmer and his family — wife, children, servants, male and female; and is heaped with the rude plenty of beans and bacon, beef and cabbage, fried potatoes and bacon, huge puddings. . . .' But the work, starting at five in the morning and continuing until dark, was hard, and, of course, varied with the age of the lad. Beginning with helping with the poultry, running errands, and doing odd jobs, he graduated up till he could 'learn to drive plough, and then to hold it; to drive the team, and finally do all the labours of a man. That is the growing up of a farm-servant. All this time he is learning his business, but he is learning nothing else, — he is growing up into a tall, long, smock-frocked, straw-hatted, ancle-booted fellow, with a gait as graceful as one of his own plough-bullocks . . . and there he is, as simple, as ignorant, and as laborious a creature as one of the wagon-horses that he drives.' His change of status comes when 'he is metamorphosed into a labourer by marrying and setting up his cottage, finding himself, and receiving weekly instead of yearly wages'.

If the young labourer had been thrifty on the £6 or £7 a year he had been earning as a farm servant, he might be so fortunate as to have a pig in a sty, which in those days was considered the best possible start for married life. He certainly had little else; nor had he much hope of living on his wages of from 8s. to 9s. a week, just over £20 a year. Statistics show that in 1823 the cost of living of a married couple with three children amounted to £20 for food, £3 for rent, and £8 for clothing, making £31 in all. If he was so fortunate as to have a potato patch attached to his cottage or, better still, a cow gait or cow pasture, the young labourer and his wife might, with what she could earn, manage for a while to make both ends meet without having recourse to the parish. But many a young couple started married life without any such prospect.

The arrival of children only increased the labourer's dependence on parish relief, but it was not long before they were made
to contribute something to their own keep. They were at least
able to do so under more healthy conditions than in the new
industrial towns where the horrors of child labour were
unspeakable. As soon as the children 'can run about', Howitt
tells us, 'they are set to watch a gate that stands at the end of the
lane or the common to stop cattle from straying, and there
through the long solitary days they pick up a few halfpence by
opening it for travellers. They are sent to scare birds. . . . They
help to glean, to gather potatoes . . . to gather mushrooms and
blackberries for market', and in many other ways they earned a
trifle for the family budget, and as they grew older they contributed more and suffered more. Here is Cobbett's description
of a party of girls at work on a Wiltshire farm early one November day in 1821 : 'There were some very pretty girls, but ragged
as colts, and as pale as ashes. The day was cold too, and frost
hardly off the ground; and their blue arms and lips, would have
made any heart ache.'

'We abound with poor,' wrote Gilbert White, 'many of
whom . . . live comfortably in good stone or brick cottages,
which are glazed, and have chambers above stairs: mud buildings we have none.' The poor of Selborne were lucky. In many
parts of England, especially in the Midlands, cottages built of
mud mixed with straw were common, and often enough they
had but one room the window of which had paper or rags in
place of glass. This is the description of a labourer's cottage by
Howitt who certainly did not exaggerate the miseries of the
poor: 'There is his tenement of, at most, one or two rooms. His
naked walls, bare brick, stone or mud floor, as it may be; a few
wooden, or rush-bottomed chairs; a deal, or old oak table; a
simple fire-place, with its oven beside it, or, in many parts of the
kingdom, no other fire-place than the hearth; a few pots and
pans and you have his whole abode, goods and chattels.' That is
probably a fair picture of a cottage such as a great many
labourers lived in at the time. In Cobbett, of course, we find
a much grimmer picture of how some labourers had to live.
This is his description of cottages which he considered typical of
Leicestershire in 1830: 'Look at these hovels, made of mud and
straw; bits of glass, or of old off-cast windows, without frames or

hinges, frequently, but merely stuck in the mud wall. Enter them, and look at the bits of chairs or stools; the wretched boards tacked together to serve for a table; the floor of pebble, broken brick, or of bare ground; look at the thing called a bed; and survey the rags on the backs of the wretched inhabitants.'

'A couple of flitches of bacon are worth fifty thousand methodist sermons and religious tracts', wrote Cobbett. 'The sight of them upon the rack tends more to keep a man from poaching and stealing than whole volumes of penal statutes, though assisted by the terrors of the hulks and the gibbet.' Bacon was of course the traditional food of the farm labourer but enclosure of the open fields and the wastes had made it very difficult for many a man to keep a pig, and bacon was expensive to buy. Fresh meat had become so dear that only the comparatively prosperous could afford it as often as once a week. There must have been many like the man who, one November day, told Cobbett he had not tasted meat since harvest. We hear of men going to work on a breakfast of cold potatoes instead of the traditional bread, bacon, and beer. Potatoes were tending to take the place of bread, especially in the West where labourers were often given a bit of potato ground, but the shortage of fuel for baking in many parts of England may have had something to do with it. How miserably low the labourer's standard of living had fallen is clearly shown by the quantity of bread allowed him when he was 'on the dole' being less than was given to felons in gaol, and even then it was sometimes made from a mixture of wheat and barley flour.

Up till about 1780 every cottage brewed its own beer, which formed an important and valuable part of the family's diet. The average consumption of a labourer's family was two quarts a day in winter, rising to five quarts in July and August. The failure of wages to keep pace with the crippling rise in the cost of food in the war years, and the heavy taxes on malting barley and hops, had combined to change the drinking habits of the village. Few could afford to brew so they drank much less beer and they drank it in the public house. In the home tea had largely taken the place of beer which, bearing in mind the shocking lack of nourishing food, must have been a change for the worse, though not as bad as the censorious Cobbett made out. He viewed 'tea drinking as a destroyer of health, and enfeebler

I *Sir John Morshead Felling his Timber to Settle his Debts*: In felling his trees at Trenant Park Sir John Morshead (wrongly called Sir Henry by Rowlandson) was conforming to the custom of impoverished landowners.

II *Gipsy Encampment*: Enclosure was a grievous blow to gipsies. The loss of common land, their traditional home, forced them to become more nomadic, and, late in the nineteenth century, to take to the caravan which till then they had scorned.

of the frame, an engenderer of effeminacy and laziness, a debaucher of youth, and a maker of misery for old age . . . the gossip of the tea table is no bad preparatory school for the brothel.' Those who could not afford tea at about 2s. 10d. a pound used rye, roasted and ground, in its place.

Another recent change in domestic habits was in the lighting of the home. The dip candle had taken the place of the home-made rush light. Candles were taxed and their manufacture at home forbidden. But lighting even with taxed candles was not a heavy expense because during the greater part of the year the labourer and his family were in bed before night fell. This was often out of sheer weariness of under-nourished bodies, but it was partly to save the expense, not of lighting, but of fuel. Throughout much of England no small part of the sufferings of the poor was due to the high cost of firing, to the problem of how to get enough fuel for cooking, let alone enough to keep themselves warm. Cobbett once wrote of the grass lands of Hampshire: 'these countries have one great draw-back: the poor day-labourers suffer from the want of fuel, and they have nothing but their *bare pay*. For these reasons they are greatly worse off than those of the *woodland countries*; and it is really surprising what a difference there is between the faces that you see here, and the round, red faces that you see in the *wealds* and the *forests*, particularly in Sussex, where the labourers *will* have a *meat-pudding* of some sort or other; and where they *will* have *a fire* to sit by in winter.' It was a theme on which he liked to dwell. 'The richer the soil, and the more destitute the woods; that is to say, the more purely a corn country, the more miserable the labourers', he wrote on another occasion. 'No hedges, no ditches, no commons, no grassy lanes . . . a few trees surround the great farm-house. All the rest is bare of trees; and the wretched labourer has not a stick of wood, and has no place for a pig or a cow to graze, or even lie down upon. The rabbit countries are the countries for labouring men.' So wrote Cobbett in 1825. But he attributed the comparative well-being of the labourer in woodland countries much more to 'that great blessing, abundance of fuel at all times of the year', than to abundance of rabbits.

In those days, when most hedges were no more than thin lines of young quick, and most hedgerow trees were mere

c

saplings, all vigilantly guarded, fuel was an acute problem wherever there were not woodlands close at hand to draw on. In the south-east, where the land had long been enclosed, the occasional trees in the old hedgerows were often pollarded to provide fuel for the labourers on farms, a practice which Cobbett, for all his passionate concern for the poor, strongly condemned. 'Here is the great disfigurement of all these three eastern counties', he wrote. 'Almost every bank of every field is studded with *pollards*, that is to say, trees that have been *beheaded*, at from six to twelve feet from the ground, than which nothing in nature can be more ugly. They send out shoots from the head, which are lopped off once in ten or a dozen years for fuel, or other purposes. To add to the deformity, the ivy is suffered to grow on them, which, at the same time, checks the growth of the shoots. These pollards become hollow very soon, and, as timber, are fit for nothing but gate-posts, even before they are hollow. Upon a farm of a hundred acres these pollards, by root and shade, spoil at least six acres of the ground, besides being most destructive to the fences. Why not plant six acres of the ground with timber and underwood? Half an acre a year would most amply supply the farm with poles and brush, and with every thing wanted in the way of fuel.' Many of these old ivy-clad hedgerow pollards still survive to remind us of the acute fuel problem of 150 years ago.[1]

Enclosure aggravated the fuel shortage very considerably, not so much by reducing the woodlands as by reducing the wastes on which the rural population had always depended for alternative fuels. The chief of these, outside the limited areas of hill and fen where peat was obtainable, were turf, gorse, and reeds or sedge. Turf was used, under the commoners' right of turbary, wherever heather grew on the common waste. This was burnt off in summer or autumn, leaving a charred turf which could be cut and carried in for winter use. Gorse or furze, whenever available, was much used as fuel, and sometimes sedge. It would be difficult to think of any less satisfactory domestic fuel than sedge (though it was preferred by some for bread ovens) had we not Cobbett's note, made near Marlborough in 1821, of 'girls

---

[1] In some forests the commoners had the right to pollard or lop. In parts of Epping Forest, for example, the branches of oak, beech, elm, and hornbeam trees might be cut at 6 or 7 feet from the ground during the winter months. Lower branches were reserved by the Crown as food for the deer.

carrying home bean and wheat stubble for fuel'. But fern can hardly have been much better. In 1809 Horace Walpole's Miss Berry, sheltering in a Cumberland cottage, found the wife making girdle cakes 'over a fire of fern, by which we dried our clothes'.

Enclosure, by robbing the cottagers of their cows, sometimes helped to deny the poor their traditional fuel in a grazing country. This was cow-dung which was mixed with short straw, kneaded into lumps, and dried. Since the beginning of the eighteenth century progressive agriculturists had condemned the practice as a waste of good manure, and it had been suggested that leases should include a restrictive covenant forbidding the burning of cow dung. But as cow dung would never have been burnt had any other fuel been available the practice continued unchecked, particularly in the Midlands and the North, until, towards the middle of the nineteenth century, railways made cheap coal widely available.

Before enclosure many wastes or commons were annually allotted to the local villagers who had a legal right to cut fuel; those without legal rights frequently exercised a right of custom, perhaps dating back over the centuries. When a parish was enclosed the former received some compensation but the latter seldom got anything. How disastrous even to those with legal rights an Enclosure Act could be is well illustrated by the unhappy experience of Ewelme in Oxfordshire. 'One of the commons enclosed', Gilbert Slater tells us, 'was known as the "Furze Common", and it supplied the poor of the neighbourhood with their fuel, for *every* inhabitant had the right of cutting furze on it. After enclosure the Furze Common was allotted to one man, who allowed no trespass on it, and the *owners* of cottages were awarded allotments of land in consideration of the rights which the *cottagers* had exercised. The lands so allotted became part of ordinary farms, and the poor simply lost their supply of fuel without any compensation whatever.'

At Salisbury, Cobbett tells us, 'the poor take by turns, the making of fires at their houses, to boil four or five tea-kettles. What a winter-life must these lead, whose turn it is not to make the fire! At Launceston in Cornwall, a man, a tradesman too, told me that the people in general could not afford to have fire in ordinary, and that he himself paid 3d for boiling a leg of mutton at another man's fire!'

In those days every cottager customarily baked his own bread, but sometimes, for lack of fuel, he had to buy it ready baked at the village bake-house, or eat potatoes instead. In the grazing countries of the Midlands the labourers dried their bacon for want of wood with which to smoke it.

'If we suppose', wrote Cobbett, 'the great Creator to condescend to survey his works in detail, what object can be so pleasing to him as that of the labourer, after his return from the toils of a cold winter day, sitting with his wife and children round a cheerful fire, while the wind whistles in the chimney and the rain pelts the roof? But, of all God's creation what is so miserable to behold or to think of as a wretched, half-starved family creeping to their nest of flocks or straw, there to lie shivering till sent forth by the fear of absolutely expiring from want?' A very different observer, one who was less obsessed than Cobbett with the distress of the poor, gave a very similar description of human misery in cottage homes at this time. Benjamin Disraeli, in *Sybil*, also described the return of the labourer from his toils 'to the squalid hovel which profaned the name of home. To that home, over which Malaria hovered, and round whose shivering hearth were clustered other guests besides the exhausted family of toil — Fever, in every form, pale Consumption, exhausting Synochus, and trembling Ague, — returned after cultivating the broad fields of merry England the bold British peasant, returned to encounter the worst of diseases with a frame the least qualified to oppose them; a frame that subdued by toil was never sustained by animal food; drenched by the tempest could not change its dripping rags; and was indebted for its scanty fuel to the windfalls of the woods.'

Some years earlier, in 1788, John Byng had painted a curiously similar picture of cottage life in a Sussex village which had suffered the loss of its kindly squire. 'How wretched', he wrote, 'do the miseries of a cottage appear! (and this was only of comparative distress); want of food, want of fuel, want of clothing! Children perishing of an ague! and an unhappy mother unable to attend to, or relieve their wants, or assuage their pains; nor to allow time sufficient even for the reparation of their rags; — whilst the worn-down melancholy father (perhaps a shepherd) pinch'd by cold, and pining with despair, returns at evening close, to a hut devoid of comfort, or the smallest renovation of hope: for no longer are left the fost'ring, forgiving hand of his landlord, or the once bountiful buttery of the manor house, to apply to!'

All the advantages of enclosure forecast by Arthur Young — improved methods of agriculture, increased production, and a strengthening of the country's economy — had been realized. Moreover, but for enclosure, England might well not have survived the Napoleonic wars. But Young fully recognized the disastrous consequences of the mismanagement of enclosure, the failure to protect the interests of the poor, and the aggravation of their distress by what was called the Speenhamland Act. 'Go to an alehouse kitchen of an old enclosed country', he wrote, 'and there you will see the origin of poverty and poor rates. For whom are they to be sober? For whom are they to save? (such are their questions). For the parish? If I am diligent, shall I have leave to build a cottage? If I am sober, shall I have land for a cow? If I am frugal, shall I have half an acre of potatoes? You offer no motives; you have nothing but a parish officer and a workhouse! — Bring me another pot — '

It has been suggested from time to time that the landowners and large farmers sponsored Enclosure Bills with the deliberate intention of enriching themselves at the expense of the poor. This was manifestly not so. Where they failed, and failed lamentably, was in permitting enclosure to be so hopelessly mismanaged, in not seeing that the rights of the poor were properly protected. For this they had little excuse. Enclosure by Act of Parliament started to become general in about 1760, and its evil consequences to the poor soon became obvious. Yet seldom was any attempt made to provide for those to whom the loss of their rights in the common field and common waste was ruination. All that was required was to fix a minimum holding to ensure that none went wholly landless. But no one thought of that.

'Has Meriden Common been long enclosed?' asked John Byng of a Warwickshire labourer.

'Ah, lackaday, Sir, that was a sad job; and ruin'd all us poor volk: and those who then gave into it, now repent it.'

'Why so?'

'Because, we had our garden, our bees, our share of a flock of sheep, the feeding of our geese; and could cut turf for our fuel. — Now all that is gone!'

Among the many humble sufferers from the Enclosure Acts were the gipsies who had long made the commons their principal home. They already called themselves Travellers, but they lived wholly in tents, and held the half-bred caravan-dwelling gorgio in great contempt. Readers of *The Romany Rye* will recall Ursula's sympathy for gipsy children who had the misfortune to fall 'into the company of gorgios, trampers, and basket-makers, who live in caravans. . . . I hate to talk of the matter, brother; but so comes this race of half and halfs.' Maggie's gipsies, in *The Mill on the Floss*, lived 'in a little brown tent on the commons'. It was probably the loss of their traditional camping grounds that compelled the true gipsies, at the end of the nineteenth century, to take to the caravan.

For the larger farmers events were taking a course which suited them admirably. What they wanted, and what enclosure was giving them, was a proletariat wholly dependent on them, whom they could employ or lay off as they chose. But the promoters of Enclosure Bills were not usually farmers; they were the squires, the large landowners, who traditionally did not lack sympathy for their humble neighbours. Their callousness at this time was mainly due to the prevailing anti-Jacobin spirit which the French Revolution had engendered. The poor had to be repressed — kept in their place — and taught to be content with their lot, not that they needed much teaching—for the most part they accepted it without question. From time to time there had been disturbances, but there was no serious trouble until 1830 when the new threshing machines threatened to aggravate the distress which had already become unendurable, and provoked the famous 'Swing' riots in the southern counties. In the early years of the century there was nothing to disturb the peace of mind of the rich and make them realize the need to protect the poor against the evil consequences of enclosure. On the rare occasions on which farm labourers are even mentioned in contemporary literature they are usually referred to contemptuously as mere 'chawbacons' or 'hawbucks'.

While little effort was made to remove the causes of poverty or curb the growing numbers of the poor, charity was not lacking. Too often, however, it took a course which afforded no relief to present distress. For example, there was a vogue for establishing village schools, but their founders appear to have encountered a good deal of frustration. Although Howitt thought education was the greatest need of the countryside, the liberal-minded Cobbett was dead against village schools. 'The child', he wrote, 'is spoiled as a labourer; his book-learning has only made him conceited; into some course of desperation he falls. . . . I am wholly against children wasting their time in the idleness of what is called *education*; and particularly in schools . . . where nothing is taught but the rudiments of servility, pauperism and slavery.' When the worthy Mr. William Allen started building his School of Industry at Lindfield in Sussex he was suspected by those he was seeking to help of a diabolical plot to incarcerate their children preparatory to kidnapping them and shipping them away to foreign parts, for which the sea at Brighton was so conveniently close. But the greatest obstacle to the education of the poor was the natural reluctance of impoverished parents to forgo the few pence their children, so long as they remained at home, could earn for the family budget.

III

Captain Swing

THE Enclosure Acts, which afforded opportunities to acquire the holdings and stock of small men at knock-out prices, had enabled the big farmers to grow bigger. The boom prices of the Napoleonic wars brought them wealth. It might have been better for them and for the country had this not been so. In their new easy circumstances, which they thought would last for ever, most farmers saw no reason to change their ways in favour of the new and greatly improved methods of agriculture which had now become bountifully available. Only the few who took to the new machines, new crops, new methods of drainage, and new fertilizers were able to weather the coming slump with comparatively light hearts. The battle of Waterloo was followed by the sad spectacle of the farmers of England struggling to maintain a grand manner of living in the face of threatening bankruptcy.

Then, as ever since, the small holder was the man who had the greatest struggle. The plight of those who, by a narrow margin, had contrived to survive enclosure as independent cultivators was well described by Arthur Young. 'The small farmer', he wrote, 'is forced to be laborious to an extreme degree; he works harder and fares harder than the common labourer; and yet with all this labour and all his fatiguing incessant exertions, seldom can he at all improve his condition or even with any degree of regularity pay his rent and preserve his present situation. He is confined to perpetual drudgery, which is the source of profound ignorance, the parent of obstinacy and blind perseverance in old modes and old practices, however absurd and pernicious. He is in a manner shut out from that intercourse with the world, which enlarges the mind and improves and increases knowledge. His understanding and his conversation are not at all superior to those of the common labourers, if even equal to them, as the latter, by sometimes changing their masters and working in different situations, extend the sphere of their observation and experience and make some little accession to their narrow stock of ideas.' In 1823, more than a hundred years after Jethro Tull had invented the corn-drill, Cobbett was moved to write: 'It seems strange, that men are not to be convinced of the advantage of the row-culture for turnips. They will insist upon believing, that there is some *ground lost*. They will also insist upon believing that the row-culture is the most expensive. How can there be ground lost if the crop be larger? And as to the expense, take one year with another, the broad-cast method must be twice as expensive as the other.' It had taken Cobbett's contemporary, Coke of Norfolk, sixteen years to persuade his tenants to follow his example and adopt the drill, the use of which, he estimated, spread at the rate of only a mile a year. But much of Coke's early life was spent in trying to break down the traditional conservatism of the English farmer. He had to grow wheat successfully on the sandy Norfolk soil for nine years before he could persuade anyone to do the same. For years he could not get the villagers of Holkham to eat potatoes, still less the farmers to grow them. Soon after some of his tenants had at last been persuaded to admit that perhaps ' 't wouldn't poison tha' pigs' the potato became a regular crop.

For the time being the farmer could afford to persist in his obstinate inertia to change because, thanks to enclosure and war prices, his traditional methods of agriculture had brought within his reach a standard of living far beyond his expectations. 'Before enclosure', wrote W. H. R. Curtler, 'the farmer entertained his friends with bacon fed by himself, washed down with ale brewed from his own malt, in a brown jug, or a glass if he were extravagant. He wore a coat of woollen stuff, the growth of his own flock, spun by his wife and daughters, his stockings came from the same quarter, so did the clothes of his family.' When to the advantages of enclosure were added those of war with France, his style of living began to approach that of the squire. 'The English farmer', wrote Cobbett, 'has, of late years, become a totally different character. A fox-hunting horse; polished boots; a spanking trot to market; a "get out of the way

or by G-d I'll ride over you" to every poor devil upon the road;[1]
wine at his dinner; a servant (and sometimes in *livery*) to wait at
his table; a painted lady for a wife; sons aping the young
squires and lords; a house crammed up with sofas, pianos and
all sorts of fooleries.' Elsewhere he returns to these 'fooleries', the
worst of which 'was a *parlour*. Aye, and a *carpet* and a *bell-pull*
too! . . . And, there were the decanters, the glasses, the "dinner-
set" of crockery-ware, and all just in the true stock-jobber style.'
He overlooked the harps and grand-pianos which excited the
ridicule of other contemporary chroniclers, but he does not note
that the farmer's 'wine at his dinner' was usually either gooseberry wine or currant wine. But it was not always.

There were no farmers in the country as prosperous as the
Holkham tenants. Coke, in middle age, was justly proud of
having at last, after years of precept and example, taught them
how to win wealth from a thin sandy soil on which, it had been
said before his day, 'all you will see will be one blade of grass
and two rabbits fighting for that'. 'It has been objected against
me', he once declared, 'that my tenants live too much like
gentlemen, driving their own curricles, perhaps, and drinking
their port every day. I am proud to have such a tenantry, and
heartily wish that instead of drinking their port they could afford
to drink their claret and champagne every day.'

An unfortunate but inevitable consequence of larger farms
and more prosperous farmers was the gradual disappearance of
the ancient custom of the unmarried labourer living under the
same roof as his employer. To the young labourer, coming out
of a poverty-stricken home, the advantage of enjoying for some
years solid farm-house fare was, as we have seen, immense. But
perhaps still more valuable was the social advantage of the
close intimacy which the custom created between master and
man. 'At night', wrote Howitt, 'the farmer takes his seat on the
settle, under the old wide chimney — his wife has her work-
table set near — the "wenches" darning their stockings, or
making up a cap for Sunday, and the men sitting on the other
side of the hearth, with their shoes off. He now enjoys of all
things, to talk over his labours and plans with the men, — they

---

[1] Bewick similarly condemned their behaviour on the highway. 'When these
upstart gentlemen left the market,' he wrote, 'they were ready to ride over all they
met or overtook on the way.'

canvass the best method of doing this and that — lay out the course of tomorrow — what land is to be broken up, or laid down; where barley, wheat, oats, etc. shall be sown, or if they be growing, when they shall be cut. In harvest-time, lambing-time, in potato setting and gathering time, in fact, almost all summer long, there is no sitting on the hearth — it is out of bed with the sun, and after the long hard day — supper, and to bed again. It is only in winter that there is any sitting by the fire, which is seldom diversified further than by the coming in of a neighbouring farmer or the reading of the weekly news.' But the great advantage of this system to the young labourer was, to quote a contemporary agriculturist, that he 'was regarded as one of the farmer's own family, for whose good conduct and appearance the master was in some degree accountable and for whose success in life, if he conducted himself properly, he was never entirely indifferent'.

Larger farms meant more farm workers, but not necessarily larger farm houses. Consequently it was not always possible, in these changed circumstances, for a farmer to house and feed his unmarried men. A more potent reason for abandoning the traditional custom was probably the rise in the farmer's standard of living while that of his men remained unchanged. Class consciousness was beginning to creep in; social difference was gaining emphasis and when, as now happened, the farm house became too grand for the dirty feet of the workers to be allowed in, and their manners too uncouth to be endured, it widened into a gulf which has never since been closed. This was precisely the sort of situation which Cobbett delighted to exploit and distort. He ridiculed the farmer's wife, 'stuck up in a place she calls a *parlour*, with, if she have children, the "young ladies and gentlemen" about her . . . a dinner brought in by a girl that is perhaps better "educated" than she . . . the house too neat for a dirty-shoed carter to be allowed to come into'. But behind it all he detected something much more sinister. 'Why do not farmers now *feed* and *lodge* their work-people, as they did formerly? Because they cannot keep them *upon so little* as they give them in wages.'

All these changes were very gradual. For long after the war many farmers continued in their old ways, housing and feeding their workers, ploughing with six oxen hitched to a wooden plough,[1] and broadcasting their seed instead of drilling it. But no matter whether farmers were progressive or reactionary, there were few among them, outside the always exceptional Holkham tenants, who did not find themselves overwhelmed by the disaster which was fast approaching.

England emerged from the Napoleonic wars victorious but crippled by a huge National Debt, excessive taxation, and an enormous poor rate. To these burdens others, no less grievous, were quickly added. The sudden ending of war-contracts had plunged industry into grave difficulties. This, and increasing dependence of manufacturers on machines, threw many thousands of industrial workers out of jobs, and created an unemployment problem which was greatly aggravated by the demobilization of the army and navy in which a sixth of the adult male population had been serving. Acute poverty, even among the employed (wages had doubled but the cost of living had trebled), and mass unemployment led to discontent and a steadily rising tide of bitter resentment against authority.

The plight of the country village was as grievous as that of the industrial towns, involving landlords, tenants, and labourers alike. War-prices had brought large profits but these had in part been absorbed by the growth of taxation, most of which had fallen on the agriculturists. Indeed, many of the new burdens — notably the county-, poor-, and highway-rates, the new duties on hops and barley, the taxes on farm horses, sheepdogs,[2] and leather — were almost wholly carried by the farming community. What was left of the war-time profits had mostly been reinvested in the land, in improvements and in new acres. Mansions had also been rebuilt and enlarged; expenditure on farm buildings and roads, on draining, breaking, and fencing the wastes, had been heavy. For these purposes loans and mortgages had been raised on the security of ancestral homes and farm land; they had also been raised to meet the competition for land created by the territorial aspirations of the new rich of the industrial towns. As land values rose so did the demand for

---

[1] Both Arthur Young and William Marshall preferred oxen to horses for ploughing. They cost less in food, harness, and shoeing, and they needed no grooming. At the end of their working lives they fattened well and could be sold for beef. Oxen were still widely used, either alone or with horses, for drawing waggons.

[2] The tax of 8s. on a sheepdog was a serious burden to shepherds, who were poorly paid and usually required at least two trained dogs, and one or two learners.

farms, for which prospective tenants eagerly bid against each other. With the heavy rise in rents, sometimes fourfold, had gone a similar increase in tithes. Thus when the crash came, when wheat fell from 110s. a quarter in 1813 to 66s. in 1815, the farming community found itself saddled with commitments which it could no longer meet, except out of capital of which there was usually very little in liquid form. 'Bankers pressed for their advances,' wrote Lord Ernle, 'landlords for their rents, tithe-owners for their tithe, tax-collectors for their taxes, tradesmen for their bills. Insolvencies, compositions, executions, seizures, arrests and imprisonments for debt multiplied. Farmhouses were full of sheriffs' officers. Many large farmers lost everything, and became applicants for pauper allowances.' Distress so widespread was naturally not confined to the farming community. The shopkeepers in the country towns, the village blacksmiths, wheelwrights, and saddlers, and the many others who depended for their living on the custom of squires, farmers, and labourers, all suffered.

In April 1816 a petition from Cambridgeshire to the Commons mentioned 'that in one parish, every proprietor and tenant being ruined with a single exception, the whole poor-rates of the parish, thus wholly inhabited by paupers, are now paid by an individual whose fortune, once ample, is thus swept entirely away'. Landlords could not reduce rents without defaulting on their commitments, but if the rents were not reduced their tenants went bankrupt. Tenants-at-will walked out, and some of those with long leases absconded or committed suicide.

In many cases landlords were as distressed as their tenants, so that the reduction of rents was not always easy. More often than not the landowner was at his wits' end to meet his engagements, but when he could reduce his rents he usually did so. The 4th Duke of Portland, a progressive agriculturist with a keen sense of the responsibilities attaching to his position, reduced his rents on a sliding scale which was related to the price of wheat. Commendable efforts were made by many other landowners to relieve rural distress. At Ashridge Lord Bridgwater made it a rule never to refuse work to any who applied for it, and at one time he had 800 men in his employ. It was an example which many others followed. Unfortunately the majority of landowners were in no position to increase their commitments, and the lesser ones were often themselves deserving objects of charity.

A Northumbrian squire, John Grey of Dilston, wrote to *The Times* describing the plight of the smaller landowners: 'All landowners are not in the condition of the Dukes of Northumberland and Devonshire, of Lords Grosvenor and Fitzwilliam, or Sir Francis Burdett, men who are beyond the reach of any reduction of rent to affect their credit or comfort. You ought to recollect that there is a large class of landowners of a lower rank . . . more reduced in their relative position in society than any other description of persons that you can name, — possessed of property which, in many instances, they cannot dispose of, and upon which they are mere agents between the tenants whose rents they receive, and the tax-gatherer and mortgagee to whom they are transferred; to say nothing of properties in land in certain situations, the produce of which is nearly absorbed by the poor's rates, yielding hardly any surplus to the possessor. That rents must be still further reduced there is no doubt, any more than there is that many more landed proprietors must be ruined.'

Great tracts of land went out of cultivation — no less than nineteen farms in the Isle of Ely were abandoned. In Norfolk, outside the Holkham estate, land to the value of £1½ m. was placed on the market and found no buyers. Landlords could find no tenants, not even the Duke of Bedford who had done all he could to emulate the example of his friend Coke. Holkham was, as the Duke wrote, 'a splendid exception to the rest of the Kingdom . . . you must derive infinite satisfaction in the reflection that 38 years of persevering and unwearied efforts in promoting a beneficial System of Husbandry, should have created such a mass of Capital among the Tenantry of Norfolk as to enable them to bear up against the evils which are overwhelming every part of the Empire'.

That the Duke should have seen a threat to every part of the Empire in the embarrassments with which he and his brother landlords were faced shows the depth of gloom in which rural England was plunged. That year, 1816, was certainly a very bad one; it was so wet that in October much of the harvest was still ungathered; the potato crop was a failure; sheep died in hundreds of thousands; the floods of an exceptionally wet spring and

summer were followed by an unusually severe winter. Ruin
stared everyone in the face. The succeeding years were not so
bad, but they were not good and it anyway required more than
fair harvests to restore prosperity to English farming. It also
required something more than the succession of ineffective
Select Committees which Parliament appointed to solve the
problem of rural distress. The depression continued, with
slightly fluctuating degrees of acuteness, for twenty more years.
Not till 1836 did prosperity begin to return. Long before those
twenty dreary years had passed the limit of endurance of the
wretched starving labourers had been reached and the country
had witnessed the horrors of one of the blackest chapters in the
history of rural England.

There had been serious rioting in the spring of 1816,
some months before the horrors of that terrible year had
reached their peak. The trouble had been confined to East
Anglia where bands of labourers, sometimes several hundred
strong, took to firing farm houses, barns, and stacks. Under a
banner inscribed 'Bread or Blood', and armed with loaded
staves, they terrorized the countryside, demanding cheaper
bread and meat, and extorting money. In some districts the
rioters had been appeased with higher wages, but for the most
part the rising had been crushed by the full rigour of the law
enforced by ruthless judges. The hanging of five starving rioters
and the transportation or imprisonment of many more had
sufficed to discourage similar outbreaks, but only for a time. By
1830 the effect of the terrible retribution of 1816 had spent itself,
and the long-drawn and seemingly endless years of privation
could no longer be endured. They had robbed death of half its
terrors. The winter of 1829–30 was a severe one and its miseries
determined many of those who could afford it to emigrate.
People were beginning to compare the plight of England with
that of France before the Revolution. Amongst them was
Cobbett who wrote, in April 1830, that one 'respect in which
our situation so exactly resembles that of France on the eve of
the Revolution, is, the *fleeing from the country* in every direction.
When I was in Norfolk, there were four hundred persons,
generally young men, labourers, carpenters, wheelwrights, mill-
wrights, smiths, and bricklayers. . . . These people were going to
Quebec, in timber-ships, and from Quebec, by land, into the

United States. . . . From Boston, two great barge loads had just gone off by canal, to Liverpool, most of them farmers. . . . From the North and West Riding of Yorkshire numerous waggons had gone carrying people to the canals, leading to Liverpool. . . . At Hull . . . ten large ships have gone this spring, laden with these fugitives.'

Another effect of the severe winter was a fresh outbreak of sporadic rioting and incendiarism in the southern counties. Fanned by a miserably wet spring and summer, and bitter resentment at the introduction of the threshing-machine from the North, the smouldering embers of revolt burst suddenly into flame. In August a band of four hundred Kentish labourers started smashing threshing-machines. Their hatred for these machines was not unreasonable. In some villages threshing with the flail was the only work available for labourers during the winter months, and in many more it was the only work that enabled them to earn a little more than the bare minimum essential to survival. To all such men — and they were to be numbered by hundreds of thousands — the threshing-machine spelt despair. Its destruction, therefore, became the first object of the rioters.

As the wet year dragged on and the horrors of another winter drew near, the rioting spread westwards into Dorset, north and east into Northamptonshire, Lincolnshire, and Norfolk. The numerous outbreaks were so much of a pattern that they appeared to law-abiding citizens to be inspired and directed by a single malevolent mind. Colour was lent to this supposition by the smashing of machines and the burning of ricks being often preceded by threatening letters to farmers, concluding with some such phrase as 'Beware of the fatel daggar' and usually signed 'Swing'. Who Swing was, whether he even existed, is still not known. The name had sinister implications and its holder was accorded military rank. Captain Swing became a bogey which held half England in terror.

How great this terror was, how aggravated by wild rumours, is graphically described by Mary Mitford:

No one that had the misfortune to reside during the last winter in the disturbed districts of the south of England, will ever forget the awful impression of that terrible time. The stilly gatherings of the mis-

III *Breaking the Ice*: This picture, reproduced by permission of Sheffield Corporation, shows a labourer's cottage of the period. With glazed windows and apparently two rooms, it was superior to the hovels in which many labourers lived.

IV (a) *Pack Horses:* Until far into the nineteenth century pack horses were
still used for the carriage of goods.

IV (b) *A Stage Waggon:* Pack-horse transport was supplemented, on the better
roads, by stage waggons which were required by law to have very broad
wheels.

guided peasantry amongst the wild hills, partly heath and partly woodland, of which so much of the northern part of Hampshire is composed, — dropping in one by one, and two by two, in the gloom of evening, or the dim twilight of a November morning; or the open and noisy meetings of determined men at noontide in the streets and greens of our Berkshire villages, and even sometimes in the very churchyards, sallying forth in small but resolute numbers to collect money or destroy machinery, and compelling or persuading their fellow-labourers to join them at every farm they visited; or the sudden appearance and disappearance of these large bodies, who sometimes remained together to the amount of several hundreds for many days, and sometimes dispersed, one scarcely knew how, in a few hours; their day-light marches on the high road, regular and orderly as those of an army, or their midnight visits to lonely houses, lawless and terrific as the descent of pirates, or the incursions of banditti; — all brought close to us a state of things which we never thought to have witnessed in peaceful and happy England. . . .

Nor were the preparations for defence, however necessary, less shocking than the apprehensions of attack. The hourly visits of bustling parish officers, bristling with importance (for our village, though in the centre of the insurgents, continued uncontaminated — 'faithful amidst the unfaithful found,' — and was, therefore, quite a rallying point for loyal men and true); the swearing in of whole regiments of petty constables; the stationary watchmen, who every hour, to prove their vigilance, sent in some poor wretch, beggar or match-seller, or rambling child, under the denomination of suspicious persons; the mounted patrol, whose deep 'all's well,' which ought to have been consolatory, was about the most alarming of all alarming sounds; the soldiers, transported from place to place in carts, the better to catch the rogues, whose local knowledge gave them great advantage in a dispersal; the grave processions of magistrates and gentlemen on horseback; and, above all, the nightly collecting of arms and armed men within our own dwelling, kept up a continual sense of nervous inquietude.

Fearful, however, as were the realities, the rumours were a hundred-fold more alarming. Not an hour passed but, from some quarter or other, reports came pouring in of mobs gathering, mobs assembled, mobs marching upon us. Now the high roads were blockaded by the rioters, travellers murdered, soldiers defeated, and the magistrates, who had gone out to meet and harangue them, themselves surrounded and taken by the desperate multitude. Now the artizans — the commons so to say, of B. — had risen to join the peasantry, driving out the gentry and tradespeople, while they took

D

possession of their houses and property, and only detaining the mayor and aldermen as hostages. Now that illustrious town held loyal, but was besieged. Now the mob had carried the place; and artizans, constables, tradespeople, soldiers, and magistrates, the mayor and corporation included, were murdered to a man, to say nothing of women and children; the market-place running with blood, and the town hall piled with dead bodies. This last rumour, which was much to the taste of our villagers, actually prevailed for several hours; terrified maid-servants ran shrieking about the house, and every corner of the village street realized Shakespeare's picture of 'a smith swallowing a tailor's news'.

So passed the short winter's day. With the approach of night came fresh sorrows; the red glow of fires gleaming on the horizon, and mounting into the middle sky; the tolling of bells; and the rumbling sound of the engines clattering along from place to place, and often, too often, rendered useless by the cutting of the pipes after they had begun to play — a dreadful aggravation of the calamity, since it proved that among those who assembled, professedly to help, were to be found favourers and abettors of the concealed incendiaries. Oh the horrors of those fires — breaking forth night after night, sudden, yet expected, always seeming nearer than they actually were, and always said to have been more mischievous to life and property than they actually had been!

Whoever the directing genius of the revolt may have been, his plans were formidable. 'We will destroy the corn stacks and threshing machines this year,' said one of the rioters, 'next year we will have a turn with the parsons, and the third we will have war upon the statesmen.' Nevertheless, the riots generally were governed by marked restraint, and persons and property (unless it was a rick or a threshing-machine) were seldom in peril. Indeed, the behaviour of the labourers was often remarkable for its moderation and the courtesy — one might almost say consideration — shown to their employers. Moreover, their case was often well-reasoned, and well and respectfully presented. The following is from a letter picked up by chance in a Sussex village:

We would rather appeal to the good sense of the magistracy, instead of inflaming the passions of our fellow labourers, and ask those gentlemen who have done us the favour of meeting us this day whether 7d a day is sufficient for a working man, hale and hearty, to keep up the strength necessary to the execution of the labour he has to do? We ask also, is 9s a week sufficient for a married man with a family, to provide the common necessaries of life? Have we no reason to complain that we have been obliged for so long a period to go to our daily toil with only potatoes in our satchels, and the only beverage to assuage our thirst the cold spring; on retiring to our cottages to be welcomed by the meagre and half-famished offspring of our toilworn bodies? All we ask, then, is that our wages may be advanced to such a degree as will enable us to provide for ourselves and families, without being driven to the overseer.

The parish overseers were specially hated, and particularly the salaried assistant overseers. The administration of parish relief was in the hands of honorary overseers, who were usually shopkeepers or farmers who filled the distasteful office by turn for short periods. The shopkeepers inevitably tended to favour the friends and labourers of their customers, and they were not slow to take advantage of much of the relief being orders for goods on local tradesmen. When a farmer filled the office of overseer he did not always resist the temptation to reduce his wage-bill out of the parish funds. But the injustice and corruption of the overseers was more tolerable to the poor than the treatment they commonly received from the salaried assistant overseers, Jacks-in-office who appear generally to have delighted in humiliating the poor with petty tyrannies. The letter just quoted described them as 'men callous to the ties of nature, lost to every feeling of humanity, and deaf to the voice of reason', which we gather from other sources was an understatement. The most humiliating practice of the assistant overseers, and a common one, was to harness gangs of paupers, sometimes women, to the village dung-cart. The rioters, with a pleasant sense of the appropriate, were much given, on first entering a village, to transport the assistant overseer in his own dung-cart to a neighbouring parish.

The moderation of the rioters, the patent hardness of their lot, and the modesty of their demands — usually for a wage of 2s. 6d. a day and a little ready cash — went far to win them the sympathy of the farmers. There were men among them like, to take an extreme case, a limbless Peninsular veteran who contrasted his 9d. a day with the Duke of Wellington's pension of £60,000 a year and a 'whole skin', whose case could not have failed to move the hardest heart; but there was hardly a man in their ranks who had ever known anything but grinding poverty. The farmers therefore were often ready to grant their demands and, more surprisingly, to agree to the smashing of their threshing-machines.

In agreeing to pay the higher wages demanded by rioters, some farmers were astute enough to add a warning that they would not be able to continue to do so unless rents and tithes were reduced, and in some parishes they made this a condition of the payment of a higher wage. The labourers were not slow to put pressure on the parsons, the tithe owners, and in many cases they were successful. There were parishes in which the farmers took the initiative and suggested to their law-abiding labourers that they might see whether a good fright would not induce the parson to abate his tithe. On one such occasion the labourers attended the parson's tithe audit, begging him 'to throw something off for us and our poor Children'; he did what they asked and, the chronicler records, 'we made our obedience to him and he to us, and we gave him three cheers and went and set the Bells ringing and were all as pleased as could be at what we had done'. All very English and as unlike the French Revolution as could be. Farmers not only added their signatures to the demands on the parsons, but numbers of them even joined the bands of roving law-breakers.

It was one thing to put pressure on the parsons to abate their tithes, but quite another to attempt to frighten the local landowners into reducing their rents. It was from their ranks that the magistrates were drawn, and as magistrates, on whom the government was now laying great pressure to be tough with the rioters, it was their duty to repress law-breakers, no matter how much they might sympathize with them. But the magistrates were finding it very difficult to carry out their duty. They could not induce the farmers, even when they were their own tenants, to join the yeomanry, and the tradespeople were too much in sympathy with the labourers, whose bands many of them joined, to enrol in the constabulary. To add to the magistrates' cares, their clamorous demands for help from the army were usually rejected because there were not enough troops in the country. Faced with a rising tide of rebellion, and no means to quell it, the landowners became seriously alarmed, and their fears quickly spread.

In Mrs. Arbuthnot's journal we see reflected the generally complacent attitude of the Duke and his Tory government to the increasing unrest. In March 1830 she wrote: 'It is all nonsense taking off taxes. The country is rolling in wealth & there is not a tradesman now who does not live as luxuriously now as the country squires of 4 or 5,000 a year did formerly.' At the end of the month she said there was less and less talk of distress and 'I really believe there is as little now as there ever can be in such a country as this'. By the end of October the unrest was 'but a mere imitation of France & Belgium &, as the circumstances are entirely different, so will the result be'. Not till a month later, a few days after the Duke had resigned, did Mrs. Arbuthnot show any real concern: 'The country is in a terrible state, thanks to people who have been lauding the French revolution up to the skies and dinning into the ears of the people that, if they choose to rise, nothing can resist them. The consequence has been that all over the country the peasantry, who in many parts do really suffer under great privations, have been worked upon by incendiaries & agitators & have burnt rickyards and broke machines to a great extent . . . wherever they have been stoutly resisted, they have shown great cowardice, & nothing is necessary but promptitude & energy in the magistrates to put an end to it.'[1]

But the public were less complacent than the Duke and his friends. In September Emily Eden had written that people were talking of a revolution and what they should do for a livelihood. ('If it comes to that,' said Lord Alvanley, 'I know what I shall do; keep a disorderly house.'). In October Lord Sefton had told Creevey, 'I dont believe there will be a king in Europe in 2 years' time, or that property of any kind is worth 5 years' purchase.' In November, when the Whigs came into power under Lord Grey, the new Chancellor of the Exchequer, Lord Althorp, wrote: 'We begin our administration with the whole of the south of England in a state bordering on insurrection.' In December Greville wrote from Woburn that 'a feverish anxiety about the future universally prevails, for no man can foresee what course events will take, nor how his individual circumstances may be affected by them'.

[1] On 7 December Lord Ellenborough, the son of the Chief Justice, and a member of the Committee on the Poor Laws, recorded in his diary that Bedfordshire and Kent afforded 'a sad picture of the state of the lower orders — but I think an excess of population seems to be the cause'.

Up to the autumn of 1830 conciliation had been reasonably successful. Unfortunately neither the Government nor the general mass of farmers and landowners outside the area of the disturbances had the sense to realize the need to anticipate trouble by voluntary concessions such as the rioters elsewhere were securing by threats and violence. When some far-seeing magistrates recommended a standard wage at a higher rate they were reproved by the new Home Secretary. 'Reason and experience', he wrote, 'concur in proving that a compliance with demands so unreasonable in themselves, and urged in such a manner, can only lead, and probably within a very short period of time, to the most disastrous results.' From the labourers' point of view rioting was paying very good dividends. Rioting consequently spread in an alarming manner. It had to be stopped, but no one was prepared to stop it by voluntary concessions. The only alternative was a stern policy of repression which was now adopted. From this moment bitterness entered into the struggle and tragedy became inevitable.

Despite the slender forces at their disposal, the magistrates took heart and began arresting rioters. Contrary to their expectations there was so little resistance that the prisons were soon overflowing and workhouses were being turned into gaols to hold the hundreds of rioters taken into custody. The effect of this new policy was immediate. The roving bands of machine-breakers and incendiaries quickly melted away, violence ended and, apart from some sporadic arson, there was little serious trouble. By December the disturbances were over, but the tragedy was about to begin.

In *The Village Labourer, 1760–1832*, by J. L. and Barbara Hammond, we have an admirable study of the Swing riots, but marked by a prejudice against landowners almost as bitter as that of William Cobbett. Like him, they lay all the troubles of the country, especially those of 1830, at the door of the squires. Amongst these there were certainly a few like Lord Marney in Disraeli's *Sybil*, who declared that 'a family can live well on seven shillings a-week, and on eight shillings very well indeed. The poor are well off, at least the agricultural poor, very well off indeed. Their incomes are certain, that is a great point, and they have no cares, no anxieties. . . . People without cares do not require so much food as those whose life entails anxieties.'

But, as we have seen, the sympathy of the landowners with the rioters induced so conciliatory an attitude that they were reproved by the Government and told to desist from appeasement. When called upon to resort to repression they did no more than their duty, and did it very effectively. It is possible that as magistrates some of them preferred to choose for arrest from among the local rioters those who were most obnoxious to them, and these may sometimes have been poachers. But the magistrates had little part in the terrible retribution that followed, and which forms the blackest chapter in the sad story of the Swing riots.

The chapter opened on 2 December when, with hundreds of prisoners awaiting trial, Brougham told the House of Lords, 'Within a few days from the time I am addressing your Lordships, the sword of justice shall be unsheathed to smite, if it be necessary, with a firm and vigorous hand, the rebel against the law.' The Government had of course had a bad fright and so seemingly had the judges if we may be guided by their charges to the Grand Juries now assembling in the assize towns. The general tenor of their addresses was a caution against exaggerating such distress as there might be in the country, which they seemed not to think very great.

The plight of the prisoners was grievous. Mostly labourers, nearly all were poor and illiterate, and very few could afford counsel. They were so completely ignorant of the law that many of them believed that the King or the Government had ordered the threshing-machines to be broken. The only witnesses they could call had themselves been rioters and could not give evidence without risk of prosecution. On the other side, heavy bribes were offered to prisoners to give evidence against their fellows. Hanging over their heads were the penalties prescribed in an Act of 1827 — for destroying a threshing-machine transportation for seven years, and for firing a rick it was death.

The Special Commissions appointed by the Government to try the rioters approached their task in the spirit of Brougham's announcement to the Lords. From the start the scales of justice were loaded against the prisoners. Extenuating circumstances were treated as irrelevant, and evidence about distress and wages was ruled out so far as possible. At Winchester Mr. Justice Alderson told the jury, 'We do not come here to inquire into grievances. We come here to decide law.' When in the same court a witness said of the labourers: 'The men were in very great distress; many of the men had only a few potatoes in their bag when they came to work', the judges objected to the continuance of this course of examination because 'it might happen that through drinking a man might suffer distress'. It is not surprising to learn that judges such as these found the sympathy of the juries for the prisoners an embarrassment. At Winchester, a jury known to be reluctant to convict prisoners driven to law-breaking by distress was discharged by the presiding judge, and another empanelled.

The Special Commission at Winchester convicted capitally 101 prisoners, of whom six were to be hanged; nearly all the rest were transported for life. The public were aghast and the people of Winchester were harrowed by the appalling distress which now surrounded them. 'The scenes of distress in and about the jail are most terrible', wrote *The Times* correspondent from Winchester on 7 January. 'The number of men who are to be torn from their homes and connexions is so great that there is scarcely a hamlet in the county into which anguish and tribulation have not entered. Wives, sisters, mothers, children, beset the gates daily, and the governor of the jail informs me that the scenes he is obliged to witness at the time of locking up the prison are truly heart-breaking.' Public indignation saved the lives of four of the men sentenced to be hanged.

The second Special Commission sat at Salisbury where the trials were of the same pattern as those at Winchester, and Mr. Justice Alderson was again one of the judges. Two men were sentenced to death, 154 men and boys to transportation — some for life and others for seven or fourteen years. For most prisoners there was little difference between transportation for life and transportation for a term of years, because when a convict had served his sentence he could only return to England if he had enough money to pay for his passage. 'You will leave the country, all of you: you will see your friends and relations no more,' Mr. Justice Alderson told the prisoners, 'for though you will be transported for seven years only, it is not likely that at the expiration of that term you will find yourselves in a situation to return. You will be in a distant land at the expiration of your sentence. The Land which you have disgraced will see you no more; the friends with whom you are connected will be parted from you for ever in this world.' The conclusion of the trials at Salisbury was followed by scenes as heart-rending as those at Winchester.

Trials by Special Commissions followed at Dorchester, Reading, Abingdon, and Aylesbury, but with an increasing tendency towards less severe sentences. According to the Government, the Winchester and Salisbury trials had sufficed to produce the effect they desired. 'The state of things is quite altered; great effect has been produced: the law has been clearly explained.' Both Government and judges saw that the limit of what public opinion would tolerate was drawing very near.

In the course of the disturbances the rioters had neither killed nor seriously injured anyone. Yet justice had exacted nine lives of men or boys, the transportation of 457 more, and the imprisonment at home of about 400 others.

'After the law had been thus vindicated,' wrote W. H. Hudson, of his native Wiltshire, '. . . it was generally agreed to raise the wages one shilling. But by and by when the anxiety had died out, when it was found that the men were more submissive than they had ever been . . . they cut off the extra shilling, and wages were what they had been — seven shillings a week for a hard-working seasoned labourer with a family to keep. . . . But there were no more risings.'

IV

Pikeman and Packman

THE twenty years following the battle of Waterloo, for all their misery, were not a period of unrelieved gloom and stagnation. Outside the more remote and isolated villages social life was changing for the better, and Englishmen were leading, in many respects, increasingly easier and fuller lives. This was mainly due to improvements in communications which had been gradually growing since the middle of the previous century.

So durable were the wonderful roads which the Romans had given the country that they had remained England's main thoroughfares until the end of the Middle Ages. But, the science of road-making having left the country with the Romans, there had been few attempts to preserve, still less to extend, the roads they had made. When at long last these roads fell into decay from sheer neglect England became virtually roadless, and so remained till late in the eighteenth century.

In 1770 Arthur Young cautioned travellers to avoid the Preston to Wigan road 'as they would the devil; for a thousand to one but they break their necks or their limbs, by overthrows or breakings down'. He thought equally badly of the road running south from Newcastle: 'A more dreadful road cannot be imagined. I was obliged to hire two men at one place to support my chaise from overturning. Let me persuade all travellers to avoid this terrible country, which must either dislocate their bones with broken pavements or bury them in muddy sand.' At the end of the century the Devonshire roads were still so bad that packhorses were the sole means of transport for goods; only recently had they completely superseded the still more primitive sledge. Elsewhere, in Staffordshire, we hear of waggons being taken off their wheels and dragged like sledges over the morass. Essex was notorious for its bad roads. 'Of all the cursed roads that ever disgraced this kingdom,' wrote Young, 'none ever equalled that from Billericay to ... Tilbury.' Highwaymen were a comparatively minor hazard of travel in the eighteenth century.

In many parts of the country the effect of enclosure had been to make the roads worse. Before enclosure they had been unfenced tracks along which the public enjoyed both a right of way and a right of deviation. If a road became founderous travellers and drovers could deviate from the customary track on to the adjoining land, even if it were under crops. Enclosure led to the roads being confined between quick-set hedges or stone walls with the inevitable result that many of them became bottomless morasses throughout the greater part of the year, and apt to be blocked by foundered waggons. We hear of roads so narrow that 'a mouse could barely pass a carriage', and of thirty or forty horses being required to extricate a single waggon. The purpose of the old-fashioned bells on draft-horses was to warn approaching vehicles not to enter a narrow or boggy bit of road.

Although wheeled traffic was becoming more common the greater part of the carrying trade of the country was done with packhorses. These carried packs or panniers, or, in the West Country, crooks. 'There was great skill required in packing,' wrote Baring-Gould, 'the pack-horse had crooks on its back, and the goods were hung to these crooks. The crooks were formed of two poles, about ten feet long, bent when green into the required curve, and when dried in that shape were connected by horizontal bars. A pair of crooks, thus completed, were slung over the pack-saddle, one swinging on each side, to make the balance true. The short crooks, called *crubs*, were slung in a similar manner. These were of stouter fabric, and formed an angle; these were used for carrying heavy materials.'

To meet the needs of packhorses there was often in the middle of the road, or at its side, a narrow causeway, four feet wide, covered with flags or stones, to provide sound footing for trains of packhorses travelling head to tail. Like the waggon teams, the packhorses carried bells to give warning of their approach. When two pack trains, sometimes numbering up to 40 horses, met, one had to get off the causeway into the morass at its side and often had great difficulty in getting back. In the Midlands these horse paths, or bridle paths, were less common. Josiah Wedgwood recalled packhorses and asses laden with coal, tubs full of ground flint from the mills, crates of ware, panniers of clay, 'hacked to pieces by the whip of their cruel drivers, whilst floundering knee-deep through muddy holes'. But given metalled horse paths, proper care and a good staging system, packhorse transport could be surprisingly fast. In 1710 the enterprising fishermen of Folkestone began supplying London with fish carried on galloping packhorses, travelling night and day, and very soon 320 fish-laden horses (one fisherman to eight horses) were galloping through Tonbridge daily. So successful were the Folkestone men that the rest of the south-coast fishermen were soon following their example. By 1740 Berwick had established a similar service to carry salmon to Billingsgate, and eight years later Carlisle and Workington were sending fish, 'fresh as they take them, up to London upon horses, which, changing often, go night and day without intermission, and as they say, outgo the post; so that the fish come very sweet and good to London'.

The badness of the roads contributed to the backwardness of English agriculture by making access to markets often difficult. For the most part farmers had to content themselves with producing only enough corn to satisfy local needs. Consequently there were wide local variations in the price of corn, and in the event of a bad harvest there was sometimes a real danger of famine in the more inaccessible villages. Stock breeders sometimes suffered heavy losses through being forced to sell their cattle and sheep on the road at knockout prices through inability to reach London or some other important market.

The principal reason for the badness of the roads was lack of a road authority. The duty of maintaining a highway — which amounted to no more than removing obstacles and filling in ruts and holes with faggots and unbroken stones — fell on the parishes through which it passed. Every parishioner was required by law to do six days unpaid work annually on the roads under the direction of the parish surveyor, a hateful office filled in turns by reluctant local farmers. The resentment which this *corvée* — for it was nothing else — aroused was aggravated by the apparent injustice of local people having to make good damage done by through-traffic from distant towns. It is hardly surprising that the modest amount of work the law demanded for the highway often remained undone. And where a conscientious surveyor saw that it was done, usually with pauper labour, it was still hopelessly inadequate.

Matters began to improve in the middle of the eighteenth century when turnpike trusts started to come into fashion. The turnpike system dated back to the reign of Charles II when money was first raised for the upkeep of highways by levying tolls at bars or pikes placed across the road on posts. When the system was revived in the eighteenth century toll-gates took the place of the old turnpike, and at each gate a toll-house was built for the pikeman who collected the tolls from the users of the highway. The system was operated by highway or turnpike trusts with statutory powers granted by Act of Parliament. To begin with the trusts were not very effective, partly because of their ignorance of how to mend a road and partly owing to the corruption of both trustees and their officers, but they improved with experience. At its best the turnpike system was no more than a palliative because it was not universal, even on the main thoroughfares. Where there was no turnpike trust the maintenance of the highway remained in the hands of the usually incompetent parish surveyors. A few miles of sound turnpike might be followed by fifty or more of parish roads at their worst. Readers of *Mr. Sponge* may recall Jack Spraggon's journey to Jawleyford Court. 'The route was not along one continuous trust, but here over a bit of turnpike and there over a bit of turnpike, with ever and anon long interregnums of township roads, repaired in the usual primitive style with mud and soft field-stones, that turned up like flitches of bacon.' Bad though the road was, it was far better than 'the deeply-spurlingered clayey-bottomed cross-road' or by-road, as we should call it, leading to Jawleyford Court.

Although pedestrians and local farm traffic, and waggons carrying certain agricultural requirements, were allowed to use the turnpike road toll-free, there was usually great opposition to the establishment of a new turnpike trust. People wanted better roads but did not want to pay for them. Some thought that bad roads best served their interests. Among these were landowners and farmers who happened to be well-placed for a favourable market which they wished to remain inaccessible to those less fortunate than themselves. Drovers hated turnpikes because hard roads injured animals' feet.

Most landowners appear to have been opposed to better roads because they brought more traffic, more poaching, more disturbance of game and, above all, 'foreign' ways. 'I wish with all my heart', wrote John Byng in 1781, 'that half the turnpike roads of the kingdom were plough'd up, which have imported London manners, and depopulated the country. — I meet milkmaids on the road, with the looks of strand misses; and must think that every line of Goldsmith's Deserted Village contains melancholy truths.' A little later he lamented the passing of the days 'before the baneful luxury of turnpikes was very public: when the horseman travelled in quiet and cheapness in countries fill'd with game, and timber, and when he met with civility, honesty and good cheer'.

But although a new toll-gate was sometimes pulled down, the toll-house burnt, and the pikeman put in fear of his life, the superiority of turnpike roads soon won over public opinion. During the last forty years of the eighteenth century Parliament passed about 1,100 Turnpike Acts. But the tolls were not light, and they varied from one turnpike road to another as did the powers of the highway trusts, each of which operated under its own Act of Parliament. Most of them found difficulty in making both ends meet, and the farming out of tolls — selling them by auction to the highest bidder — became usual. The tendency therefore was for tolls to rise. The tolls charged by the well-known Epping and Ongar Highway Trust in 1815 and 1822 may be taken as a general indication of what it cost the public to use a turnpike road; these are a few taken from the two schedules:

	1815		1822	
	s.	d.	s.	d.
Every one horse chaise or carriage	0	6	0	6
Every carriage drawn by four horses or beasts of draught	1	0	2	0
Every waggon or wain drawn by six horses	2	0	3	0
Every horse, mule or ass, laden or unladen	0	1	0	2
Neat cattle, by the score	0	10	2	6
Sheep and hogs, by the score	0	5	1	0

The responsibilities of users of turnpikes did not begin and end with the payment of tolls. There were numerous regulations which had to be observed at the risk of fines. On many roads, where there was a narrow causeway of stones to give footing to horses, it was forbidden to harness two horses abreast for fear of 'destroying the horse path'. Many trusts forbade the use of wheels with fellies of less than three inches in width and charged double tolls for wheels of less than six inches. The minute book of the Epping and Ongar Highway Trust records in 1802 that 'The owners of the waggon with narrow wheels drawn by two horses abreast on the turnpike road . . . were fined five shillings on their promising not to offend again.'

The turnpike trusts naturally sought to protect themselves against the damage to their roads by heavy vehicles with narrow wheels, but unfortunately wheels suitable for the metalled highway were not suitable for the miry by-roads and farm tracks. This conflict of interests caused an infinity of trouble which came to a head with the passing of the General Highway Act of 1822. This Act defined in meticulous detail what wheels might be used on a turnpike. For example, if they were six inches in width, the diameters at the inner and outer edges were not to differ by more than half an inch. But waggons and carts with wheels of less than three inches were forbidden altogether. There was much in the new Act to infuriate Cobbett, especially a clause making waggons carrying chalk and lime liable to turnpike duty. 'This is a monstrous oppression upon the owners and occupiers of clay lands', he wrote. 'But, it is the provision with regard to the *wheels* which will create the greatest injury, distress and confusion. The wheels which the law orders to be used on the turnpike roads, on pain of enormous toll, cannot be used on the *cross-roads*. . . . To make these roads and the *drove-lanes* (the private roads to farms) fit for the cylindrical wheels described in this Bill, would cost a pound an acre, upon an average, upon all the land in England.'

Turnpikes were also unpopular because of the uncertainty in the incidence of tolls. When a trust, or the farmer of its tolls, ran into difficulties it could either increase its tolls or, what was much more unpopular, increase the number of its toll-gates.[1]

---

[1] Sometimes double tolls were charged on Sundays. On the other hand, we read in the records of the Epping and Ongar Highway Trust that 'the inhabitants of Thornwood hamlet should not be asked for tolls when going to church'.

On one turnpike road one might have to pay one toll in twenty miles, but on another five or more over the same distance.[1] To the expense of multiplied toll-gates was added the annoyance of irritating delays at each of them, especially at night when, to quote Dickens, there was 'the stopping at the turnpike where the man was gone to bed, and knocking at the door until he answered with a smothered shout from under the bedclothes in the little room above, where the faint light was burning, and presently came down, night-capped and shivering, to throw the gate wide open, and wish all wagons off the road except by day.' How infuriating rustic pikemen could be even by day was well described by Surtees: 'First, Pikey had to find his glasses, as he called his spectacles, to look out a one-horse-chaise ticket . . . when he found he had all sorts except a one-horse-chaise one ready — waggons, hearses, mourning-coaches, saddle-horses, chaises and pair, mules, asses, every sort but the one that was wanted. Well, then he had to fill one up, and to do this he had, first, to find the ink-horn, and then the pen that would "mark" so that, altogether, a delay took place that would have been peculiarly edifying to a Kennington Common or Lambeth gate-keeper to witness.'

Heavy penalties attached to the evasion of tolls, but there were a great many people like Hazey in *Facey Romford* 'who never disturbed a pikeman, if he could help it'. Indeed, the avoidance of tolls[2] was easy enough to anyone on a horse, far easier than it would be today, because a horse could push through most of the new enclosure hedges. 'Of these 13 miles [from Winchester to Whitchurch],' wrote Cobbett, 'we rode about eight or nine upon the *greensward*, or over fields equally smooth. And, here is one great pleasure of living in countries of this sort: no sloughs, no ditches, no nasty dirty lanes, and the hedges, where there are any, are more for boundary marks than for fences.'

---

[1] London was naturally hedged with toll-gates. Travelling westwards along Piccadilly the first gate was at Hyde Park Corner, opposite Apsley House; there was another close to where the Marble Arch now stands.

[2] Under one local Turnpike Act of 1836 carts drawn by dogs or goats became subject to a toll of a halfpenny for each animal. As the relevant clause begins: 'Whereas it has of late become a practise for low carts drawn by a dog or dogs . . . to pass and repass along the said road', it looks very much as though dogs and goats were being used in place of horses in order to avoid the payment of tolls. The use of dogs as draught animals did not become illegal till 1854.

The turnpikes, like the railways of later days, left the greater
part of rural England untouched. As late as 1838, when there
were nearly 8,000 toll-gates and 20,000 pikemen, only 17 per
cent. of the English roads were turnpiked. 'Those that travel on
turnpike roads', wrote Cobbett in 1825, 'know nothing of
England'; and in the same year, 'In any sort of carriage, you
cannot get into the *real country places*'. The by-roads, which were
the only roads known to most country people, were still in the
uncertain care of the parish surveyors and consequently, close
to towns and villages, impassable throughout a great part of the
year. But out in the open country they were mostly the drove
roads or green lanes so many of which, happily for us, still
survive. Those were the roads, or tracks, which drovers still
used so far as they could, but which Surtees, as late as 1844,
considered already all too rare. 'It was a real green lane', he
wrote in *Hillingdon Hall*. 'Scarce a cart-rut broke its even surface, and its verdure was kept so close nipped by cattle. . . .
It was one of those continuous lines of by-roads frequented
by cattle-drovers. The woodbine-entwined and rose-bending
bushes of the high hedges in the narrow parts formed a cool
shade, while broader places, widening into patches of common
towards the hill-tops (over which these roads always pass),
furnished cheap pasture for the loitering cattle.' As Mr.
Jorrocks, in his old age, made his way down this green lane, 'he
encountered a large drove of Scotch kyloes, picking their way as
they went. There might be fifty or sixty of them, duns, browns,
mottles, reds, and blacks, with wildness depicted in the prominent eyes of their broad faces.' To Mary Mitford we owe
another pleasant glimpse of life on a drove road. 'That apparently lonely and trackless common is the very high road of the
drovers who come from different points of the west to the great
mart, London. Seldom would that green be found without a
flock of Welch sheep, footsore and weary, and yet tempted into
grazing by the short fine grass dispersed over its surface, or a
drove of gaunt Irish pigs, sleeping in a corner, or a score of
Devonshire cows straggling in all directions, picking the long
grass from the surrounding ditches; whilst dog and man, shepherd and drover, might be seen basking in the sun.'

The economic importance of these drove roads, scoring all
England, was immense, for they were the channels by which

E

London's teeming population was kept supplied with meat. From every point of the compass droves of cattle were constantly on passage, converging on the capital. On his travels John Byng encountered 'vast droves' passing through Horsebridge on their way from the Sussex marshes to London; in Yorkshire, between Askrigg and Ingleborough, he came to an inn 'call'd Grierstones, the seat of misery' where there was a Scotch fair, 'the ground in front crowded by Scotch cattle and drovers; and the house cramm'd by the buyers and sellers, most of whom were in plaids, fillibegs, &c.' A day later, at Buckfast, he found 'vast droves of Scottish cattle passing South'; in North Wales, near Bala, he met a man who told him: 'I am a trover; I trives up cattle to Barnet Vair: — I knows Englant, and have been jolly with my friends in Lonton.' There was also, every autumn, throughout England a steady movement of horned cattle towards the east for fattening. For some reason, which seems never to have been explained, the stall-feeding of cattle was at this time confined to the east coast, from as far north as Northumberland all the way down to Essex. But London was the ultimate destination of most of these cattle.

Nothing contributed more to the shocking state of the roads around London than the enormous quantity of livestock required to feed its population. At the end of the eighteenth century a hundred thousand head of cattle and three-quarters of a million sheep were slaughtered annually in Smithfield market.[1] When one recalls that these hundreds of thousands of livestock, all travelling on the hoof, formed but a small part of the traffic pouring into the capital, it is not surprising to read of Kensington Palace being cut off from Westminster by 'an impassable gulf of mud'. As late as 1819 mail and stage coach proprietors found they needed ten horses near London to do the work of eight in the provinces.

The improvement in the roads, for which the turnpike trusts were largely responsible, had made wheeled transport very much more common throughout England. But of necessity it was still largely confined to the turnpike roads. Many of the small country towns and villages, what Cobbett called 'real country places', could not be reached in any sort of carriage: in all such

---

[1] The price of mutton in London depended on the state of the roads, and in winter it was often unobtainable because the going was too deep for sheep to travel.

districts, and they comprised the greater part of England, wayfarers of every class rode on horseback, the women being on pillions.[1] Similarly the carriage of goods — whether farm produce, hardware or other household goods — was done entirely by packhorses as it always had been. This was why all down the ages the village had been, in the main, a self-supporting unit, growing its own food, brewing its own beer, weaving its own cloth and making its own clothes.

In the country the impediments to travel made all forms of trading very difficult, whether to sell surplus produce or to buy household goods. So the traders, both buyers and sellers, had to go to the people. This was the origin of the great annual fairs, which, whether at Beaucaire on the Rhône or Stourbridge on the Cam, had to be easily accessible, preferably by water. Stourbridge Fair, held annually for three weeks in September on the outskirts of Cambridge, was the greatest of the English fairs. Defoe's description of it in 1724 differs very little from that of Henry Gunning in 1789. It was subject to a curious custom: it was held in a large cornfield, doubtless an unenclosed common field, and, Defoe tells us, 'if the Husbandmen who rent the Land, do not get their corn off before a certain day in August, the fair-keepers may trample it under foot, and spoil it, to build their booths; on the other hand, to balance that severity, if the fair-keepers have not done their business of the fair and removed and cleared the field by another certain day in September, the ploughman may come in again, with plough and cart, and overthrow all and trample it into the dirt; and as for the filth, dung, straw, etc., necessarily left by the fair-keepers, the quantity of which is very great, it is the farmers' fees, and makes them full amends for the trampling, riding and carting upon, and hardening the ground.'

Like all the great fairs, Stourbridge was the meeting place for merchants from all over the kingdom wanting to do business in the goods, notably cheese and hops, for which it was especially noted. It was also the meeting place of the local country people

[1] The leather belt customarily worn by a liveried groom on horseback is, a survival of the strap which the lady held when riding on a pillion, clad in her joseph, a long riding cloak. 'Some women, I grant,' wrote George Eliot in *Silas Marner*, 'would not appear to advantage seated on a pillion, and attired in a drab joseph and a drab beaver-bonnet, with a crown resembling a small stew-pan. . . . It was all the greater triumph to Miss Nancy Lammeter's beauty that she looked thoroughly bewitching in that costume.'

who flocked there to buy, if they could afford it, their stores for
the year and to enjoy the fun of the popular entertainments
which then were an essential, albeit a minor, feature of every
fair, but which today are all that survive of most fairs.[1]

Stourbridge, Gunning tells us, 'was the great mart at which all
the dealers in cheese from Cottenham, Willingham, with other
villages in the county and isle assembled; there were also traders
from Leicestershire, Derbyshire, Cheshire, and Gloucestershire.
Not only did the inhabitants of the neighbouring counties
supply themselves with their annual stock of cheese, but great
quantities were brought and sent up to London. . . . There were
about a dozen booths, called "Ironmongers Row": these, among
a great variety of other articles, furnished the goods required by
saddlers and harness-makers, together with every description of
leather in great abundance. . . . Another row of booths . . . was
called "The Duddery". These contained woollen cloths from
Yorkshire and the western counties of England.[2] A large area
was set aside for hops, a smaller one for earthenware and china,
another for the silkmercers, linendrapers, furriers, stationers, an
immense variety of toys, and also of musical instruments. . . .
The most conspicuous person in the fair . . . came from Lime-
house, and dealt in tea, sugar, soap, candles, and every other
article in grocery that housekeepers could possibly require. His
goods were of the finest quality . . . so that any family in Cambridge, or within thirty miles of it, (who could afford the money),
laid in their annual stock at that season. He was also an extensive dealer in pickles.' He was also the father of a lovely daughter
known to the University as 'Miss Gherkin' until, alas, she lost
her figure and became 'Miss Mango'. Gunning continues:
'Besides the tradesmen, there was the usual mixture of dwarfs
and giants, conjurers and learned pigs. . . . There were a great
number of drinking-booths. One on a very large scale. . . .
In this booth (if the weather was fine) men from the country,
with their wives and families, used to feast on geese, pork, and
herrings.' Finally there was a theatre which produced Shake-

[1] Harlow Bush Fair, noted as a market for horses and cattle, was, under the terms
of its ancient charter, purely a business fair; but the pursuit of pleasure had always
been an essential part of it. When, in 1879, the fair was officially abolished, only
the business fair came to an end; the pleasure fair continued well into the present
century. Probably many surviving pleasure fairs have a similar history.

[2] In Defoe's day the goods Manchester contributed to the Duddery amounted
to 'near a thousand horse-packs'.

spearian and other plays for crowded houses throughout the three
weeks the fair lasted, and, incidentally, thus provided the University with the only opportunity it then had to see a stage play.

Lesser fairs, many of purely local interest, were held throughout the country, so that there were few country people who were
not able to attend at least one fair a year. To the well-to-do they
provided an opportunity to buy all they needed for the year
over and above what was produced locally. To the poor their
only attraction was 'the fun of the fair', and for many the
greatest day of the year was their annual visit to the local
fair. It began, to quote Mary Mitford, with the excitement
of joining the throng on the turnpike. 'Carts crammed as full as
they could be stowed, gigs with one, two, three, and four inside
passengers; waggons laden with men instead of corn; droves of
pigs; flocks of sheep; herds of cattle; strings of horses; with their
several drovers . . . all bound to the fair. Here an Italian boy
with his tray of images; there a Savoyard with her hurdy-
gurdy; and lastly, struggling through the midst of the throng,
that painful minister of pleasure, an itinerant shewman, with
his box of puppets and his tawdry wife. . . . No end to the people!
no end to the din! The turnpike-man opened his gate and shut
his ears in despairing resignation.' Arrived at the fair-ground
the yokel forgot his troubles 'in the solid luxuries of tarts and
gingerbread; in the pleasant business of purchasing and receiving petty presents'. When evening came he was 'still untired
of stuffing and staring . . . he had seen well nigh all the sights
of the fair; — the tall man, and the short woman, and the calf
with two heads . . . the dancing dogs and two raree-shows;
and lastly, had visited and admired the wonders of the
menagerie.'

The labourer's modest needs in 'foreign' goods — what his
village did not produce — could not be bought at the fair
because he had not the money. They were supplied by the
packman or pedlar who, with his train of packhorses, visited the
village about twice a year. The packman's arrival caused a
flutter of excitement in every village he visited, not so much for
the goods he carried as for the news he brought of the outside
world. We have a delightful contemporary description of these
itinerant traders by W. B. Donne which will stand quotation
at length. Deploring their passing during his lifetime he wrote:

Pedlars and packhorses were a necessary accompaniment of bad and narrow roads. The latter have long disappeared from our highways; the former linger in less-frequented districts of the country, but miserably shorn of their former importance. A licensed hawker is now a very unromantic personage. His comings and goings attract no more attention among rustics or at the squire's hall than the passing by of a plough or a sheep. The fixed shop has deprived him of his utility, and daily newspapers of his attractions. He is content to sell his waistcoat or handkerchief pieces; but he is no longer the oracle of the village inn or the housekeeper's room. In the days however when neither draper's nor haberdasher's wares could be purchased without taking a day's journey at the least through miry ways to some considerable market-town, the pedlar was the merchant and newsman of the neighbourhood. He was as loquacious as a barber. He was nearly as ubiquitous as the Wandering Jew. He had his winter circuit and his summer circuit. He was as regular in the delivery of news as the postman; nay, he often forestalled that government official in bringing down the latest intelligence of a landing on the French coast; of an execution at Tyburn; of a meteor in the sky; of a strike at Spitalfields; and of prices in the London markets. He was a favourite with the village crones, for he brought down with him the latest medicines for ague, rheumatism, and the evil. He wrote love-letters for the village beauties. He instructed alehouse politicians in the last speech of Bolingbroke, Walpole, or Pitt. His tea, which often had paid no duty, emitted a savour and fragrance unknown to the dried sloe-leaves vended by ordinary grocers. He was the milliner of rural belles. He was the purveyor for village songsters, having ever in his pack the most modern and captivating lace and ribbons, and the newest song and madrigal. He was competent by his experience to advise in the adjustment of top-knots and farthingales, and to show rustic beaux the last cock of the hat and the most approved method of wielding a cane.

Small wonder that Wordsworth made the packman the hero of his *Excursion*. Readers of Surtees may recall that Pickering Nook, 'one of the quietest places in the kingdom', depended on an occasional pedlar for the latest London fashions.

The survival of the packman depended on the continuance of bad roads. As they improved a new feature crept into village life which cut seriously into the packman's trade. This was the village shop which was unknown to most villages until the end of the eighteenth century. So long as communications were so bad that a village shop could not replenish its shelves from a local town at frequent intervals it could hardly survive, for few shopkeepers had enough capital to stock up for months ahead. When better roads made the country town accessible the village shop became practicable. It derived added encouragement from both industrialization and enclosure. The former drove industry from the villages and made them less self-supporting; the latter killed the small holders who, unlike large farmers, carried on a retail trade in butter, milk, and eggs with their fellow villagers. But, like most new things, the village shop was abhorred by Cobbett. '*Shops* have devoured *markets and fairs*,' he wrote, 'and this, too, to the infinite injury of the most numerous classes of the people. Shop-keeping, merely as shop-keeping, is injurious to any community. What are the shop and the shop-keeper for? To receive and distribute the produce of the land. There are other articles, certainly, but the main part is the produce of the land. The shop must be paid for; the shop-keeper must be kept; and the one must be paid for and the other must be kept by the consumer of the produce. . . . When fairs were frequent, shops were not needed.'

Despite Cobbett the village shop not only survived but became one of the most valued features of country life. Nor has it greatly changed. The shop of his and Mary Mitford's day was very like that of ours. Here is her description of one in Berkshire early in the nineteenth century. 'At one end of the cluster of cottages . . . stood the shop of Judith Kent, widow, "Licensed" — as the legend imported, "to vend tea, coffee, tobacco and snuff". Tea, coffee, tobacco, and snuff formed, however, but a small part of the multifarious merchandise of Mrs. Kent; whose shop . . . might have seemed an epitome of the wants and luxuries of humble life. In her window, candles, bacon, sugar, mustard, and soap, flourished amidst calicoes, oranges, dolls, ribbons, and gingerbread. Crockery ware was piled on one side of her door-way. Dutch cheese and Irish butter encumbered the other; brooms and brushes rested against the wall; and ropes of onions and bunches of red herrings hung from the ceiling. She sold bread, butcher's meat, and garden-stuff, on commission; and engrossed, at a word, the whole trade of Hilton Cross.'

Both before and after the coming of village shops, rural trade depended a great deal on the services of the bagmen, who were to be found in every roadside inn. 'As posterity may be ignorant of what a bag-man is,' wrote John Byng with remarkable prescience, 'let them learn that he is a rider, who travels, with saddle bags, to receive of shop keepers a list of what goods are wanting from manufactories, and wholesale dealers; and to collect the debts.' As industry became concentrated in manufacturing towns the bagman became a vital link between the country towns and villages and their sources of supply.

An important event in the history of English communications was the opening of James Brindley's Manchester–Worsley canal in 1761. It inaugurated the canal era from which, for a short period, immense benefits flowed. The development of inland navigation, primarily designed for the carriage of coal, helped considerably to ease the fuel problem of the towns and villages through which the new waterways passed. But in the absence of efficient ancillary transport services the canals had little impact on the ordinary country village. The value of inland navigation was industrial rather than domestic.

V

The Squires

In the eighteenth century the squires, as we may conveniently call the landed gentry (whether great or small, peers or commoners), were still in full enjoyment of a monopoly of power and wealth. Parliament was composed almost entirely of themselves or their nominees, often in virtue of their position as borough-mongers; in the country where, as Justices of the Peace, they performed all the functions of local government as well as most of those of the judicature, they were politically and of course socially supreme. Moreover, in an age when the less fortunate classes still meekly accepted their lot in life, however hard, as part of the order of things, to question which (their clergy told them) was impious, there was none to challenge the squires' monopoly of power and few to question it. Not many would have dared to echo the words of the postillion in *Lavengro*: 'If he had had borough interest, he wouldn't have been poor, nor honourable, though perhaps a right honourable.' Indeed, the economy of the country being based on agriculture from which the landed gentry derived their wealth, who better than they to control the destinies of the country? What was to their interest was to the interest of everyone else.

At the end of the century the squires were still omnipotent, but their monopoly of wealth and power was being challenged by forces which were destined ultimately to prevail and change the whole pattern of political and social life. These were the Industrial Revolution, Methodism, and Radicalism.

Pressure of population, scientific invention, and an expanding overseas trade had combined to launch a revolution in industry which was gathering ever-increasing impetus as one new invention led to another. The invention of the steam-engine and the discovery of how to use coal, in place of wood-charcoal, for the smelting of iron had led to the concentration of industry where coal and iron were both readily available, notably in the Midlands and the North. There old towns were becoming cities and new towns were being built. A great urban population was being created, and with it new sources of wealth for people to whom the countryside was no more than the stamping ground of rural squires who unjustly, through Parliament, controlled their destinies, while holding them and their new towns in contempt. Thus, for the first time in its history, was the country divided, as in many respects it still is, between two sharply contrasted social systems, the one patriarchal and rural, and the other democratic and urban, the one wanting dear wheat and able to exact it, the other clamouring for cheap flour but powerless to enforce its demand; the one obstructing the making of canals, new roads, and, later on, the railways, which were so vital to the other; the one, in the main, reactionary, and the other progressive.

Shocking though, as we have seen, were the living conditions of the labouring classes in the country, they were generally far better than those in the new industrial towns. Of the many thousands of farm labourers who had been driven by poverty to seek employment in industry, there were few who did not look back regretfully at their village life which, for all its hardness, was mellowed by blessings they could no longer enjoy. The cottage gardens, the green fields and trees, the games on the village green, the Mayings and the fairs, even the field sports of their betters — coursing and shooting and hunting — had brightened village life in ways which had no counterparts in the new industrial towns. There the employers were mostly men of humble origin who saw no reason, especially in a period of under-employment, to give their 'hands' more than the barest necessities, such as had sufficed for themselves in their childhood, nor to impose on them, and their tiny children, shorter working hours than the minimum essential to survival. The grim pictures we have drawn of contemporary village life pale before the unspeakable horrors of life in the new slums with no sewers but the alley-ways, which were never cleansed, and cloaked in a pall of smoke which the sun never penetrated.

The Industrial Revolution was creating, besides a rich middle class, a discontented proletariat, both of which, before many years had passed, were to challenge the squires' monopoly of wealth and power. The industrial workers did not share the farm labourers' complacent attitude to the hardness of their lot. Both sought solace in drink, but only the townsman sought it also in religion to which the new Methodism pointed the way. In those hard times it was the Methodists, rather than the Church of England, who concerned themselves with the souls of the lowest and most depraved grades of society, who saw what opportunities 'neglected heathendom' offered them. From the middle classes, always the principal stronghold of dissent, Methodism spread downwards to the industrial workers whom it began to educate and teach not to be content with their lot, a dangerous heresy in direct contradiction to the teachings of most country clergy.

The natural consequence of this fostering of discontent by the Methodists was a demand for parliamentary reform, directed towards depriving the squires of their monopoly of political power, from which sprang the Radicals whose idea of parliamentary reform already extended even to universal suffrage. The association between the new rich of the Industrial Revolution, the Methodists, and the Radicals was very close and presented a combination of power wholly opposed to the rule of the squires which time served only to strengthen.

It is not easy to reconcile the opprobrium heaped on the heads of the country gentry (and not only by the townsmen) with their astonishing record of service to the community and the affection in which they were held locally by the rural population. This apparent inconsistency was partly due to their being so extraordinarily diverse. There was no such thing as a typical squire. Our novelists, of course, would have us think otherwise. The tradition of William Fielding's Squire Western and Dr. Johnson's Squire Bluster still lives. Ever since the middle of the eighteenth century readers of fiction have been presented with an endless succession of uncouth, bucolic oafs as fair examples of a country squire. It would seem that the Sir Roger de Coverleys had died with Joseph Addison. This, as we shall see, was far from being the case.

But even today rural England is not without its Westerns and its Blusters. That they were common enough early in the nineteenth century is apparent from the frequency with which they appeared in contemporary fiction. There was Thackeray's Sir Pitt Crawley who was drunk every night, beat his wife, spoke 'in the coarsest and vulgarest Hampshire accent', and, in the words of Becky Sharp, was 'an old, stumpy, short, vulgar, and very dirty man, in old clothes and shabby old gaiters . . . and cooks his own horrid supper in a saucepan'; there was Surtees's Lord Scamperdale, 'stumpy, and clumsy, and ugly', who lived in the steward's room of his mansion on tripe, cow-heel, and beefsteak, and never spent a penny on anyone or anything but foxhunting. Then there was Mrs. Gaskell's Squire Hamley, a half-educated, rough-spoken but not un-pleasing character who, 'by continuing the primitive manners and customs of his forefathers the squires of the eighteenth century, did live more as a yeoman, when such a class existed, than as a squire of this generation'. Such characters, all admir-able material for a novelist, had many counterparts in real life. Both Sir Pitt Crawley and Lord Scamperdale are said to have been modelled on Surtees's neighbour Sir William Chaytor of Witton Castle, of whom history, unfortunately, preserves no portrait. Of a similar type was Sir Tatton Sykes who talked broad Yorkshire and, like Squire Hamley, affected the manners and habits of a yeoman. Much less unattractive and more representative of the lesser squires was the Mr. Hallowes whom Elizabeth Grant met in Nottinghamshire in the eighteen-twenties: 'A regular country squire, fit for a novel — short, chubby, good-looking, shooting, fishing, hunting, hospitable, kindly, a magistrate, and not an ounce of brains!'

Cobbett would have us believe that such men were typical of the landed gentry of those days. History teaches us a very different lesson, especially the history of agriculture. Jethro Tull, the inventor of the corn-drill, Lord Townsend in Norfolk, Lord Ducie in Gloucestershire, Lord Halifax in Berkshire (all of whom did so much to foster and encourage Tull's work), Arthur Young, the greatest and most influential of English writers on agriculture, the incomparable Coke of Norfolk,[1] and Sir John Lawes of Rothamstead, the pioneer of agricultural chemistry, were all sons of squires and all born in the eighteenth

---

[1] Even Cobbett admired Coke, of whom he wrote after a visit to Holkham in 1818: 'Every one made use of the expressions towards him which affectionate children use towards their parents.'

century.¹ The lessons they taught, and especially the example
set by Coke at Holkham, were an inspiration to the rest of the
great landed proprietors of the day. The 5th Duke of Bedford,
Lord Stafford, the 4th Duke of Portland, the 4th Duke of Richmond, Lord Althorp, Lord Rockingham, and Lord Egremont all
devoted themselves to the improvement of their estates and to
bettering the conditions of their tenants and their labourers. Up
and down the country there were lesser men making their
contributions, by study, experiment, and practice, at great
expense in time and money, to bettering the principal industry
of the country. These men, English country squires, led the
world in scientific agriculture.

Let no one suppose, though so many do, that the vulgar and
bucolic John Jorrocks was typical of the masters of foxhounds
of those days. Four of the most famous, whose names will
always live in the history of sport, were men who commanded
respect on grounds other than their services to foxhunting.
John Warde of Squerries, 'the father of fox-hunters', a master of
hounds from 1778 to 1825, was considered a model for all
landowners; the critical Surtees described him as 'the most
perfect example of the old English gentleman'. The equally
famous Ralph Lambton, who hunted his own hounds for thirty-
four years, represented Durham in Parliament for even longer,
and was one of the best loved landowners in the North; Tom
Smith, for many years master of the Craven and the Pytchley,
was a progressive agriculturist and a gifted engineer; Thomas
Assheton Smith, for fifty-nine years a master of hounds, was a
member of Parliament, a man of science, and a good classical
scholar who could quote Horace and Shakespeare at length with
equal facility. Each of these four great masters of hounds, all
dearly loved in their own countryside, would have won
distinction in any field.

The interests of the landed gentry were not confined to
agriculture, foxhunting, and politics, nor their culture to the
reading of Horace and Shakespeare. The Grand Tour on which
the sons of wealthy squires were sent to broaden their minds and

¹ In the same progressive period the vast professional farming community
produced only four men whose names are still remembered in the history of
English agriculture: Robert Bakewell, Charles and Robert Colling, the three
pioneers of scientific stock-breeding, and Joseph Elkington, a pioneer of land
drainage.

study the arts was still in fashion and did much to give the
wealthy a taste for travel and intellectual pursuits. At no period
were England's stately homes more enriched with works of art
and fine books than in the late eighteenth and early nineteenth
centuries. Europe's innumerable Hotel Bristols are a monument to one of the greatest of England's aristocratic dilettantes,
the 4th Earl of Bristol, who spent much of his life, in the late
eighteenth century, searching Europe for works of art for his
stately mansions, of which the most beautiful, Ickworth in
Suffolk, was his own creation. Those were the days when pictures by the great masters, Greek and Roman antiquities, and a
fine library were considered essential to the proper equipment
of a gentleman's home. But there was no doubt much justification for John Byng's acid remark that one of the advantages of
foreign travel was 'to come home with a vamp'd Correggio, and
some shabby marbles, and then neglect the real antiquities, and
old pictures at your family seat!' Byng was probably equally
correct in condemning the *nouveaux riches* for omitting a library
from their pretentious homes. 'Your hasty wealth thinks not of
that.'

But our concern here is with the part the squires played in
country life, especially in relation to their neighbours who
looked up to them as their leaders in all matters of local concern.
That the gentry were deeply conscious of their obligations is
made clear by their readiness to censure those who neglected
them. 'I believe that the first ingredient in the happiness of a
people', declared Lord George Bentinck, 'is that the gentry
should reside on their native soil, and spend their rents among
those from whom they receive them.' Surtees, himself a dutiful
squire, held up 'as a model of his order' the wealthy J. J.
Farquharson of Langton in Dorset: 'He resides nearly the whole
year on his estate, spending his large income in the county
whence he draws it, promoting the amusement of his friends and
neighbours and discharging all the public duties that pertain to
his position.' It was in the same spirit that Assheton Smith, as a
young man, abandoned a brilliant career as a master of hounds
in the Shires to hunt the cold-scenting woodlands of his native
Hampshire.

The most serious charge brought against the many rich men
who left their houses to spend the winter months hunting at

Melton was that they were neglecting their duty to their neighbours. One of the objections raised to the turnpike system was that better roads would lead to landowners spending their money in London instead of where they lived. This is in fact what the new roads did, and consequently, in later years, railways were opposed for the same reason but with far greater vehemence. Howitt, however, who had a greater appreciation of culture than most of the landed gentry, found much to be said in favour of the wealthy spending some of their time in London where they met men of culture who taught them to appreciate art and literature. 'If they spend large sums in splendid houses and establishments in town', he wrote, 'such houses and such establishments become equally necessary to them in the country; and it is by this means that, instead of old and dreary castles and chateaus, we have such beautiful mansions, so filled with rich paintings and elegant furniture, dispersed all over England. From these places . . . similar tastes are spread through the less wealthy classes, and the elegances of life flow into the parsonages, cottages, and abodes of persons of less income and less intercourse with society. In town, undoubtedly, a vast number of the aristocracy spend their time and money very foolishly, but it is equally true, that many others spend theirs very beneficially to the country.'

Nevertheless, most of the gentry thought their money was better spent in the country than in London. With everything to do with local government wholly dependent on them, it was of course desirable that they should remain on their estates. Unfortunately hard times and sometimes extravagant living compelled many of the gentry to abandon their homes, while the allurements of London and Brighton induced not a few to spend much of their time and money away from home to the detriment of their estates and dependents. Mary Mitford sadly complained that in Hampshire 'All our mansions are let, or to be let. The old manorial Hall, where squire succeeded squire from generation to generation, is cut down into a villa, or a hunting-lodge, and transferred season after season, from tenant to tenant, with as little remorse as if it were a lodging-house at Brighton. The lords of the soil are almost as universally absentees as if our fair country were part and parcel of the Sister Kingdom.' So strongly did the gentry themselves feel

about their obligations that they would condemn a landowner
who let his shooting on the ground that it was anti-social.

Of the many evils that flowed from squires abandoning their
homes, whether of necessity or voluntarily, not the least was the
consequent neglect of the sick and the poor. 'I cannot help
deploring', wrote John Byng, 'the desertion of the country, by
the gentlemen. . . . These were the supporters of the poor, and
of their rights; and their wives were the Lady Bountifuls of the
parish: there was then a good country neighbourhood, whose
families intermarried with each other. But since the increase of
luxury, and turn-pike roads, and that all gentlemen have the
gout, and all ladies the bile, it has been found necessary to fly
to the bath, and to sea-bathing for relief.' A few months later
he asked: 'How should the poor exist, when the landlord that
should protect, and support them, is gone off to reside in Mary-
bone-Parish; whilst of his formerly squirelike place nothing
remains but some decay'd garden walls? . . . To whom now are
they to look up? The curate cannot befriend them; the steward
will not!'

The same trouble arose when, as sometimes happened, a large
landowner with two or more estates favoured the one where he
lived, or spent most of his time, at the expense of the others.
'Two or three men of rank in life', complained the rector of
Abbess Roding in 1807, 'carry off all the produce of their landed
estates to a distant part of the country, not leaving a guinea
behind them. Hopeless is the prospect that our children can
spiritually differ from the wild life and colts.'

Worse than a landowner starving his dependents in one part
of the country for the sake of those in another was, in John
Byng's eyes, what happened when an English heiress was so
unwise as to marry a Scot. It was a matter on which he felt
very strongly. 'Within my memory,' he wrote, 'a *certain nation*,
from their shrewdness, and cunning, have by marriages, and
management so riggled themselves into the South, that like their
native thistles, they can never be weeded out. . . . Our boroughs
have they got; our heiresses have they married; and the possessions of this land will they obtain . . . would they reside here; —
would they fraternize; would they naturalize. No; never; — the
crop is carried off by them to manure the meagre North: They
will not be thought Englishmen; they are not at home here;

V (a) *Tyburn Turnpike:* On the left is the toll house which stood on the site of the old permanent gallows, close to where Marble Arch now stands.

V (b) *Toll Gate:* In the country many turnpikes or toll gates were crude, but effective. The toll house was usually a cottage in which the pikeman lived.

VI *Harlow Bush Fair*: Owing to the difficulties of travel, country people depended on the annual fairs for goods not produced locally. Fairs provided vital services of which entertainment was a traditional part.

they hate us; they are miserable in our society; they will send a bailiff from the North to collect their rents, but they will not grow upon the soil. . . . Upon my honor, I think that the great should be forced to country residence for so many months in the year; and that an Act should be passed to prevent heiresses from marrying aliens.'

In 1821 Cobbett, who had not by then acquired the venomous hatred for squires which marked his later years, had a very keen appreciation of the difference between resident and absentee landlords: 'The difference between a resident *native* gentry, attached to the soil, known to every farmer and labourer from their childhood, frequently mixing with them in those pursuits where all artificial distinctions are lost, practising hospitality without ceremony, from habit and not on calculation; and a gentry, only now-and-then residing at all, having no relish for country-delights, foreign in their manners, distant and haughty in their behaviour, looking to the soil only for its rents, viewing it as a mere object of speculation, unacquainted with its cultivators, despising them and their pursuits, and relying, for influence, not upon the good will of the vicinage, but upon the dread of their power.'

There is nothing to quarrel with there. Five years later, however, it was a very different story. 'There is in the men calling themselves "English country gentlemen" something superlatively base. They are, I sincerely believe, the most cruel, the most unfeeling, the most brutally insolent: but I know, I can prove, I can safely take my oath, that they are the most base of all the creatures that God ever suffered to disgrace the human shape.' A month later his invective reached its peak: 'Of all the mean, all the cowardly reptiles, that ever crawled on the face of the earth, the *English land-owners* are the most mean. . . . Never was there in this world, a set of reptiles so base as this.'

What, it may be fairly asked, had happened to Cobbett between 1821 and 1826? Why, during those five years, had he developed this venomous hatred of the landed gentry? It is a pertinent question for, in spite of his many obsessions and absurd prejudices, Cobbett was a man of considerable influence. In 1823 some of his friends and admirers had unsuccessfully formed a committee to secure him the seat in Parliament for

F

which he craved. It may well be that their failure had something to do with his changed attitude to the landed gentry. For
it was the latter who virtually controlled Parliament, and his
hatred was aimed at them as legislators, far more than as country
squires. He held them responsible, and not without justification,
for the crushing burden of taxation and tithes on which he
blamed all rural poverty and distress. 'The base wretches', he
raged, 'know well, that the *taxes* amount to more than *sixty
millions* a year, and that the *poor-rates* amount to about *seven
millions*; yet, while the cowardly reptiles never utter a word
against the taxes, they are incessantly railing against the poor-
rates, though it is, (and they know it) the taxes that make the
paupers.' And again: 'the carrion baseness of these wretches, is
that . . . they never even whisper a word against pensioners,
placemen, soldiers, parsons, fund-holders, tax-gatherers, or
tax-eaters!' Cobbett's hatred was so pervasive (it embraced all
Scots), that one can but marvel that he was taken so seriously
and was so influential. Nevertheless, there was good reason for
his fulminations against pensioners and placemen who together
constituted the greatest public scandal of the age.

It had been customary to grant allowances to public servants
on their retirement, but it was not until 1810 that an Act was
passed entitling them to pensions. This opened the way for the
abuse of patronage on a remarkable scale, and at immense
cost to the Exchequer. At the time of the passing of the Act the
allowances to retired officers of the Customs amounted annually
to £7,800 but by 1820 they had increased to £90,000 — and the
Customs was only a small part of the public service. An officer
would be retired on pension, not because he had reached retiring age or on account of unfitness, but because a Minister
wanted his place for a friend or relation who might very soon
also be retired, on pension of course, to make way for another.
Given the backing of an influential and pliable patron it was
possible to retire from office after office on account of unfitness
and be granted a pension on each retirement. Thus in 1818 the
well-known Yorkshire baronet Sir Bellingham Graham was
receiving pensions from four different offices for each of which
he had been declared unfit. In addition, many appointments
were mere sinecures, perhaps even created for the benefit of a
tiresomely importunate protégé who could not otherwise be

provided for. The classic placeman was Lord Camden (to Cobbett 'this great and awful sinecure placeman') who drew £23,000
annually as Teller of the Exchequer, a sinecure appointment. He was said to have drawn altogether over £1,000,000
of government money from this and similar appointments.[1]

The Whig Opposition was at one with Cobbett in his railings
against the malign influence of the landed gentry at Westminster, and none was more critical than Coke of Norfolk, the
greatest of them all. In later years, when the passing of the
Reform Bill was drawing near, Coke declared that the House of
Commons was 'the representative of the aristocracy rather than
the people', and that 'the landed-interest in the House of
Commons was the great supporter of extravagance and profusion, and the landed proprietors had only themselves to thank
when it reacted on themselves'. His friend the Duke of Bedford
held identical views.

Nevertheless, when the Whigs came into power in 1830 and
were expected to end the jobbery and nepotism against which
they had railed when in opposition, they disappointed the
country. On becoming Prime Minister, Lord Grey provided his
three sons-in-law and two brothers-in-law with office, and made
his old but impoverished friend Thomas Creevey, then aged
sixty-two, Treasurer of the Ordnance, a sinecure appointment
worth £1,200 a year with free quarters in the Tower. Nor did
Creevey, hitherto a bitter enemy of jobbery, hesitate to squeeze
all he could out of his appointment to which, it seems, the
coveted privilege of the franking of letters unfortunately did not
attach. 'I can't suppose', he wrote, 'that the Treasurer *franks* by
virtue of his office, but *that* is always managed some way or
other in every publick office.'[2] It cannot be doubted that he was
right.

The demand for parliamentary reform, engendered by the
urban masses of the Industrial Revolution and fostered by

---

[1] Church patronage was a very profitable field for jobbery. For example, Dr.
Sparke, Bishop of Ely, had acquired by 1831 for himself, his two sons, and his son-
in-law a total income of £39,942 (to say nothing of the appointments he had secured
for more distant relatives) by means of 'shiftings, resignations, movings about, and
heaping up of offices'.
[2] Letter postage, which was payable by the recipient, varied from 10d. to 2s.
according to distance, except in the London area where it was only 2d. Anyone
enjoying the privilege of franking usually franked his friends' letters as well as his
own and his family's.

Methodism and Radicalism, was, as we have seen, a growing threat to the squires' monopoly of power. But they were on the defensive for other reasons. The first dated from the French Revolution which had filled the English governing classes with an intense fear of Jacobinism. Although it was, as we shall see later, a purely imaginary danger, there were agitators going round England telling the workers that what the *ouvriers* of France had done could be done also in England. This was frightening and it certainly coloured the attitude of the landed gentry, anyway of the less imaginative and more reactionary among them, to the labouring classes. To all such there was a growing need for repression, for keeping the labourers in their place. To show undue sympathy for the hardness of their lot, or even to admit its existence, might be very dangerous. It was an attitude of mind which lent a ready ear to the teachings of the Rev. Thomas Malthus. Poverty, he declared, was inevitable on account of natural increase in population; in England the increase was due to poor-rates; the right of the poor to support should be repudiated; no illegitimate child should be entitled to parish relief. That sort of talk, which commanded wide attention, naturally encouraged a hardening of the attitude of the rich to the poor lest they should ultimately overwhelm their betters by sheer weight of numbers.

The fear of Jacobinism and the teachings of Malthus were partly responsible for the lamentable failure of successive Tory ministers to relieve rural distress, but they do not appear to have disturbed personal relationships in village life. From the litera-ture of the period, whether chronicles or fiction, it is abundantly clear that there was no abatement of the traditional interest of the squires and their families in the sick and the poor, and in the welfare of old retainers. In England's stately homes no family jubilation, such as the birth or coming-of-age of an heir, or a wedding, was complete without the villagers of the surrounding countryside being entertained and associated with the happy event. Richard Rush, the American ambassador, could have heard at morning prayers in many other country houses the prayer that pleased him so much at Hagley — 'Teach us to be just to those dependent on us'. Whatever their shortcomings as legislators, in their home life the governing classes still pre-served their customary regard for their less fortunate neighbours.

Their methods of dispensing charity were perhaps not very enlightened, and on the Bench their administration of justice may sometimes have been biased, but in Cobbett we find a striking example of how imaginative, one might say how twentieth-century, a squire could be. Mr. Drummond of Albury, in Surrey, he tells us, 'instead of hunting down an unfortunate creature who has exposed himself to the lash of the law; instead of regarding a crime committed as proof of an inherent disposition to commit crime; instead of rendering the poor creatures desperate by this species of *proscription*, and forcing them to the *gallows* . . . instead of this, which is the common practice throughout the country, he rather seeks for such unfortunate creatures to take them into his employ, and thus to reclaim them, and make them repent of their former courses.'

In 1800 George Villiers,[1] finding that his labourers were being shockingly exploited by the local shops — then not at all unusual in the country —provided them with bread and meat at prices far below the shopkeepers'. He was also planning to supply them with cheese, bought wholesale in London, at cost price. Seven years later the Duke of Buccleuch gave up his annual visit to London in order to devote himself to relieving unemployment which was then acute in the North. He found work for 947 men over and above those he normally employed. In 1822 Lord Bridgwater, as we have seen, made it a rule at Ashridge never to refuse work to anyone.

Unfortunately there were still plenty of black sheep among the gentry, too many Squire Westerns, especially on the Bench where they were not subject to any sort of supervision, and where a tyrant, often sitting in judgement in his own house, could terrorize a whole district. A growing menace to the rural areas surrounding the expanding industrial towns was the new rich who were infiltrating into the countryside, worming their way into the seats of the gentry and setting themselves up as squires, and often bringing with them the heartless and tyrannical methods which characterized their attitude to the workpeople in their factories. Cobbett saw clearly the difference between the *nouveaux riches* of the towns and the country squires in whose sports he so loved to join. 'An aristocracy of *title and privilege*,' he wrote, 'when kept within due and constitutional

[1] The future 4th Earl of Clarendon.

bounds, brings none of the oppression upon the people which is always brought upon them by a *damned aristocracy* of *money*.'

Had not the relations between the landed gentry and the lower classes been in general one of mutual respect and confidence the story of the Swing riots would have been very different. From their start there was no lack of agitators anxious to promote a class war, who hoped so to inflame the masses against the squires that the rising would assume the pattern of the French Revolution and culminate in the destruction of the landowning classes. As we have seen, not only did nothing of the sort happen, not only was class bitterness almost entirely absent, but in presenting their grievances the starving labourers preserved their customary deference and courtesy to those whom they were urged to regard as their oppressors.

The reason why a bloody revolution after the French pattern was impossible in England was that most of the English country gentry, unlike the French nobility, lived on their estates, spent their money locally, took the lead in all local activities, shared the joys of field sports and games with their humble neighbours, and ruled their districts as benevolent patriarchs. The tyrants and dissolute wasters, such as the notorious John Mytton, were far too few to leaven the whole, or even to tip the balance ever so slightly against the class of which they boasted but disgraced. In rural England it is character, not wealth, that commands esteem. The lauding of the rich, because of their wealth, belongs to the towns, especially to their suburbs.

All this was clearly apparent to a foreign visitor, a French aristocrat who, having witnessed the revolution in his own country, was able to compare the aristocracy of England with that to which he belonged. 'The true strength of the English Aristocracy and nationality', wrote the Comte de Montalembert, 'abides in the many thousands of families of Landed Proprietors, and who, in virtue of their property, are the magistrates, and . . . *administrators of the country*. They do not disdain, as the old French nobility did, to accept administrative, legislative, and judicial functions. Far from it — they have almost monopolized them, and by so doing have maintained themselves at the head of all the developments of society.'

One of the commonest, and least just, of the charges brought against the landed gentry was social exclusiveness. It was unjust because they were no more exclusive than any other class; the middle-class William Howitt inferred that they were less so. 'The lower you descend in the scale,' he wrote, 'the more exacting becomes the spirit of exclusiveness.' But then Howitt had no social aspirations; at the time when he wrote a great many other people had, and more than ever before. This was because war had enriched so many industrialists and business people of humble origin. Finding that the popular esteem for which they had hoped attached to the possession of land and not of money, their one unsatisfied ambition, short of a title, was to become a country landowner with a seat on the Bench. It was the recognition of this simple fact, of the special esteem in which a squire was held, that led Lord George Bentinck to induce Disraeli, of whom he so rightly expected great achievements, to buy Hughenden and set himself up as a landowner.

The impoverishment of so many of the landed gentry made the acquisition of a country estate comparatively easy. The seat on the Bench was much more difficult. Before a man could become a Justice of the Peace he had to win social acceptance into the ranks of the gentry, which was no easier for him than it was for the shopkeeper's wife to take tea with the doctor's, or the labourer's with the farmer's. But if and when, at long last, the gentry did pay calls on the urban squire he still had far to go before he could realize his fondest wish. The Commission of the Peace was a very close corporation.

At the end of the eighteenth century the likelihood of a Lord-Lieutenant recommending the appointment of a Justice of the Peace who was unacceptable to the Bench concerned was remote. In practice most nominations originated with the Justices themselves who, with rare exceptions, were country gentlemen with strong prejudices. They set their faces against anyone of their own class whose politics they disliked, and against virtually everyone of an inferior class, especially if he were connected with any form of trade or manufacture.[1] Exclusive and bad as many of the Benches were, it is significant that their badness tended to be blamed on their being insufficiently exclusive. For all their many faults and the consequent mis-

---

[1] In 1813 the Home Secretary told the Commons that he had no objection to the appointment as magistrates for Lancashire of 'wealthy and respectable persons engaged in trade, but not in manufacture'.

carriage of justice, the landed gentry were the people the countryside expected to sit in justice over them. In 1788 someone wrote to the *Gentleman's Magazine* urging that the Lord-Lieutenants should be 'more attentive to the birth, parentage and education' of those they recommended for appointment as magistrates, and he went on to complain of a Justice who neglected his duties and, 'though naturally a good kind of man . . . gives up his neighbours to pettifoggers and half-gentlemen, who torture the laws to base purposes of petty quarrels, low prejudices, and mercenary cabal'.

Although some squires were judicial tyrants, especially in the severity with which they enforced the game laws, the country people preferred to have them as magistrates on account of their knowledge of country ways and their placing the law above the 'base purposes of petty quarrels'. We owe to Smollett a memorable portrait of a retired London tradesman, Mr. Justice Gobble, who, having bribed his way on to the local Bench, 'committed a thousand acts of cruelty and injustice against the poorer sort of people'. When, in 1833, some county magistrates actually went on strike in protest against a new appointment to their Bench, the Commissioner sent by the Whig Government to look into the trouble produced a dictum which, though astonishing to modern ears, probably reflected the consensus of rural opinion in those days. 'The refusal of the County Magistrates', he wrote, 'to act with a man who has been a grocer and is a Methodist is the dictate of genuine patriotism; the spirit of aristocracy in the county magistracy is the salt which alone preserves the whole mass from inevitable corruption.'

At a time when a plebeian landowner was a rarity the invasion of the countryside by wealthy self-made townspeople was naturally disturbing to rural society. The landowning class, like every other social stratum, had always been recruited from the class below, but new blood had usually been absorbed almost unconsciously, from families like Mr. Weston's in *Emma*, 'which for the last two or three generations had been rising into gentility and property'. The county families of the early nineteenth century were faced with a mass attack against which, they ruefully found, their exclusiveness was not the protection they had thought.

The new rich were able to secure the social advancement of

their sons by sending them to public schools, as Thackeray's
Osbornes and Sedleys did, or, like his Bludyers of Mincing Lane,
by buying them commissions in the army. But most of them were
as much interested in securing their own advancement as their
sons', and, after the manner of their kind, they usually set
about it in the wrong way. A not unusual one was architectural
self-advertisement, to which the fashionable Gothic revival was
so admirably suited. While some contented themselves with
doing no more than Thomas Peacock's Mr. Crotchet, who
changed the name of his villa to Crotchet Castle, there were
many like Surtees's Marmaduke Muleygrubs who sought to
aggrandize himself by adding to his villa, which had started as a
farmhouse, 'massive stone towers, with loop-holed battle-
ments . . . imitation guns peered through a heavy iron palisade
along the top'. But the pretentious splendour of Cockalorum
Hall paled before the 'immeasurable folly', as Emily Eden called
it, of Fonthill Abbey which the *parvenu* William Beckford
erected in one of the loveliest parts of Wiltshire. Near Newbury,
in 1821, Cobbett came to the park of a Mr. Montague: 'Of all
the ridiculous things I ever saw in my life', he wrote, 'this place
is the most ridiculous. . . . I do not know who the gentleman is.
I suppose he is some honest person from the 'Change . . . and
that these *Gothic arches* are to denote *the antiquity of his origin.*'

In fairness to these pretentious urban squires it must be
conceded that architecturally they were only following an
example set by the aristocracy. At the same time that Cobbett's
Mr. Montague was building his Gothic arches Lord Grosvenor
was turning his comparatively modest Eaton Hall into what
Greville described as 'a vast pile of mongrel Gothic, which cost
some hundreds of thousands, and is a monument of wealth,
ignorance and bad taste'. Not long afterwards Lord Stuart of
Rothesay was astonishing his neighbours with the strange
castellations of his Highcliffe Castle. Many others, notably
the owners of Toddington Park in Gloucestershire and Hawar-
den in Wales, were doing the same thing on a less flamboyant
scale. What was mere bad taste in the aristocracy was pretentious vulgarity in the new rich, but naturally they could not see
it.

The efforts of the *nouveaux riches* to ape or surpass the houses of
the gentry did not get them very far, but even then, although

wealth did not command rural esteem, it could, carefully used, unlock many doors. This had been clearly demonstrated by Mrs. Coutts, late of Drury Lane, whom Mrs. Arbuthnot described as a 'memorable example of the power of money. She lived with Mr. Coutts many years before his first wife died, was an actress & now, because he has left her his whole fortune, she gives balls and breakfasts & is invited by every body.'

In the country there must have been many a distressed landowner who found it difficult, when the bailiffs were knocking at the door, not to pocket his pride and accept the profferred loan. It was some such circumstances that had secured a seat on the Bench for Smollett's Mr. Gobble. And it was not very easy to ignore altogether those who subscribed lavishly to local good causes.

When the Napoleonic wars ended the urban squires were presented with a ladder to social heights which they had never before enjoyed. In circumstances to be recounted in a later chapter, foxhunting was ceasing to be exclusively a private pastime of rich landowners and was becoming a national and highly democratic sport in which anyone might join. Moreover, the new subscription packs of hounds were nearly always short of money. In the hunting field the new rich could spend their days rubbing shoulders with their social superiors whose good opinion they might win by good horsemanship, courage, and unselfishness (especially in taking their fences and caring for casualties). Those who were too old or too fat or too timid to ride to hounds could always subscribe; few masters were in a position to go on snubbing the regular subscriber of a hundred guineas. These heaven-sent opportunities were quickly seized by the urban squires to whom we owe half the fun of Surtees's novels. It also gave foxhunting some very fine sportsmen, like the great John Cook, the son of a Hampshire corn-chandler.

The gradual acceptance of the new urban landowners into rural society, culminating in their absorption into it, led to increased emphasis on lineage. Pride of ancestry had always been a trait of the county families, especially of the untitled ones who were often the more ancient. There were many places like Mrs. Gaskell's Hollingford where the ancient Hamleys of Hamley, who had owned their paltry eight hundred acres since the Conquest, were rather overshadowed by the Earl and

Countess of Cumnor who had had their great estate for no more than a hundred years. 'Mere muck of yesterday', old Hamley called them. The usual comment of a friend of Delmé Ratcliffe's, an octogenarian divine, on a gentleman of whom he disapproved, was: 'Rely upon it that fellow never had a grandfather.' It is impossible to read the exclusive Nimrod, a classic snob, without being nauseated by his adulation of ancient lineage, but even the democratic Surtees, the complete reverse of Nimrod, has to tell us that Ralph Lambton was 'one of the most highly bred men in the Kingdom'. Nevertheless, without going so far as Montalembert who thought that the *marchand enrichi* was the hope of England, the infusion of plebeian blood into rural society was timely and beneficial.

The astonishing privileges which, down the ages, the peers had secured for themselves in part accounted for the unattractive habit of the untitled but high-born to draw attention to their ancient lineage. A peer, unlike a commoner, could not be arrested for debt, made bankrupt, or have his estates sequestrated — he could defraud his creditors with impunity. He paid less stamp duty and taxes than a commoner, and on the turnpike he paid far lighter tolls. He sent and received letters postage free, and customarily franked also the letters of his friends and relations. His person was also privileged. 'You may knock down Nathan Rothschild, though he is a very rich man,' reads *The Black Book*, 'or a worshipful alderman, or even a right honourable lord mayor, and the justices will only charge you a few shillings for the liberty you have taken; but if you knock down a peer, though he is ever so insolent, it is almost as bad as murder.' While a commoner sitting in judgement had to give his verdict upon his oath, a peer was required to give his only on his honour, 'just as if a peer alone had *honour*, and all others were base perfidious slaves, from whom truth could only be extorted when they had been forced into the presence of their Creator'. At a time when ancestry mattered more than a title, the enjoyment of such extraordinary privileges by upstart peers naturally excited jealousy.

VI

The England of Emily Eden

THE Comte de Montalembert, who thought so highly of the English aristocracy compared with his own, was not the only distinguished foreigner to be impressed by their love of the country. 'The enthusiastic fondness of the English for the country, is the effect of their laws', wrote Richard Rush, the American ambassador. 'Primogeniture is at the root of it. Scarcely any persons who hold a leading place in the circles of their society live in London. They have *houses* in London, in which they stay while Parliament sits, and occasionally visit at other seasons; but their *homes* are in the country. Their turreted mansions are there, with all that denotes perpetuity — heirlooms, family memorials, pictures, tombs. This spreads the ambition among other classes, and the taste for rural life, however diversified or graduated the scale, becomes widely diffused. Those who live on their estates through successive generations, not merely those who have titles, but thousands besides, acquire, if they have the proper qualities of character, an influence throughout their neighbourhood. It is not an influence always enlisted on the side of power and privilege. On the contrary, there are numerous instances in which it has for ages been strenuously used for the furtherance of popular rights. These are the feelings and objects that cause the desertion of the west-end of the town when Parliament rises. The permanent interests and affections of the most opulent classes, centre almost universally in the country. Heads of families go there to resume their stand in the midst of these feelings; and all, to partake of the pastimes of the country life, where they flourish in pomp and joy.'

The stately homes of the old aristocracy belonged to a world of their own and usually opened their doors to the lesser county

families only on special occasions. Nevertheless, it is improbable
that outside the still feudal North, anyone, however great, dared
to follow the example set at Alnwick. When the Duke of
Northumberland, wrote Elizabeth, Lady Holland, after a visit
to the castle in 1798, 'is willing to receive the visits of the neighbouring gentry, a flag is hung upon the highest turret as a signal
that he may be approached'. She was excusably a little doubtful about how much notice was taken of 'this aristocratical
summons'.

One senses that more pleasure was taken in feasting the poor
than entertaining the lesser gentry who were less easy to please
and probably regarded as rather dull. In 1834 Charles Greville
was staying with the aged Lord Egremont at Petworth for what
he called 'the finest *fête* that could be given', an annual event for
the entertainment of the poor. About 4,000 were bidden 'but,
as many more came, the old Peer could not endure that there
should be anybody hungering outside his gates, and he went
out himself and ordered the barriers to be taken down and ad-
mittance given to all. They think 6,000 were fed. Gentlemen
from the neighbourhood carved for them, and waiters were
provided from among the peasantry.' This vast gathering was
fed at tables set out on the lawn. 'Plum puddings and loaves were
piled like cannon balls, and innumerable joints of boiled and
roast beef were spread out, while hot joints were prepared in the
kitchen, and sent forth as soon as the firing of guns announced
the hour of the feast.' At night, when the crowd had swollen
to 10,000, there were fireworks. 'It was altogether one of the
gayest and most beautiful spectacles I ever saw', concludes
Greville, 'and there was something affecting in the contempla-
tion of that old man . . . rejoicing in the diffusion of happiness
and finding keen gratification in relieving the distresses and
contributing to the pleasures of the poor.'

In the early years of the nineteenth century the greatest
annual event in rural England was Coke's Sheep-Shearings at
Holkham. They had begun as far back as 1778 when Coke
called together a number of local farmers to discuss farming
matters and to give him, then an inexperienced young landowner, their advice on the problems of developing his great
estate. As years passed and Holkham, under Coke's gifted hand,
became a model estate on which agricultural practice was far

ahead of the rest of England, the gatherings were swelled by farmers and landowners from all over the country, come no longer to give, but to seek, advice, and they lasted four days. By the turn of the century they had become world-famous and were regularly attracting practical agriculturists and scientists from as far as America in the west and Russia in the east. Not the least attractive feature of these gatherings, or Coke's Clippings, as they were called, which eventually as many as 7,000 people would attend, was their simplicity and the entire absence of class distinctions. At the daily discussions, which were always preceded by a tour of some part of the Holkham estate, and occupied several hours, the smallest tenant farmer was given as ready a hearing as any of the great territorial magnates who regularly attended. Prominent among the latter was Coke's friend the Duke of Bedford who copied his Clippings at Woburn. While these famous shearings owed the whole of their success to Coke's magnetic personality, his pre-eminence as a practical farmer, and his inexhaustible energy, they could never have been held but for the lavish hospitality which the size of Holkham and the wealth and generosity of its owner made possible.

'He does it handsomely', Arthur Young commented in 1802. 'Two hundred dined on plate. The dinner better than at Woburn, I think from the vicinity of the sea, which gives plenty of fish.' Dinner at 3 o'clock, the principal event of each day, was followed by speeches and discussions. At the last of the Clippings, in 1821, between 500 and 700 guests were entertained to dinner each day, seated at tables in adjoining rooms. That year there were no less than eighty guests staying in the house, most of whom, as was customary, lingered on some days after the sheep-shearings were officially over.

The Woburn Shearings seem to have followed closely the Holkham pattern. The guests were no less distinguished, and the hospitality was equally lavish. In 1800 the company included the Duke of Gloucester, a German baron, and 'four gentlemen from Ireland'. On the first day 'about three o'clock the company adjourned to dinner; and his Grace entertained near 200 noblemen, gentlemen, and yeomen, in the large hall, in the ancient part of the Abbey. His Grace presided. Prince William of Gloucester sat as Croupier.

'About six o'clock they left the Abbey, and proceeded to the farm-yard again, when a very fine hog ... was shewn, which was supposed to weigh about an hundred stone. During the whole of this time, the men continued shearing the sheep.' On the fourth and last day, by which time the staff may well have grown rather weary, the guests all assembled as usual for dinner at 3 o'clock, but they had to wait two hours before they got it. What with the lack of fish and having to wait so long for dinner we are left feeling, seemingly with Arthur Young, that they did it slightly better at Holkham.

Archery at this time was very much in fashion, and brought together immense house parties. There was an annual meeting at Acton Park, near Wrexham, where Sir Foster Cunliffe entertained 'sixty to a hundred persons with the best of everything, together with their servants and horses'. Nearby, at Greddington Hall, a similar party used to be held by Thomas Kenyon at which, Nimrod tells us, 'the company, amounting to upwards of two hundred persons, partook of a dinner consisting of almost everything that could please the eye or gratify the palate'.

In those days of slow and difficult travelling, visits to country houses usually lasted from one to two or more weeks,[1] and most of the guests brought servants with them. As it was usual to ask a number of guests at a time, according to the size of the house, entertaining must have imposed a considerable strain on host and hostess; nevertheless, as the fashion continued they seem to have taken it in their stride. But not so the guests. The chronicles of the time clearly show that dull company and discomforts which were tolerable for a week-end became insupportable for longer, more particularly for women. They passed the evenings pleasantly enough, taking part with the men in cards, dancing, music, and theatricals, but in the daytime, especially in winter, when the men shot, hunted, or played billiards, time was apt to hang heavily on their hands. Their principal amusements were country drives and sight-seeing visits to other houses. Many of these bored guests were like Elizabeth in *Pride and Prejudice* who complained 'that she was tired of great houses;

---

[1] The Duke of Sussex, son of George III, perhaps unconscious of the strain a royal visit places on a host, used to spend a couple of months at Holkham most winters.

after going over so many, she really had no pleasure in fine carpets or satin curtains'. But the men were not always satisfied. In 1815 Lord Auckland sent his sister Emily Eden[1] the following terse account of a visit to the Grenvilles at Dropmore: 'Mary in such a fright you never saw — such a silence you never heard — room so hot you never felt — dinner so cold you never tasted — dogs so tiresome you never smelt.'

His sister Emily, young, amusing, and attractive, was intolerant of bores. Following a visit to Studley Royal, where she was taken ill, she wrote: 'My illness was remarkably opportune, inasmuch as it began at Studley, and which was so uncommonly dull, that the impossibility of dining down was an immense advantage that I had over the rest of society.' Visits to Chatsworth, under the 6th Duke of Devonshire, were a sore trial to her. 'I shall continue to think a visit to Chatsworth a very great trouble', she wrote in 1825. 'You are probably right in thinking the Duke takes pleasure in making people do what they don't like, and that accounts for his asking me so often. We have now made a rule to accept one invitation out of two. We go there with the best dispositions, wishing to be amused, liking the people we meet there . . . supported by the knowledge that in the eyes of the neighbourhood we are covering ourselves with glory by frequenting the *great house*; but with all these helps we have never been able to stay above two days there without finding change of air absolutely necessary, — never could turn the corner of the third day, — at the end of the second the great depths of *bore* were broken up and carried all before them: we were obliged to pretend that some christening, or a grand funeral, or some pressing case of wedding (in this country it is sometimes expedient to hurry the performance of the marriage ceremony) required Robert's immediate return home, and so we departed yawning.'

On the other hand, four years later, Greville found Chatsworth very much to his liking: 'The party was immense; 40 people sat down to dinner every day, and about 150 servants in the steward's room and servants' hall. . . . Nothing could be more agreeable from the gaiety of numbers and the entire liberty that prevails; all the resources of the house — horses,

---

[1] The Honble. Emily Eden and her brother were children of the 1st Baron Auckland.

VII *Woburn Sheepshearing*: The 5th Duke of Bedford copied at Woburn the more famous Holkham shearings. Coke is shown on the left talking to Sir Joseph Banks; behind him stands Professor (afterwards Sir Humphry) Davy. The Duke, mounted, is in the centre foreground.

VIII *Lord Dysart Treating his Tenantry*: This scene at Ham House illustrates the pleasant custom of owners of great houses entertaining their poorer neighbours, sometimes to the number of several thousand, either annually or on special occasions.

carriages, keepers, &c. — are placed at the disposal of the
guests, and everyone does what they like best. In the evening
they acted charades or danced, and there was plenty of whist
and *écarté* high and low.' On his next visit, less than a year later,
he found Chatsworth 'rather dull', and as he was not easily
bored one is left with the feeling that perhaps Emily Eden had
been right.

She found Newby Hall, Lord Grantham's, 'excessively
comfortable, with a stove in every passage, and a fire in every
room, servants' and all, an excellent library, and a very pretty
statue gallery, heaps of amusing books, and an arm chair for
every limb. I foresee a great probability of my being very happy
here.' Emily was a young woman of culture as well as charm,
and seems to have been happy wherever she found food for her
intellect. The Alexander Barings' house, The Grange, Alresford,
was 'delicious now it is finished, and heaps of new books and
good pictures'. She went to Hatfield for some amateur theatricals
which she evidently dreaded, but they were a great success.
'I went expecting to find the *gentlefolk* all tolerable sticks on the
stage, awkward, affected, and only helped through by an indul-
gent public, and I found I never had laughed more heartily,
never had seen a play really well acted in all its parts before.'
She thought the young Lady Salisbury the least good but 'only
objectionable because she was like an actress on the real
stage'. Panshanger, 'full to the brim of vice and agreeableness,
foreigners and roués' when she stayed there in 1832, was 'all
very pleasant'. Of the many great houses she stayed in, Bowood
seems to have pleased her most, and not only on account of her
devotion to the Lansdownes. She once wrote to George Villiers
that she and her brother had 'been for a fortnight at Bowood. The
house was full of people and we enjoyed ourselves amazingly. It
is always rather surprising society in point of talk: there is less
said about people, and more about books, than in most country
houses.' Maria Edgeworth also found the Lansdownes charming
people to stay with. 'This visit to Bowood', she wrote in 1818,
'has surpassed my expectations in every respect. I much enjoy
the sight of Lady Lansdowne's happiness with her husband and
her children: beauty, fortune, cultivated society, in short
everything that the most reasonable and unreasonable could
wish.'

G

Unfortunately Emily Eden was too young and Lord Egremont too old for her to be asked to Petworth. She would have found much to make up for its lack of comfort and the eccentricities of the host. 'It is a very grand place,' Greville tells us, 'house magnificent and full of fine objects, both ancient and modern; the Sir Joshuas and Vandykes particularly interesting, and a great deal of all sorts that is worth seeing. Lord Egremont ... has reigned here for sixty years with great authority and influence. He is shrewd, eccentric, and benevolent, and has always been munificent and charitable in his own way; he patronizes the arts and fosters rising genius. Painters and sculptors find employment and welcome in his house.'

Belvoir would not have pleased her. When Greville stayed there in 1833 for the Duke of Rutland's birthday he was one of a party which was 'very large and sufficiently dull'. Apart from the Duke of Wellington and a few others they were 'a rabble of fine people, without beauty or wit among them. . . . The establishment is kept up with extraordinary splendour. In the morning we are roused by the strains of martial music, and the band (of his regiment of militia) marches round the terrace, awakening or quickening the guests with lively airs. All the men hunt or shoot. At dinner there is a different display of plate every day, and in the evening some play at whist or amuse themselves as they please, and some walk about the staircases and corridors to hear the band, which plays the whole evening in the hall. On the Duke's birthday there was a great feast in the Castle; 200 people dined in the servants' hall alone, without counting the other tables. We were about 40 at dinner.'

The visitors to the great houses of the day naturally, though unfortunately for posterity, seldom recorded in their letters and journals what to them was commonplace but which to us would be interesting. Lord William Pitt Lennox, however, has left us a brief account of how a male guest was received: 'As the hour strikes six . . . you drive up to the well-kept lodge. The gate is thrown open — in less than a mile you approach the house, through a finely-wooded park; the carriage stops at a grand portico, a peal at the bell is given, and in a few seconds the doors are thrown open, and the butler, attended by the groom of the chambers, and a couple of tall, six feet two, powdered, pampered footmen, are in readiness to receive you.

'Ushered into the library, you find your host writing against time, for the post. He gives you a hearty welcome, and hopes to show you some excellent sport in the morning. . . . The dressing-bell is rung; the host, who still retains one of the most courteous customs of the old school, shows you to your room, desiring the groom of the chambers to see that everything is comfortably prepared for your reception.

'In due time your toilet is made; "the tocsin of the soul", the dinner-bell sounds, and you descend to the drawing-room, where the well-bred, and of course charming, hostess receives you with a warm shake of the hand, and smiles a welcome; the folding doors are shortly afterwards opened, and a dignified butler announces dinner . . . the company stand upon "the order of their going"; selecting your partner therefore in rank, you run the gauntlet through a line of liveried servants, the rear rank being formed of lords' and gentlemen's "gentlemen", as the steward's room phraseology describes them.'

Prince Pückler-Muskau, who was at this time touring England on an unsuccessful quest for a rich and aristocratic wife,[1] gives us this account of 'the routine of an English dinner' — but evidently in a less smart house than that described by Lord William: 'The gentlemen lead the ladies into the dining-room, not as in France, by the hand, but by the arm. . . . After soup is removed and the covers are taken off, every man helps the dish before him, and offers some of it to his neighbour; if he wishes for anything else, he must ask across the table, or send a servant for it; — a very troublesome custom, in place of which, some of the most elegant travelled gentlemen have adopted the German fashion of sending the servants round with the dishes.

'It is not usual to take wine without drinking to another person. When you raise your glass, you look fixedly at the one with whom you are drinking, bow your head, and then drink with the greatest gravity. . . . If the company is small, and a man has drunk with everybody, but happens to wish for more wine, he must wait for the dessert. . . .

'At the conclusion of the second course comes a sort of intermediate dessert of cheese, butter, salad, raw celery, and the like; after which ale, sometimes thirty of forty years old, and so strong that when thrown on the fire it blazes like spirit, is handed

[1] He was jilted by Mary Arabella, widow of the 1st Marquis of Lansdowne.

about. The tablecloth is then removed: under it at the best
tables, is a finer, upon which the dessert is set. . . . It consists of
all sorts of hot-house fruits, which here are of the finest quality,
Indian and native preserves, stomachic ginger, confitures
and the like. Clean glasses are set before every guest. Three
decanters are usually placed before the master of the house,
generally containing claret, port, and sherry, or madeira. The
host pushes these in stands, or in a little silver waggon on wheels,
to his neighbour on the left. . . . After the dessert is set on, all the
servants leave the room: if more is wanted the bell is rung, and
the butler alone brings it in. The ladies sit a quarter of an hour
longer, during which time sweet wines are sometimes served,
and then rise from the table.'

From another foreigner, Mr. Willis, the American ambassador, we learn more of how parties in great houses were entertained. This is from his account of a visit to Gordon Castle early
in the century: 'The drawing-room was crowded like a *soirée*.
The Duchess . . . with a smile of the most winning sweetness,
received me at the door, and I was presented successively to
every person present. Dinner was announced immediately, and
the difficult question of precedence being sooner settled than I
had ever seen it before in so large a party, we passed through files
of servants to the dining-room. . . . The band ceased playing
when the ladies left the table; the gentlemen closed up, conversation assumed a merrier cast, coffee and *liqueurs* were
brought in when the wines began to be circulated more slowly,
and at eleven there was a general move to the drawing-room.
Cards, tea, music, filled up the time till twelve, and then the
ladies took their departure, and the gentlemen sat down to
supper. I got to bed somewhere about two o'clock; and thus
ended an evening, which I had anticipated as stiff and embar-
rassing, but which is marked in my tablets as one of the most
social and kindly I have had the good fortune to record in my
travels.'

On coming down to breakfast the next morning the ambassador was a little surprised to find a scene in marked contrast
with that of the previous evening, and for which, one fears, he
must have been most unsuitably dressed. 'The troops of liveried
servants, the glitter of plate, the music, that had contributed to
the splendour of the scene of the night before, were all gone.'

The Duke, in a coarse shooting coat, sat at the head of the table reading a newspaper; the Duchess 'was in a plain morning dress and cap of the simplest character'; none of the women wore jewellery and 'the ten or twelve noblemen present were engrossed with their letters or newspapers over tea and toast', and dressed in fustian and hob-nailed shoes. He felt his country-men would have found it difficult to believe that 'that plain party . . . was composed of the proudest nobility and the highest fashion of England'.

'The routine at Gordon Castle', he continues, 'was what each one chose to make it. Between breakfast and lunch, the ladies were generally invisible, and the gentlemen rode or shot, or played billiards, or kept in their rooms. At two o'clock, a dish or two of hot game and a profusion of cold meats, were set on the small tables in the dining room, and everybody came in for a sort of lounging half-meal, which occupied perhaps an hour. Thence all adjourned to the drawing-room, under the windows of which were drawn up carriages of all descriptions, with grooms, outriders, footmen, and saddle-horses for gentlemen and ladies. Parties were then made up for driving or riding. . . .

'The number at the dinner-table of Gordon Castle was seldom less than thirty; but the company was continually varied by departures and arrivals. No sensation was made by either one or the other. A travelling-carriage dashed up to the door, was disburdened of its load, and drove round to the stables, and the question was seldom asked, "Who is arrived?" You are sure to see at dinner — an addition of half a dozen to the party, made no perceptible difference in anything. Leave-takings were managed in the same quiet way.'

This constant coming and going of guests, which was typical of the great houses of the day — and so remained for nearly a century — would have reduced country-house visits to some-thing approaching hotel life had not most of the guests, usually drawn from the same aristocratic circle, known, or known of, each other. At Petworth, where the company was more varied, it may have been different for, as Greville tells us, 'Lord Egre-mont hates ceremony, and can't bear to be personally meddled with; he likes people to come and go as it suits them, and say nothing about it, never to take leave of him.'

When one considers the size of these great house parties —

80 at Holkham, 40 at Chatsworth, 40 at Belvoir and, as Emily
Eden tells us, as many at Knowsley and other great houses —
with every guest accompanied by one or more servants — and
how well they were managed, one can but marvel at the capa-
city of the aristocracy of those days for organization. They had
of course been bred and born to the management of great
estates, to each of which was usually attached a big London
house, and many of them carried great outside responsibilities.
(Cabinet ministers, ambassadors, great officers of state, colonial
governors or governors-general for example, were mostly drawn
from the aristocracy.) Entertaining on so generous a scale would
clearly have been impossible but for excellent servants. But no
matter how good stewards and housekeepers might be, they
alone could not have successfully managed these vast households with scores of guests to be entertained, and up to 200
servants to be fed. When, through incapacity or age, the master
lost control the guests could be very uncomfortable. At Petworth the aged Lord Egremont was surrounded by servants who
were 'rustic and uncouth'. Oatlands Park, then the home of the
Duke of York, was, Greville tells us, 'the worst managed
establishment in England; there were a great many servants,
and nobody waits on you; a vast number of horses, and none to
ride or drive'. Royalty had not yet acquired the magic touch of
the aristocracy.

But life in aristocratic homes was not an endless round of
entertaining in a grand manner. Every now and then we get a
glimpse of very homely occupations, not the least of which was
gardening, then very much the fashion, and not by any means
left entirely to the head gardener and his staff. We hear of Lord
Auckland, a future Governor-General of India, working in his
garden from breakfast to dinner and quarrelling with his sister
Emily about where their favourite plants were to go. She
complained that 'he does not care a straw for the flower itself,
but merely for the cutting, or the root, or the seed. However, I
must say he contrives always to have quantities of beautiful
flowers, hurrying on one after the other.'

Then we have Emily's charming picture of how the pretty
young Lady Lansdowne sometimes employed her time at
Bowood. 'She has got some receipts for dyeing muslins, sattins
and silks any colours, and has been all this morning up to the

elbows in soap-suds, starch and blue, and then on her knees for
an hour ironing on the floor, — the work of the morning.'
At Oatlands, when the servants were so bad, the Duke of York
provided his guests with very simple pleasures. 'On Sunday',
wrote Greville, 'we amused ourselves with eating fruit in the
garden, and shooting at a mark with pistols, and playing with
the monkeys.'

The owners of less grand houses followed so far as they could,
in proportion to their means and the size of their establishments,
the example of the stately mansions in both their manner of life
and their entertainment of guests. The novels of the day,
notably Mrs. Gaskell's *Wives and Daughters*, give us a very good
idea of the every-day life of an ordinary country squire and his
family.

Social life in the country was of course wholly dependent on
the adequacy and efficiency of domestic servants. Life in the
great houses, with immense staffs controlled by admirable
upper servants, was probably seldom disturbed by the sort of
domestic problems to which small establishments were vulner-
able, such as Emily Eden experienced at Park Lodge, Greenwich, the house she shared with her brother.[1] 'Yesterday', she
wrote, 'was a day of misfortunes. . . . The footman was suddenly
laid up by a violent attack of gout; one of the maid-servants was
taken dangerously ill; one of the horses took to kicking *itself*, of
all things in the world! and hurt itself very much, which it
deserves, but it is very inconvenient to us; the cream was sour
at breakfast; we got quite wet through going to church . . . the
puppy and kitten fought; there was no mint-sauce to the lamb at
dinner.' A few weeks later a party of unexpected guests made a
most untimely appearance. 'Think of our going to sit down to
dinner the other day, in our accustomed domestic manner, soup
and a mutton-pie; and Lord and Lady Jersey, F. Villiers, and
Lord Castlereagh arrived *at* seven for dinner. No entrées, no
fish, no nothing, and the cook ill. However, it turned out very
pleasant.'

[1] In 1829 Lord Auckland was made a Commissioner of Greenwich Hospital.

VII
Below Stairs

ENTERTAINING on the immense and grand scale described in the previous chapter was only made possible by much easier travelling, to which we will return later, and a plentiful supply of highly efficient servants. Nevertheless, there was at this time a serious servant problem. With the increasing wealth of the industrial classes and the consequent rise in the standards of living of the lower social strata, there was an unprecedented demand for servants, especially in London and the big towns. In the former there was a strong prejudice against London-born servants who were regarded as dishonest and insubordinate. So marked was it that we hear of London girls leaving for the country in order to establish a rural domicile as the only way of getting a good place in London.

There was naturally an eager response to this demand for country-bred servants for, as someone asked at the time, 'What lass, in the rural village, that hears the name of London, but wishes to be there? What young Damsel that knows of the Lord Mayor's show, that don't wish to be a witness of its splendour?' The ambition of so many young people to get to London was greatly encouraged by the alluring pictures painted by servants who paid annual visits to the capital with their employers. Consequently there were, to quote the *Gentleman's Magazine* of 1793, 'vast numbers continually drawing off from the country ... to the metropolis to the service of noblemen and gentlemen'. Time served only to swell the flow of young people into London with the result that it became increasingly difficult for country houses to get the servants they needed.

 To modern readers, most of whom have never known what it is to have no servant problems, the constant references in early nineteenth-century literature to the lack of servants and the

badness of most of them sound strange. Good servants were
scarce enough even then to be called 'treasures'. By the middle
of the century, judging by Surtees's constant allusions to the
problem, the shortage had become acute. 'The breed of old
attached family servants', he wrote, 'will be almost extinct with
their generation. Few new ones are rising up to supply their
places.' Again, 'He was one of the old-fashioned breed of servants, now nearly extinct, who passed their lives in one family.'
Picnics, another odd product of the Gothic revival then much in
fashion, were considered excellent training for young ladies
who, 'as servants go', needed to know how to wait on themselves.
'Can any of your correspondents inform me', inquired someone
of *The Lady's Monthly Museum* in 1801, 'what is become of the
race of plain-dressing, docile and obedient beings who formerly
served as cooks, or housemaids, or maids of all work, in a
family?'

In the country domestic servants, like farm servants, used to
be engaged at the annual fairs where servants out of a place
gathered, each bearing a distinctive mark to advertise his particular skill. Cooks, for example, wore a red ribbon and carried
a basting spoon; housemaids wore blue and held a broom. Large
houses mostly recruited their staff through advertisements in the
newspapers, but no doubt some were occasionally driven to use
the London registry offices. These offices, carrying on an old
trade, had a bad reputation for victimizing servant girls, usually
by taking fees under false pretences and for deceiving employers
with the forged characters in which they traded. The worst of
them were chiefly interested in the procurement of girls for
prostitution — 'markets for pimps and procuresses', one writer
called them, and he was probably right. In the country, John
Byng complained, you seldom saw handsome young men or
women, 'for the army gets one, and Bond Street the other'.
These registry offices also acted as agents for the press gang by
luring young men into lockups. These abuses led to the formation of a free registry run by the London Society for the Encouragement of Faithful Servants; the servants paid no fee but
could not get their names on to the books unless they had been
two years in one place, or had not been out to service
before.

Big houses drew most of their servants from the families of

their own estate employees, for whose daughters there was little alternative employment and many of whose sons had no greater ambition than the servants' hall of the mansion from which it was possible to attain a position of high authority and great dignity. Thackeray's Raggles, it will be recalled, rose 'from the knife-board to the footboard of the carriage, from the footboard to the butler's pantry', and perhaps, for all we know, to a stewardship.

Life below stairs reflected in many ways that of the employer and his family, the upper servants exacting from the lower the same deference that they themselves accorded to their master and mistress. An upper servant's social position derived from that of his master. 'You will be known by your master's rank and fortune' reads an eighteenth-century guide to domestic service. 'I lost caste terribly amongst the servants', said the ex-footman in *Lavengro* who had left the service of a baronet for that of the editor of a review, 'for entering the service of a person connected with a profession so mean as literature; and it was proposed at the Servants' Club, in Park Lane, to eject me from that society.'

In the servant hierarchy there was a very well-defined line of cleavage between upper and under servants, but both above and below that line there were a number of gradations, depending on the size of the household, the strict observance of which governed social life below stairs.

A few noble families possibly still employed a gentleman-in-waiting and some a comptroller, but in most of the great houses of the day the head of the domestic household was the steward, who was responsible for the whole staff and answerable only to his master. He kept the household accounts, paid the wages, engaged the menservants, and did much of the ordering. He probably had three rooms in the house to himself, a bedroom, sitting-room, and an office, and he took his meals in the steward's room, sitting at the head of what was called the second table, as opposed to the first in the master's dining-room. If there was no steward the head of the household was the housekeeper, also with three rooms to herself, and the second table was in the housekeeper's room over which she presided. The clerk of the kitchen ranked next to the steward among the menservants, then the *chef*, then the butler, the valet and the groom of the chambers.[1] These men were all out of livery and took their meals at the second table. Of the women the lady's maid ranked next to the housekeeper, and took her meals at the second table. These were the upper servants who ate together in the steward's or housekeeper's room, as the case might be, where they were waited on by either the steward's-room boy, the still-room maid or an under housemaid. They sat at table in order of seniority, not of age or length of service, but according to the office or function of each. Professional men, such as doctors and lawyers, who had to visit the mansion on business also took their meals in the steward's room.

The steward's or housekeeper's room, known as the Pug's Parlour to the irreverent under servants who took their meals at the third table in the servants' hall, was also where the visitors' servants took their meals. Etiquette accorded them the precedence of their employers which governed where they sat at table. One of two visitors to a country house was once asked by the valet they were sharing whose servant he was. 'Well Henry,' he was told, 'you were engaged to look after both of us.' 'Yes, Sir,' he replied, 'but you see, Sir, if I'm his Lordship's servant I sit next to the housekeeper, and if I'm your servant I sit next to the Hon. Miss —'s maid, which I should much prefer, Sir.'

Prince Pückler-Muskau was much surprised by the 'slavish reverence' that English upper servants preserved in the presence of their masters. This was in marked contrast with their attitude below stairs where their hauteur was proverbial, and the more illustrious their masters the greater their hauteur. 'What Wretches are ordinary Servants that go on in the same Vulgar Track ev'ry day . . .' James Townley makes one of them say in his *High Life Below Stairs*. 'But we, who have the Honor to serve the Nobility, are of another Species. We are above the common Forms, have Servants to wait upon us, and are as lazy and luxurious as our Masters.' The closer the association of a servant with his employer the greater the airs he gave himself, hence the traditional affectations of valets and lady's maids. 'Do you make no difference between a servant in livery, and a

---

[1] The first responsibility of the groom of the chambers was to look after the furniture. Among his other duties were the care of the fires in the main sitting-rooms, the snuffing of candles, making the house fast at night, and putting out all lights and fires when the rest of the household had gone to bed.

gentleman's gentleman?' inquires a valet in O'Keeffe's *Tony Lumpkin in Town*; '. . . here, Sir, we are delicate, nice in our distinctions; for a valet moves in a sphere, and lives in a style as superior to a footman, as a Pall-mall groom porter to the marker of a tennis-court.'

In the lesser country houses all the servants took their meals, or anyway their dinner, together in the servants' hall where, according to Samuel and Sarah Adams, the authors of *The Complete Servant* of 1825,[1] 'they preserve an order at table like the following: The housekeeper usually takes her seat at the head, and the butler at the lower end of the table; the cook at the right of the housekeeper, and the lady's maid on her left; the under butler on the right, and the coachman on the left of the butler; the house-maid next to the cook, and the kitchen-maid next to the lady's maid; and the men servants always occupying the lower end of the table. The dinner is set on the table by the cook, and the beer is drawn by the under butler.

'The servants' table', they continue, 'is usually provided with solid dishes, and with ale and table beer. . . . In well-regulated families, the servants' hall is distinguished by its decorum, good order, and even good manners, which the servants who wait in the parlour imbibe, and convey to the kitchen. Servants of coarse manners, vulgar habits, or profane discourse, and malicious dispositions, are shunned by the others, and never make good their footing or rise in first-rate families.'

The servants on whom the comfort of the family and that of their guests particularly depended were the footmen. On them too — on their build and height (they were expected to be at least 6 feet tall), their liveries, their manners, even the shape of the calves of their legs, and above all on their numbers — depended the prestige of their employers. This and the competitive spirit of the age led to the extraordinary practice of bringing into the house on big occasions uncouth outdoor servants dressed up in livery. It was much done by the vulgar urban squires, as we learn from Surtees's novels, but not by them alone. Elizabeth Grant tells us how, in 1802, at dinner parties at Castle Grant, the home of her chief, there was a 'footman in the

---

[1] Samuel Adams started, in 1770, as a footboy and became successively groom, footman, valet, butler, and finally house steward. His wife Sarah beginning as a maid-of-all-work, was in turn housemaid, laundrymaid, under-cook, lady's maid, and finally housekeeper for twenty years 'in a very large establishment'.

gorgeous green and scarlet livery behind every chair, but they were mere gillies, lads quite untutored, sons of small tenants, brought in for the occasion . . . fitted into the suit that they best filled'.

As his name implies, the footman's duties were originally those of an escort who accompanied his master or mistress on foot, whether riding, walking or, in London, in a sedan-chair. When carriages came into general use and lawlessness had grown less he was still wanted, but more as an attendant to open and shut the carriage door and to carry messages than as an escort; so he then either stood on the back of the carriage or sat on the box. This change afforded a yet greater opportunity for display. 'One great point of emulation', wrote Benjamin Silliman, an American visitor to England in 1805, 'is to excel all rivals in the number of footmen. Some of the coaches had two, three, or even four footmen, standing up, and holding on behind the carriage, not to mention a supernumerary one on the coachman's box.' When the footman was out with the carriage he was not, according to Samuel and Sarah Adams, to content himself with passively adding to the prestige of his master by the splendour of his appearance. 'Though he may', they wrote, 'indicate the importance of the family by his style of knocking at a door, he ought to have some regard to the nerves of the family and the peace of the neighbourhood.' There was good reason for these cautionary words for footmen were much given to exaggerating their employer's importance, and therefore their own, by excessively loud knocking.[1] So prevalent was this that when people were ill they had the knockers taken off their front doors. Thus in *Vanity Fair* we read of 'the street laid knee-deep with straw, and the knocker put by', when Miss Crawley was critically ill. Among the footman's outdoor duties was one that survived into our own times, that of accompanying his mistress to church to carry her books. By the beginning of the nineteenth century the greater part of a footman's time was spent in the house where no maid servant was ever allowed to be seen in the downstairs rooms. His multifarious duties, like those of the butler, are too well known to need recounting here.

[1] Below stairs much importance attached to the proper knocking at front doors, and we read of country footmen being taught the 'London knock'.

Still in fashion and very *chic*, but seen more often in London than in the country, was the negro footman. Negro servants appear to have been first introduced into England, in important numbers, early in the eighteenth century. Most of them were West Indian slaves, brought home by retired planters, naval and military officers, traders and ships' captains. From the first they were particularly associated with wealthy planters who, on returning to England, set up pretentious and luxurious establishments to which their negro slaves lent a pleasing touch of the exotic. With everything exotic much in favour, people who wanted both to attain the height of fashion and advertise their wealth, as many did, began adding a negro footman or page to their personal retinue, and sometimes a black coachman. As Charles Dunster wrote in 1790, they served as an 'Index of Rank or Opulence supreme', which is just what the fashionable world liked. While most of these negro servants came from the West Indies, not a few had been shipped as slaves from Guinea and bought from Liverpool business houses. This trade, however, had ceased in 1772 when the courts ruled that no law permitted one man to deprive another of his liberty. By that time, however, there were between 15,000 and 20,000 negroes in London alone, and they continued to come in from the West Indies.

To the impressiveness of the negro footman's appearance, which never failed to attract desirable attention, was added the not inconsiderable advantage of his requiring no wages. Decked out in splendid livery (the silver dog-collar round the neck of the early eighteenth-century negro servants was now out of fashion) and given a pretentious classical name (Pompey was much in favour), the negro footman cut a very fine figure, and was much petted by his employer, probably either a great lady or a fashionable prostitute, and often treated almost as one of the family. 'A black footman', wrote Benjamin Silliman, 'is considered a great acquisition, and consequently, negro servants are sought for and caressed. An ill-dressed or starving negro is never seen in England.' The Duchess of Devonshire was much distressed at having to get rid of her black boy: 'eleven years old', she wrote to her mother, 'and very honest, but the duke dont like me having a black, and yet I cannot bear the poor wretch being ill-used; if you liked him instead of Michel I will send him, he will be a cheap servant and you will make a Christian of him and a good boy; if you dont like him they say Lady Rockingham wants one.' It was said that at Kenwood Lord Mansfield and the whole of his establishment were ruled by his negro maid who came into the drawing-room after dinner and took coffee with the ladies. Lord Milford, Horace Walpole tells us, had a 'favourite black' who also was admitted to the drawing-room and joined in the conversation. At Knole, ever since the days of James I, the staff had included a black page, always known as John Morocco. He was finally replaced with a Chinese, Hwang-a-Tung, whom the Duke of Dorset educated at Sevenoaks Grammar School and who was painted by Sir Joshua Reynolds. Dr. Johnson's negro, Frank Barber, also sat to Sir Joshua. At Tichborne there was Andrew Bogle, the Jamaican negro who arrived there as a boy of eleven in 1818. He was a most trusted family servant who afterwards became famous as an important witness in the Tichborne Trial. He married two English wives, Lady Doughty's nurse and the village schoolmistress at Tichborne.

Trouble sometimes arose through women growing much too fond of their negro servants. Silliman was excusably shocked at seeing 'a well dressed white girl ... and even handsome, walking arm in arm, and conversing very sociably, with a negro man, who was as well dressed as she'. Greatly to the credit of these pampered menials they were, generally speaking, well liked in the servants' hall.

A curious survival from the eighteenth century was the running footman who, like the black, seems to have been valued less for the services he performed than for his spectacular appearance and the glory this reflected on his master. As his name implies, he was used as a courier who, in the days of bad and miry roads, ran ahead of his master's coach to prepare the inn to receive him; he was also employed to carry messages. One of his occasional duties was to run races with other running footmen for the diversion of his master, often for heavy wagers. We hear of the Duke of Wharton backing his man to outdistance another's in a race from Woodstock to Tyburn for 1,000 guineas, and of a similar race from Rochester to Westminster.

The dress of the running footman varied in detail, like the

ordinary footman's livery, from family to family, but he usually wore a velvet cap (sometimes with a tassel), a white jacket, and a coloured sash round the waist. In the previous century he had worn a sort of kilt, but in our period this seems to have given place to breeches, probably because, to quote a writer of 1725, 'our Village Maids delight to see the Running Footman fly bare-ars'd o'er the dusty Road'. He always carried a great staff, ornamented with a silver knob.

As roads and communications improved the running footman ceased to serve any useful purpose, and it was only love of ostentation and betting that kept him in service. The last private employer of a running footman was probably the 4th Duke of Queensberry who died in 1810.[1] Before engaging a running footman he used to race the applicants up and down Piccadilly, timing them with a watch from the balcony of his house.[2]

It would be tedious to dwell on the duties of each of the many servants in a big country house, which Samuel and Sarah set out in great detail, but something must be said of the cook on whom so much depended, and of whom we hear very little, for, as the *Almanach des Gourmands* said, 'the most consummate Cook is, alas! seldom noticed by the master, or heard of by the guests; who, while they are eagerly devouring his Turtle, and drinking his Wine, — care very little who dressed the one, or sent the other!' 'This observation', comments *The Cook's Oracle*, 'applies especially to the Second Cook, or *first Kitchen Maid*, in large families, who have by far the hardest place in the house, and are worse paid, and truly verify the old adage, *"the more work, the less wages"*. — If there is any thing right, the Cook has the praise—when there is any thing wrong, as surely, the *Kitchen maid* has the blame. — Be it known, then, to honest John Bull, that this humble domestic, is expected by the Cook to take the entire management of all Roasts and Boils, Fish and Vegetables — i.e. *the principal part of an Englishman's dinner.'*

But the cook's reputation did not depend only on her assistant. 'On first coming into a family,' advises *The Cook's Oracle*, 'lose no time in immediately getting into the good graces of your

---

[1] Two running footmen remained part of the retinue of the High Sheriff of Northumberland until the second half of the nineteenth century.

[2] In London there is a public house called The Running Footman, just where one would expect to find it, in the heart of Mayfair — Charles Street, Berkeley Square.

fellow-servants. . . . Take care, to be on good terms with the
servant who waits at table; — you may make use of him as your
Sentinel to inform you how your work has pleased in the parlour, and by his report you may be enabled in some measure to
rectify any mistake.'

In large establishments the upper servants occupied well-
furnished rooms on the ground floor, and the under ones slept at
the top of the house, where the sharing of beds was not unusual,
and the furniture limited to the barest necessities. Yet the
discomfort was probably less than what most young servants
had been brought up to in their own homes.

There was a great difference between the meals served in the
steward's or housekeeper's room and those in the servants' hall.
The former approached those of the dining-room and were
supplemented by what was left over there, so much so that
footmen sometimes took care to see that the family and their
guests did not eat too much of a favourite dish. In some great
houses the upper servants were given wine regularly. 'This
table', boasted the Duke of Kingston's valet, 'would not disgrace
a gentleman of ten thousand a year.'

In the servants' hall the under servants were naturally given
much simpler food, and they were apt to suffer from the greed
and arrogance of the second table. There are frequent complaints of the under servants being starved by the upper, both
to supplement their own sumptuous meals and to have something over to give to the many friends they liked to entertain in
the house. In spite of there being a lavish allowance of beer and
ale to every member of the household, the young servants often
had to go short, again largely because of the entertaining of friends
in the steward's room. 'We your Graces servants', wrote seventeen under servants at Welbeck to the Duke of Portland, 'beg
leave to petition for Ale; not for our selves particular, but for the
Servants of Your Grace's friends, which we have frequently
been refus'd by Mr. Martini, Your Grace's Butler, without
giving any reason for the same, but in saying I am Master and
you shall have none.' Housekeepers could be equally difficult.
'Great Complainings at Weston-House,' wrote Parson Woodforde in 1801, 'Servants complaining to their Master that they
had not victuals enough owing to the House-Keeper, Hetty
Yallop, keeping them very short.'

H

Although the work was hard and the hours very long, the servants of the rich, especially of those who entertained a great deal, did not lead particularly dull lives. The family's friends brought their servants with them, and some of the gaiety of dining-room and drawing-room spread downstairs. The rich, too, paid long visits to each other's houses, so that there were often long periods with comparatively little work to do. These absences of the family naturally benefited the under servants less than the upper because the latter made them an opportunity to do no work at all, and to entertain their own friends at the expense, in time, labour, food, and ale, of the unfortunate younger members of the staff. For valets and lady's maids, coachmen and footmen, who frequently accompanied their masters and mistresses to other houses where they were warmly welcomed, life must often have been very pleasant.

When one reads of the tyranny exercised by upper servants over the under ones one is left wondering that so many young people went into private service. This was partly due to the prestige they acquired, in the eyes of their own class, from the social status of their employers, and partly to the opportunities for advancement which private service afforded. Moreover, with everything, or nearly everything, found for them by their masters and mistresses, they were better sheltered from the hazards of life than any other class, so long as, of course, they remained in employment. *The Cook's Oracle* of 1822 reminds employers how little out of her wages 'a *poor Girl* will have remaining to place to her account in the Saving Bank, — for help *in Sickness*, — when *Out of Place*, — and for her support in *Old Age*. — Here, — is the source, — of the swarms of distressed females which we daily meet in our streets.' The Adamses were most insistent on the need for servants to use the Savings Banks to make provision for the uncertainties of domestic service.

In addition to their wages[1] and tea-money the upper servants enjoyed considerable perquisites. The butler was allowed to

---

[1] In 1825 wages for menservants varied from 80 guineas a year for a French *chef*, and 50 for a butler, down to 9 for a scullion. Women got much less: a housekeeper 24 guineas, a lady's maid 20, and the nurserymaid 7. At the bottom of the scale was the nursery room boy who had to be content with his clothes and a gratuity. The men were allowed a pot of ale a day, and the women a pint, but there seems to have been no limit on the 'table-beer' that might be drunk. Wages were paid yearly or half yearly.

keep the candle ends[1] and empty bottles, the cook the dripping which, as in our day, she sold to the village, and the coachman the worn-out carriage wheels. Valets and lady's maids got, and often sold, the cast-off clothing of their employers, and footmen were allowed to keep their old suits of livery.[2] Then there were the tips, or vails as they called them, left behind by visitors who, in great houses, could usually afford to be generous.

In such houses, too, especially if they were of historic interest, servants benefited from the not inconsiderable tips from sight-seeing tourists, who were much given to ringing the front-door bell and asking to be shown the house. So much was this the fashion that some of the more popular houses were open to the public on a certain day each week. Woburn, for example, was always open on Monday. From John Byng, who on his frequent tours in the last quarter of the eighteenth century never missed a 'sight' if he could help it, we learn a good deal about the varied experiences of those who wanted to see over other people's houses. A visit to Hagley set him 'thinking that no one shou'd suffer his place to be visited, but with intention to make those visitors happy; and shou'd likewise equip his servants with attention and civility: at Hagley there is a particular want of these articles'. He was annoyed when Lord Guildford, in very excusable circumstances, refused to allow him to see over Wroxton. 'Very rude this, and unlike an old courtly lord! Let him either forbid his place entirely; open it allways; or else fix a day of admission: but, for shame, don't refuse travellers,

---

[1] Candle ends could be a valuable perquisite for, to the grief of the poor, candles were heavily taxed and expensive. Wax candles were a great luxury. One of the pleasures to which Parson Woodforde treated himself on Christmas Day 1799, after a dinner of 'roast beef, plumb Pudding and Mince Pies', was to burn his 'old Wax Candle . . . about half an Hour, it is almost finished, it might last for once more, & that is all it can do'. On the following Christmas Day he wrote: 'I lighted my Great Wax-Candle as usual on this High-day, but it is almost burnt up.'

There were several other kinds of candles. Next to the very expensive wax ones came spermaceti candles which seem to have been nearly as good; composite candles, or 'compos' as they were called, appear to have been reserved for servants; tallow-dips were used in the kitchen; mutton-fats and moulds went to the stables.

Free candles, presumably of wax, formed part of the emoluments of some public servants. For example, Lord Auckland's remuneration as a Commissioner of Greenwich Hospital was £600 a year with coals and candles.

When Queen Victoria married not only were the thousands of candles used to light Buckingham Palace never lit a second time, but, whether they had been used or not, they were replaced daily with new. Those that were taken away, both used and unused, were the perquisites of the servants.

[2] The footman had to provide his own stockings unless they were required to be of silk, in which case his employer supplied them.

who may have come 20 miles out of their way for a sight of the place.' A note provoked by a visit to Battle Abbey has a curiously modern ring about it: 'I allways wonder', wrote Byng, 'that an owner of a real antiquity does not print a short account of his possession; which all visitors wou'd purchase with grateful avidity.'

The duty of showing visitors over a house usually fell on the housekeeper who seems seldom to have been seen at her best by tourists. The Belvoir housekeeper, according to Byng, was 'of a very drunken, dawdling appearance', but she was possibly more endurable than the one at Warwick Castle: 'An old growling superannuated housekeeper attended us; but her manners!' But he was not always lucky when a lesser mortal deputized for the haughty housekeeper. At Scrivelsby Hall, near Horncastle, a housemaid was 'stupid to an extreme' and 'ill merited our two shillings'.

The kitchen gardens and their glass houses were also an attraction to tourists, particularly to John Byng who loved to inspect a kitchen garden. But he did not like, or expect, to leave it empty-handed. At Fairford Park, we read, 'the gardener shou'd not have led me thro the hot-houses, shewing me ripe grapes, nectarines, pines, &c. without making me a single offer:— suppose a woman had been with me! In other respects he was a civil fellow; and no Scotchman!!' At Ashburnham Park he went 'to view the kitchen-garden, from the hope of getting fruit; but here we were most uncivilly disappointed, for tho' in abundance the gardener made no offer, nor wou'd even permit us a handful from the profusion of Morello cherries: so we turn'd out in dudgeon!' On one of his visits to Blenheim he was shown the gardens by a boy of twelve, 'whom I fee'd, as they do at Hampton-Court, to the great emolument of the housekeeper'. On a previous visit he had complained that 'the expence of seeing Blenheim is very great; the servants of the poor D—of M. being very attentive in gleaning money from rich travellers'.

Servants supplemented all too often their legitimate perquisites with illicit gains. One of the commonest was the acceptance of bribes, often as poundage, from tradesmen. In order to swell these surreptitious payments the more dishonest servants would connive at overcharges and short weight. As the ordering was often left to the upper servants, who could place their employer's custom where they chose, the blackmailing of tradesmen heavily dependent on a great house was easy enough. The acceptance of Christmas boxes from tradesmen had become permissible but it also led to blackmail. On one occasion the London grocers decided to protect themselves against the rapacity of their customers' servants by stopping Christmas boxes. The servants retaliated by giving up drinking tea.

There was not a little deliberate thieving by servants. Butlers, who were wholly in charge of the immense wine-cellars of those days, were much given to selling their masters' wine. Emily Eden's friend Lady Campbell was one of the victims of organized theft involving three great houses, Bowood, Longleat, and Albury Park. Lady Campbell's maid Bridget, recommended to her by Lady Lansdowne, stole £70 worth of her things. 'Never trust Jane Kingston, Lady Bath's laundress,' wrote Lady Campbell, 'for Bridget declares upon oath having sent the things to her — my best lace among the rest.' With them also was 'a fine brodée handkerchief . . . with Harriet embroidered in the corner . . . perhaps the House of Drummond might wish to make reclamation'. It is hardly surprising that servants followed their masters' example of getting drunk. A drunken footman was apt to be found out by his falling off the back of the carriage.

But in the main good employers, as ever, had good servants, and these realized that their obligations to their employers extended far beyond the mere work required of them. 'Always remember', wrote the Adamses in their advice to young servants, 'to *hold the secrets of the family sacred*, as none, not even the least of *these*, may be divulged with impunity.' The hall porter, always on duty in the entrance hall of great London houses, was required to be the soul of tact and discretion. 'The public character of a nobleman or gentleman often depends on this servant. Rude or contemptuous language, to the meanest applicant, will frequently prove injurious to the interest of his master . . . his best qualities are patience and good temper, to which may be added, secrecy in regard to the affairs, connexions, and intercourse of the family. A close tongue, and an inflexible countenance, are, therefore, indispensable, and he should practise the maxim of hearing and seeing all, but saying nothing.' History, unfortunately, has failed to record the families in which the Adamses learnt the importance of 'hearing and see-ing all, but saying nothing'.

Another good piece of advice to young servants was never to 'accept the invitations of other servants, nor go to feast at the expense of their masters or mistresses . . . it lays you under an obligation to return the treat, and induces you . . . to make free with the property of your own employers'. Above all young servants must 'manifest a MEEK and QUIET SPIRIT. . . . Act therefore with submission to the will and judgment of your superiors.' Their immediate superiors were of course the all-powerful upper servants.

From the moment he entered service the whole of a servant's time was supposed to be at the entire disposal of his master. 'When you hired yourselves', wrote Thomas Broughton in his *Serious Advice and Warning to Servants*, 'you sold all your time to your masters, except what God and Nature more immediately require to be reserved.' But it was realized that such abject service imposed considerable obligations on the employer who was expected to regard his servants as members of his family, and for whose physical and moral welfare, in the fullest sense, he was responsible.[1] Although we hear very little about servants and how they were treated in contemporary chronicles, country houses cannot have been so efficiently run as they evidently were had not the servants been well treated.

It equally cannot be doubted that there were very bad employers, and the Apperley family appear to have been among them. Nimrod (C. J. Apperley) tells us how his father, finding a footman stealing money, stripped him to the waist, hoisted him over the servants' hall door, and gave him a good flogging. The punishment may have been well deserved, but so deplorable was Nimrod's own attitude to servants that doubt is permissible. In *The Life of a Sportsman* which, Nimrod tells us, purported 'to portray the character of an English gentleman', he makes his odious hero, a wealthy and aristocratic young man, behave to servants in a way of which no gentleman, then or now, would

---

[1] An appendix to *The Complete Servant* of 1825 reads:

'Servants must go to Church

'Masters can insist on their servants going to church; and every person whose servant shall be absent from church, for one month, at a time, without a reasonable excuse, forfeits 10*l* for every month he so keeps that servant.'

have been guilty. He tells the old housekeeper she 'is really past enduring', and the old cook, 'it is time to put you on the shelf'; the gamekeeper is addressed as 'you slow old fool', and so on. In fairness to Nimrod it must be recorded that the cook was heard aptly muttering 'Gentlemen isn't what they used to be'. Nevertheless, he saw nothing blameworthy in the way he made his young hero behave to his father's old servants.

That employers usually showed great consideration for their servants is clear enough from the frequent complaints in contemporary newspapers and magazines of the reluctance of masters and mistresses to give a dismissed servant a bad character. The number of dishonest servants who had no difficulty in getting situations was invariably blamed on to this misplaced kindness which was no less prevalent then than it has been ever since. The reluctance to dismiss old servants just because they had become difficult and tyrannical, as old retainers so often do, also showed kindness and consideration. 'We were permitted', wrote John Byng of his visit to Battle Abbey, 'to run into the house, catching a glimpse of the lofty hall, and one old chamber; and saw, yet a greater curiosity, the family butler, Mr Ingall, 103 years of age, who had been a post-boy in York, in Queen Annes reign; and now, frequently, in a passion, gives warning, and threatens to quit his place: he was very deaf, else I wou'd have spoken to him; but we both bow'd to him; and his age bow'd him to us!'

When servants did retire they were usually well cared for. Many old menservants became publicans in one of the inns belonging to the estate. Pensions to old and valued servants were often followed by legacies. There must have been many a country squire who felt as Horace Walpole did when, in his old age, he wrote, 'I know . . . how pleasant it is to have laid up a little for those I love, for those that depend on me, and for old servants.'

VIII

The Slow March of Progress

It would be wrong to assume that Emily Eden's and the other contemporary accounts of visits to the mansions of the wealthiest of the aristocracy tell the whole story of social life in that lofty sphere. They inevitably leave untold a great deal that was unattractive, and much that was repellent. The aristocracy shared with all other classes the mid-eighteenth century's unpleasant legacy of debauchery and brutality, though to a diminishing degree. In the upper classes standards were rising and paving the way for the era of dull respectability and domestic virtue which we associate with the names of Victoria and Albert. But not much could be expected of a generation that had witnessed a duel between a Prime Minister and the Leader of the Opposition on Wimbledon Common, another between two Dukes in Kensington Gardens, and a third at Battersea when no less a man than the Iron Duke called out a fellow peer.

In the early years of the nineteenth century the most unattractive feature of social life was drunkenness. The Regent, wrote Creevey, describing a visit to the Pavilion, 'was certainly tipsey, and so, of course, was I.' A year or so later at a dance at Lady Hopetown's the Prince, wrote Lady Louisa Stuart, 'was most gloriously drunk and riotous indeed. He posted himself in the doorway to the terror of everybody that went by, flung his arms round the Dutchess of Ancaster's neck and kissed her with a great smack, threatened to pull Lord Galloway's wig off and knock out his false teeth. . . .'

'When the ladies left the dining-room,' wrote Lord John Russell,[1] describing a typical dinner party of this period, 'fresh bottles of port would be brought in, the host would arise

[1] Lord John was known as the Widow's Mite because he was a very small man and had married the widow of the 2nd Lord Ribblesdale.

and lock the door, and almost every man drank until he was under the table. With the exception of one or two men who kept sober, they never joined the ladies again, and a page, towards the end of the drinking, as the men slipped from their seats, would loosen the neck-cloths of the prostrate guests, and it was a regular custom for the valets to come in, carry out their masters, put them in their coaches, and escort them home. Some curious incidents arose when some of the valets were not themselves too sober, and substitutes had to take their places, and some of the masters were put into the wrong coaches and carried to the wrong houses about midnight or later, much to the astonishment . . . of the wives and other members of the households.'

Such orgies were not peculiar to the upper classes. 'At the close of last century,' wrote an Essex doctor, 'and in the beginning of this, the 19th., excessive drinking prevailed throughout all classes, and not least amongst the aristocracy. It seemed to be a mark of distinction in favour of the man who could drink the largest quantity of wine without being quite drunk; many were put under the table and some carried to bed in a helpless condition. Farmers followed the example at their parish dinners — the chair commonly taken by the Parson — and at their private home parties. Their drink was usually Punch, made of brandy and rum. The artizans and labourers were content with beer.'

The habit of drunkenness found encouragement in both the example set by the highest in the land, and the easy opportunities of early youth. The dissolute Jack Mytton, who was said never to have been sober during the last twelve years of his short life, learnt to drink when at school at Rugby, which some boys left as confirmed drunkards. It was thought unmanly, if not effeminate, for a man not to get drunk, and this led to the encouragement of early drinking. Nimrod tells us that he had been educated in 'hunting, shooting, fishing and drinking'. Born a gentleman but at heart a cad, Nimrod had a very unbalanced sense of social values. Nevertheless, he was certainly not alone in his admiration for a man who, frequently falling down drunk in drawing-rooms, was 'drunk or sober always the gentleman'; nor in his failure to censure a parson lying dead drunk on his back in a friend's garden. Then there was his friend Mr. Leche who was not a drunkard, he tells us, but never left the table sober. It is still more bewildering to hear of a stage coachman being told that he 'was not drunk for a gentleman but you were damned drunk for a coachman'. George IV's fondness for making other people drunk was certainly shared by many of his subjects. There were many country houses in which not only the host but also the butler thought it a reproach on their hospitality to allow a guest, whether a gentleman or his servant, to leave the house sober.[1]

Excessive drinking was closely associated with smuggling. The war with France, by stopping legitimate trade with the Continent, had greatly encouraged smuggling which was made easy for the English by their command of the sea. The large profits to be made and the ready access smuggling afforded to unlimited supplies of liquor, drew both the gentry and the farmers of the coastal districts into the business. It kept the country well supplied with hollands, gin and brandy, to the great encouragement of hard drinking, especially of spirits, which were far more harmful than the beer to which excessive drinking among the working classes was of necessity, and to their advantage, confined.

But light French wines were becoming popular, and we repeatedly hear of more champagne and claret and less port being drunk. This led to less drunkenness and increasing respect for sobriety. Even Nimrod, an admirer of hard drinkers, had to record approvingly that 'a pint of wine is the usual limit with many of the best men at Melton'. A few people set their faces very strongly against drunkenness. At Sir Foster Cunliffe's, Acton Park, no one was ever known to leave the dining-room drunk, and he also contrived to keep his servants' hall sober. But he was popular with neither his neighbours nor his servants. In polite society smoking was still taboo. In the country a man might smoke only out of doors or in the saddle-room, in London only outside on the balcony.

If people were drinking less wine they were not moderating their consumption of food. The gargantuan meals of the eighteenth century were not only still in fashion but were destined to remain so, as we know from the novels of Dickens and

[1] The 1st Duke of Cleveland, who died in 1842, 'always had his wine-glasses made without a foot', wrote Augustus Hare, 'so that they would not stand, and you were obliged to drink off the whole glass when you dined with him.'

Surtees, until the second half of the nineteenth. These novelists tell us little of the expensive native delicacies then to be found on the tables of the rich. As salmon ceased to run up the Thames at the turn of the century epicures were having to content themselves with Severn salmon, not quite as good but the next best. We hear nearly as often of Dunstable larks[1] as we do of Whitstable oysters. Two native luxuries still in fashion at the beginning of the century, but increasingly difficult to get, were wheatears, and ruffs and reeves.

Wheatears were caught on the Sussex Downs in turf traps, whatever they may have been. A pleasant custom allowed the epicure to help himself from the traps provided he left a penny for each bird he took away. At the Castle Inn at Brighton John Byng 'sigh'd for more wheatears after the many we had eaten dress'd to perfection'. Ruffs and reeves were caught and fattened for the London market in the Fens where Spalding was the chief centre of the small and unusual trade which hardly survived into the nineteenth century. 'There is a *glover* in this town,' wrote Byng at Spalding in 1791, 'who fattens those dainty birds, call'd ruffs and rees, for the tables of the great; but the number of these birds is much decreas'd by the drainage of the fens: however, he sells about 1200 dozen during the summer; and to the King regularly, the Duke of Portland, &c &c &c. These birds, being pinion'd, are render'd very tame, very fat, and very dear; a couple of them I sent as a present to London.' When he was at Spalding in the previous year fat ruffs and reeves were selling at '5 shillings the couple, male and female'.

The gentry closely associated themselves with the masses in racing and pugilism, in both of which the whole country took a passionate interest. It was the age of the great heroes of the prize ring — such men as Tom Cribb, Tom Spring and Langan. The great fights were usually financed and umpired by the aristocracy whose illustrious names added greatly to the attractions of these contests. But many of those who thronged the ring were drawn from the criminal classes with consequences

---

[1] Dunstable's trade in larks dated back to at least the seventeenth century. 'Dunstable larks', wrote 'Dunno', the local historian, in about 1820, 'are served up in great perfection at some of the inns in this town (owing to a peculiar and secret method in the process of cooking them); they are admired as a luxury by the nobility and gentry who travel through Dunstable in the Lark-season.'

which made prize-fighting one of the most degrading of sports. A fight between Tom Spring and Langan in 1824, umpired by Lord Deerhurst and Sir Harry Goodricke, the wealthy Yorkshire baronet and a future master of the Quorn, well illustrates how low the ring had fallen. The fight lasted two and a half hours, during the last hour of which the distinguished umpires had to quit the ring because 'it was crowded to excess by men kicking, pushing and striking with whips and sticks, Langan receiving more than his share of the blows'. From this passionate interest in the ring, and pride in being able to take as well as give 'punishment', sprang one of the more unattractive habits of the time. This was the settlement of disputes between men of the upper and lower classes by resort to fisticuffs. Men like Thackeray's Rev. Bute Crawley, who had 'thrashed all the best bruisers of the town', were local heroes. Thomas Assheton Smith, on all counts a model squire, feeling himself insulted by a very powerful coalheaver in Leicester, challenged him, and fought him up and down the street till the constables separated them. But the aggressors were not always the gentry. Prince Pückler-Muskau had the misfortune to affront a 'huge gigantic carter' in the City who at once challenged him, but he was not given the satisfaction he would have expected from an English country squire.

The principal amusements of the gentry were shooting and foxhunting, both of which had recently acquired a popularity they had never before enjoyed. The circumstances in which this came about will be described in later chapters. Both, however, were open, in contemporary opinion, to the objection that they gave so little opportunity for betting, then a ruling passion with all classes. Much of the attraction of racing and the prize-ring lay in the opportunities they afforded for gambling, which also kept alive such cruel sports as cock-fighting, dog-fighting, bull-baiting, bear-baiting and the rest. Cock-fighting was a traditional sport of the rural aristocracy whose cock-pits, Howitt declared, 'have been the nuisances of their neighbourhoods, and their game-cock caravans, travelling from place to place with these cocks, have offended the public eye'. In 1802 an unsuccessful attempt was made in Parliament to abolish bull- and bear-baiting, but soon after Waterloo public feeling began to turn against all cruel sports. This was largely due to

the preaching of the Methodists of the industrial towns, and
provided one of those very rare examples of urban influence
bettering rural society. By 1831 feeling against cruel sports had
become sufficiently strong for the prospectus of Surtees's *New
Sporting Magazine* to announce that its pages would be closed to
such 'low and demoralizing pursuits' as prize-fighting, bull-
baiting, and cock-fighting. But four years more had to pass
before cruel sports became illegal, and even then, to the regret
of many, dog-fighting was excluded.

Nevertheless, barbarity still survived in the nursery. Children's nannies threatened them with witches and shut them up in
terrifyingly dark cupboards when they were naughty; uneaten
and nauseating food came back, meal after meal — and day
after day in case of need — till it was finished. Elizabeth Grant
has left us a horrifying account of what went on in the nursery
of her father, J. P. Grant of Rothiemurchus and Thorley Hall,
in 1806, in his London and Hertfordshire houses. Elizabeth
herself was nine, her brother William eight, and her sister
Jane six. Their day started with being carried down in their
night gowns and plunged into a tub of water standing in
the kitchen court, 'the ice on the top of which had often to be
broken before our horrid plunge into it. . . . How I screamed,
begged, prayed, entreated to be saved, half the tender-hearted
maids in tears beside me; all no use, Millar [the nurse] had her
orders.' Their next ordeal was a breakfast of 'dry bread and cold
milk the year round with the exception of the three winter
months, when in honour of our Scotch blood we were favoured
with porridge'. Unfortunately for these three small children milk
nauseated them. 'My stomach entirely rejecting milk, bread
and tears generally did for me.' The cold bath and the horrible
breakfast, forced down unwilling throats, seem to have been
customary for small children in those days. It is to be hoped,
however, that the part the future Sir Peter Grant played in the
up-bringing of his children was unusual. He decided to stop the
daily fuss over the nursery breakfast. 'The milk rebellion was
crushed immediately', continues Elizabeth's story; 'in his
dressing-gown, with his whip in his hand, he attended our
breakfast. . . . He began with me; my beseeching look was
answered by a sharp cut, followed by as many more as were
necessary to empty the basin; Jane obeyed at once, and

William after one good hint.' At their mid-day meal it was the same. 'The stomachs which rejected milk could not easily manage fat except when we were under the lash, then indeed the fat and the tears were swallowed together.' There was a fourth child, Mary, who was only three and for whom her father had devised a special punishment. 'She used to be set on the lowest step of the stair . . . and not allowed to move from there till permission was given. One night my father forgot her, so, I suppose, had every one else, for on ringing for wine and water at midnight, the footman who brought it up found the poor little thing lying there asleep.' The mother of these unhappy children never visited her nursery: 'when she wanted her children or her maids she rang for them'.

In pleasant and striking contrast with the coarseness and brutality of the age was the new craze for gardening. When the Duke of Wellington and Mrs. Arbuthnot visited Blenheim in 1822 they found the Duke of Marlborough 'gardening mad'. No one was more devoted to her garden than Miss Berry, and none worked harder in it. We hear of her trundling her wheelbarrow, spending long hours in her greenhouse, and, like every good gardener, finding pleasure in making herself 'heartily tired'. One November day in 1809 her journal recorded: 'I spent the whole day in my garden and greenhouse, completely enjoying myself and forgetting everything but the pots I was arranging and the roots I was transplanting . . . I never regret a day like this.' Nearly thirty years later, when she was an old lady of seventy-five, she was longing to get back to her 'quiet garden' in which she could work so long as her strength lasted.

Emily Eden, who shared her brother Lord Auckland's love of their garden, was once reduced to tears by having to give up a day to go to Epsom Races. 'We went all the same; but, as for gardening, what was the good of cultivating flowers for other people's nosegays! So there I sat under the verandah crying. What else could be done, with the roses all out, and the sweet-peas, and our orange-trees, and the whole garden looking perfectly lovely; and George was nearly as low as I was.' On another occasion she wrote: 'We must go soon to that vile London for that foolish Parliament, and our little garden is so full of flowers, and gives so much occupation in collecting seeds, and making cuttings, that I grudge leaving it, even for a day.' A few days later she wrote: 'I have had the delight of sowing seeds to a great amount since Monday. I wish gardening were not so fatiguing. I like it so very much, but I am dead tired every night.'

This passionate love for a garden was not peculiar to the Edens, nor to their aristocratic circle. 'As the coach passes the residence of Colonel Howard at Leven's Bridge, in West-moreland', wrote Howitt, 'it stops, the passengers get out, and mount upon its top, and there behold a fine old Elizabethan house, standing in the midst of a garden of that age, with all its topiary-work, its fountains, statues, and lawns.' To Howitt it seemed that in the gardens of the gentry perfection had been reached. 'Nothing', he continued, 'can be more delicious than the rural paradises which now surround our country houses.' The beauty of English gardens owed much to the Scotch gardeners who were to be found at the head of most of the big gardens of the day, but they would not have achieved what they did but for the pride and interest of their employers in their work. This love of a garden was of course inherent in the English, but it did not blossom and fructify till the beginning of the nineteenth century. With it came the *cottage ornée*, the conservatory, and inside the house, *jardinières*, simultaneously with water-closets. We shall do well to pause and consider the circumstances that led to an enrichment of country life which not only did not fade, but has never ceased to grow.

One of the great events in the history of English gardening was when, in the middle of the eighteenth century, William Kent, to quote Horace Walpole, 'leaped the fence, and saw that all Nature was a garden'. In doing so he brought Nature into the garden and created landscape gardening. 'The leading step to all that has followed', to quote Walpole again, 'was . . . the destruction of walls for boundaries, and the invention of fosses[1] . . . an attempt then deemed so astonishing, that the common people called them Ha! Ha's! to express their surprise at finding a sudden and unperceived check to their walk.'[2] As

---

[1] According to Dr. Johnson a park wall cost £1,000 a mile. Ha-has were about £300 a mile cheaper.

[2] This seemingly improbable theory is unwittingly confirmed by Cobbett. The valleys of Wiltshire, he tells us, 'are, as to the downs, what *ah-ahs*! are, in parks or lawns. . . . You look *over* the valleys, as in the case of the *ah-ah*; and, if you be not acquainted with the country, your surprise, when you come to the edge of the hill, is very great.' Cobbett's exclamation mark (!) and the word 'surprise' are surely conclusive.

Nature came in, flowery parterres gave place to sweeping lawns,[1] adorned with statues, urns and monuments; ancient avenues were felled to make way for lakes, and cascades, and informal clumps of trees and shrubs, half concealing classical temples and, that curious product of the Gothic revival, artificial ruins — often, as a crowning absurdity, made of plaster or canvas.

The work of Kent was further developed by Lancelot or 'Capability' Brown who, from a humble beginning in the gardens at Stowe, rose to such fame that he left his mark, as both a destroyer and a creator, on most of the great gardens in England, not least on those at Blenheim. But his successor in the landscape school, Humphry Repton, was the man who did most to create the country-house garden as we know it and as it is known to fame in half the world. Perceiving the threat of landscaping to horticulture, he called a halt and brought the flower garden back to the front of the house, allowing it to merge naturally into the landscape. In doing this, in marrying horticulture to landscaping, he opened the way for gardening to become the great hobby it has ever since remained.

By the end of the century nearly every garden of importance in England had been transformed or altered by Kent, Brown or Repton and their disciples, and few owners of large estates had failed to respond to the intense interest in gardens which these three remarkable men had awakened. This new interest in gardens created an insatiable demand for new plants which collectors all over the world sought to satisfy. We owe many of our most popular garden plants to this period. The first wistaria from China to arrive in England was planted at Chiswick in 1818. Also from the Far East came at this time a host of new roses, notably the Banksia Rose, the Tea Rose, and the multifloras. By 1826 a leading nurseryman was listing over 1,400 different rose species and varieties. Other important introductions of the time were dahlias, petunias, calceolarias, lupins, pentstemons, and the garden *ribes*. With all these came a host of

---

[1] The shaving of these lawns with scythes involved immense labour. At Syon House, the Duke of Northumberland's, Prince Pückler-Muskau tells us, 'in the vast pleasure-ground twelve men are daily mowing from five till nine o'clock'. The mowing machine was invented in about 1830 but was slow to come into general use; it was claimed that it provided country gentlemen with 'amusing, useful and healthy exercise'.

IX *Frank Barber, Dr. Johnson's Negro Servant:* Negro footmen made excellent servants, received no wages, and, dressed up in gorgeous livery, attracted desirable attention.

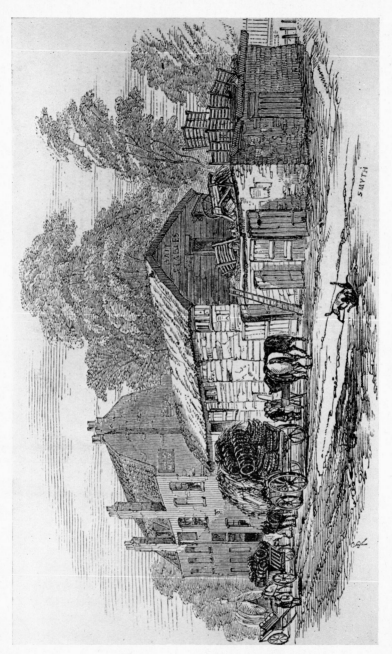

X   *The Half-Way House, between Knightsbridge and Kensington*: This typical country inn, standing in the centre of the highway opposite where the Prince of Wales Gate was later built, was considered an 'unseemly building' and a grave disfigurement to 'the western entrance to the Metropolis'.

ornamental trees, notably the Douglas fir and Sitka spruce introduced by David Douglas from the Pacific coast of North America. In 1833 the orchid collection at Chatsworth, with Joseph Paxton as head gardener, was begun. The crowding of greenhouses with new species led, in 1820, to 'bedding out', for which geometrical beds were cut in the sweeping lawns of the landscapists, and the Italian garden was created.

Such were the circumstances in which the Royal Horticultural Society was founded in 1804, and gardening became a favourite pastime of the country squires and their ladies. But not only of them. The middle classes, never slow to imitate the aristocracy, were also taking to gardening. Amid the laburnums and lilacs of their villa gardens there was now beginning to appear 'a goodly assemblage of large stones, and perhaps old roots and trunks of trees, lying loosely together on a mound of earth'. Some preferred 'hillocks of flints and fused bricks'. Thus was begotten one of the greatest of garden horrors; another, rustic furniture, also dates from this period.

To see the current fashion for the grotesque at its worst you had to go out to the country. John Byng was shown a Lincolnshire parson's garden which was 'almost cover'd with cloisters, seats, &c, all made of roots of trees, and moss, to correspond with an hermitage in the centre, finish'd with curious taste, and trouble: therein are several rooms, recesses, and chapels, all lighted by old stain'd, glass, (once in Tattershall Church;) the ornamental parts are of fir cones; the tables of polish'd horse bones. . . . I wonder'd that no country-people would endeavour to make such comfortable chairs, and tables, as he had form'd from sticks and pieces of wood: for every thing is in correspondent taste; even the ink stands are of curious roots. . . . There are books in several apartments, and on the floors many inscriptions of praise, work'd in wood, pebbles, or horse-bones; but not one cross: probably he might fear to give offence. Most of the doors are composed of fir-cones, or of roots curiously woven together.'

It was not long before the artisans of the sooty industrial towns began to realize that in the new fashion for gardening lay a mental escape from the dreariness of their surroundings, and recreation which was both outdoor and absorbingly interesting. With little space in which to practise the new art, they quickly

I

learnt to specialize in a few favourites which, with loving care, could be grown to perfection in a yard or two of carefully prepared soil. In the little back-yard gardens of the industrial Midlands and North such flowers as auriculas, tulips, carnations and pinks attained a grace and beauty they had seldom known in the gardens of the gentry. Thus did the manufacturing towns become the stronghold of the florists' societies. Certain great towns specialized in a single flower. Paisley, for example, became famous for its pinks. A strange and unaccountable aberration from the common form were the Lancashire towns which in our period were already holding the gooseberry shows which are not yet out of fashion.

English country houses were already distinguished for their kitchen gardens. Walled, and usually kept locked, they were not confined to the growing of vegetables. Their magnificent walls were covered with a wide variety of carefully trained fruit trees, and flower borders were an essential feature. In 1823 Miss Berry declared that Sir John Stanley's kitchen garden at Alderley was 'by far the prettiest I know, including tufts of trees, terraces, and a quantity of flowers'. In August the following year she was disappointed by the kitchen garden at Chatsworth: 'Magnificent in its size, and in its walls, but cruelly neglected, and positively nothing in it, even in this season of fruits and flowers.'

The steady improvement in the habits of the country gentry — notably their increasing sobriety and revulsion against cruel sports — and their growing taste for gentler pursuits and intellectual interests were part of the natural process of cultural evolution which was affecting every class. People were becoming more civilized, and none quite so fast as the landed gentry. This was largely due to the improvement in communications which, by making travelling easier, was widening their horizon, broadening their minds, and eliminating the more uncouth of the old-fashioned country squires who never left their homes and spoke the language of their tenants. Nothing benefited them more than the growing habit, which better roads encouraged, of an annual visit to London for the season. Hitherto, and for long past, this had been the custom of many of the wealthier landowners, most of whom had their own houses in London, but after the French wars it became

much more usual. Those who had no house in London rented
one, or took rooms or stayed in a hotel. The growth of this
habit was frowned upon by all those who still thought, and with
some reason, that the landowner should spend his ample rent
roll among those from whom he derived his income, but there
was a growing awareness of another side of the picture.

'One of the chief features of the life of the nobility and gentry
of England', wrote William Howitt, 'is their annual visit to the
metropolis; and it is one which has a most essential influence
upon the general character of rural life itself. The greater part
of the families of rank and fortune, flock up to town annually,
as punctually as the Jews flocked up to Jerusalem at the time of
the Passover; and it may be said for the purpose of worship too,
though worship of a different kind — that of fashion. A considerable portion of them being, more or less, connected with
one or other House of Parliament, go up at the opening of
Parliament, generally in February, and remain there till the
adjournment, often in July; but the true season does not commence till April. . . .

'Much has been said of the evil effect of this aristocratic
habit, of spending so much time in the metropolis; of the vast
sums there spent in ostentatious rivalry, in equipage and
establishments; in the dissipations of theatres, operas, routes,
and gaming-houses; and unquestionably, there is much truth
in it. On the other hand, it cannot be denied that this annual
assembling together has some advantages. A great degree of
knowledge and refinement results from it, amid all the attendant folly and extravagance. The wealthy are brought into
contact with vast numbers of their equals and superiors, and
that sullen and haughty habit of reserve is worn off, which is
always contracted by those who live in solitary seclusion, in the
midst of vast estates, with none but tenants and dependents
around them. They are also brought into contact with men of
talent and intelligence. They move amongst books and works of
art, and are induced by different motives to become patrons
and possessors of these things. . . . They make acquaintances, and
these acquaintances lead to visits, in which they observe, and
copy all that can add to the embellishment of their abodes,
and the value and productiveness of their gardens and estates. If
many acquire a relish only for Newmarket, and the gaming-

club, and a strong distaste for the quiet enjoyments of the country; many, on the other hand, come down to their estates after a season of hurry and over-excitement, with a fresh feeling for the beauty and repose of their country abodes.'

In the early months of the year, from January to the end of May, there was a migration to London from all over England, of county families coming up to present daughters or daughters-in-law at Drawing Rooms, and to attend balls, concerts, plays, to visit Astley's Circus and Vauxhall Gardens, and the many private parties which then, as much as now, were a feature of the Season. As most of the visitors rented houses which had to be staffed, the migration was swelled by hordes of servants, and of course troops of horses, for both riding and driving, and carriages. Not the least anxious of the travellers who at this time thronged the roads leading to London were the family butlers, preceding their masters and mistresses by some days, with chests of plate and linen under their special care.

One of the attractions of the Season to country people, especially if they were young, was that London, now under the transforming hand of John Nash, was still so small that many country pleasures were within easy reach. In the east it ended at Wapping, in the west at Trevor Square and Knightsbridge Barracks,[1] and in the north at Bloomsbury. Kensington and Fulham were almost wholly market gardens, growing fruit and vegetables for the London market. Brompton was a village in the leafy lanes of which Thackeray's Amelia Osborne took her walks. Belgravia was undeveloped and Chalk Farm was still a farm. Thus from the West End one had to ride no more than a mile or two to the north or west to reach unspoilt country. 'After dinner', wrote Miss Berry in her journal one June day in 1809, 'walked with my father and sister to the fields between Paddington and Bayswater. The haymaking, a beautiful warm quiet evening; we sat for some time on the cocks of hay, which I really enjoyed.'

Less rural, but even closer for pleasant riding and driving, was Hyde Park with its already fashionable Rotten Row where,

---

[1] Just beyond the Barracks was the notorious Half-Way House, a typical country inn and still in a rural setting. It was held in low repute because it had been a haunt of highwaymen late in the eighteenth century. 'This unseemly building', we read, 'which for so long disfigured the western entrance to the Metropolis', was not demolished until 1846.

Elizabeth Grant tells us, 'the amusement consisted in one long file of carriages at a foot's pace going one way, passing another long file of carriages at a foot's pace going the other, bows gravely exchanged between the occupants, when any of the busy starers were acquainted.' Then there was Kensington Gardens, to which 'soldiers, liveried servants and the great unwashed' were not admitted. Nothing brings home to us more clearly how comparatively rural London still was than the frequency with which hunting impinged upon, and sometimes invaded, the capital. The Old Berkeley hounds must have hunted right up to Kensington Gardens for we hear a complaint of no fox having been found there since 1798 when the gardeners destroyed two litters of cubs. One day early in the eighteen-twenties the respectable inhabitants of Bloomsbury witnessed an astonishing scene, within a few yards of where the British Museum now stands, which was described by Grantley Berkeley: 'We ran our stag up to No. 1. Montague Street, Russell Square. . . . A crowd had, of course, collected round me and the three or four hounds that had not been stopped on the verge of the streets. I had dismounted in my orange plush coat and hunting cap, and was standing on the pavement in front of the stag, keeping back the hounds, the deer having backed up the steps and set his haunches against the street door.'

Riding horses were taken up to London for hunting as well as hacking, and there were many Londoners, like John Jorrocks, who regularly hunted with the neighbouring packs. The Old Berkeley, secretive about their meets and not over friendly, was the best of the packs within hacking distance, but for business men like John Jorrocks, who wanted to get home in time to sign their letters for the post, the Surrey or Lord Derby's staghounds, both hunting round Croydon, were preferred. While some of the keener foxhunters who came up to London after Christmas may have hunted from London, it is probable that nearly all of them kept their hunters at one of the several convenient hunting centres, all with large livery stables, just outside the capital. Of these the principal were Pinner, for the O.B.H., and Croydon (the Melton of the South as they called it), where you could choose from three packs of foxhounds, two of harriers, and the Derby staghounds. There was also a popular pack of staghounds hunting the country round Hounslow and

Twickenham where, it seems, market gardens were a hindrance; 'Melon and asparagus beds devilish heavy', complained Lord Alvanley, 'up to our hocks in glass all day'.

The annual influx of wealthy landowners had one especially marked and lasting effect on London. This was the encouragement it gave to clubs and club life. Clubs were an institution for which Surtees had unbounded admiration, and the merits which commended them so strongly to him characterized them for another century. The man who has a club, he wrote, 'feels that he has a real substantial home — a home containing every imaginable luxury, without the trouble of management or forethought — a home that goes on as steadily in his absence as during his presence. . . . No preparation, no effort, no lamps expiring from want of work; good fires always going, good servants always in attendance, everything anticipated to his hand. . . . Clubs, in fact, are the greatest and cheapest luxuries of modern times.'

Late in July the return to the country began, and with the departing visitors went, to the dismay of foreign diplomatists, most of those who carried on the government of the country. 'In the west end of London during the autumn', wrote Richard Rush, 'little is seen but uninhabited houses. . . . The adjournment of Parliament is the first signal for desertion. You see post-chaises and travelling carriages, with their light and liveried postillions, issuing from the squares and sweeping round corners. . . . The next great egress is on the approach of the 1st September. That day is an era in England. Partridge-shooting begins. All who have not left town with the first flight, now follow. Ministers of state, even lord-chancellors, can hardly be kept from going.'[1]

These visits to London for the season, where most of the wealthiest people in the country were thrown together, encouraged extravagance because they afforded exceptional opportunities for spending money. A not inconsiderable social event of the London season of 1827 was a remarkable party given at Boyle Farm, Lord Henry Fitzgerald's house at Thames Ditton. 'The great "Carousal" of the year has been the fête at Boyle Farm on Saturday last,' wrote Emily Eden, 'I could fill

---

[1] 'Partridge-shooting', wrote Thackeray in *Vanity Fair*, 'is as it were the duty of an English gentleman of statesmanlike propensities.'

these letters to give you any account of this entertainment, and of all the impertinences which preceded and accompanied it. It was exclusive to the last degree; the founders of the feast, Alvanley, Chesterfield, H. de Roos, and Robert Grosvenor, balloted, it is said, for every name proposed for invitation. The wags say that Lord and Lady Grosvenor had four black balls; on which Robert Grosvenor said that really he could not be of it if he were not to ask Papa and Mama. Upon this he was allowed to invite them, but on an *engagement* that they should not come. People who were shabby enough to ask for invitations were well served in the answers they usually got; the men were rejected because they were old or vulgar, and the ladies because they were ugly.

'It was really amusing to hear at the Opera the reasons which the excluded ladies gave for being seen at so unfashionable a place as the Opera was that night. I will not make you stare with all the fables which are reported, roads watered with Eau de Cologne, 500 pair of white satin shoes from Paris to counter-act the damp of the green turf. More gallons of Roman Punch than Meux's great brewing vats would hold. Fireworks ordered on this scale. The Vauxhall man was asked what was the greatest expense he could go to, and then ordered to double it. And so I need hardly add that I was not invited, but it really, and without exaggeration, was a most splendid fête. Alex. Baring calculated the expense at £15,000; but no one else that I have heard carries it higher than £3,000 or £3,500.'

Most of the extravagance of this period was not of a sort that could be blamed on to the London Season. There were plenty of rich and irresponsible young men who would have had no difficulty in squandering their fortunes without London to help them. Men like Jack Mytton, with his 152 pairs of breeches and trousers, who, seeking the favours of a popular singer, sent her a cheque for 500 guineas although, Nimrod tells us, the lady, as 'all the world knows, would have been quite satisfied with a ten-pound note'. On a different plane, and outside our province, were the *parvenu* plutocrats, like William Beckford, who impoverished themselves by indulging extravagant whims and their love of vulgar ostentation. Foxhunting was the ruin of many a squire who took a pack of hounds he could not afford; down in Hampshire there was a Mr. Ridge who ruined himself in this way in which Cobbett, always ready to abuse a squire, rather surprisingly saw nothing to criticize. The magnificence of Lord Chesterfield's mastership of the Pytchley in rather later years, with the whole of the very large hunt staff mounted on the best horses money could buy, resulted in the pack, to the dismay of the followers, being seized by the bailiffs for debt.

The principal reason for the sorry tale of bankruptcies among the country squires was gambling in all its forms, especially on the turf. The craze for betting, indulged in every conceivable way, led to wagers, often of the most puerile kind, becoming a regular feature of everyday life. A Mr. Ireland bet a Mr. Jones he could not cover 100 yards in less than 30 hops and won. Someone else ate 20 fried eggs in less than five minutes for a bet. Athletics in every form was a wonderful field for match making. The famous Capt. Barclay walked 1,000 miles in 1,000 successive hours for a bet. In 1815 someone walked 50 miles a day for 20 days on Blackheath. In the famous betting book at Brooks's an entry of 1819 reads: 'Lord Yarmouth gives Lord Glengall four guineas to receive one hundred guineas if Mr. G. Brummell returns to London before Bonaparte returns to Paris.' The London gaming rooms of course thrived. The most famous of them, Crockfords, where Lord Rivers lost £23,000 one evening, was built by Wyatt in 1828 and equipped with opulent splendour. General Scott, Canning's father-in-law, won £200,000 playing whist at Whites.

Probably the greatest maker of matches and layer of wagers was George Osbaldeston, the famous Squire, who in his youth played whist for £100 a trick and £1,000 a rubber. In a trotting match over five miles on the Cambridge to Royston road he backed his horse for £1,000 against £500. On another match, over 36 miles, he lost £4,000. 'I'll take £10,000 to £3,000', he announced, 'or £20,000 to £6,000, that I ride 200 miles in 8 hours', but there were no takers. And so he went on all through life, ready to bet on anything, of course ending up a bankrupt. In his declining years he was given a pound a day to bet with at his club, and one of the last bets he took, and won, was to sit still in his chair for 24 hours. Then, as now, the turf was as easy a way as any to lose money, indeed easier because racing was much more crooked, as the Squire learnt to his cost. 'It is a well-known fact', he wrote in later years, 'that . . . five or six of the betting men have £400,000 or £500,000 among them. . . . Several of the jockeys also have £30,000; one has £40,000; one or two of them £20,000, though only twenty-two years old. Perhaps five or six others have from £10,000 to £20,000. As it is impossible that they could have realised these sums by their profession alone, it is a natural conclusion that they have "worked the oracle", as they call it, and are confederates with the betting men.' Osbaldeston's losses on the turf alone were estimated at over £200,000.

The resort of many a young man in financial difficulties was a post-obit, borrowing against the hope or the expectation of inheriting wealth from a rich relative. The existence of these unsecured loans was often disclosed by the otherwise unaccountable interest of moneylenders in the health and expectation of life of an ageing and wealthy father or other relative. In real life there were probably not a few like the young man in Nimrod's *Life of a Sportsman* who 'lost £100,000, at least, by talking of post-obiting his aunt. He called out, publicly, in the ring at Newmarket, *"what odds will anyone bet me, that I don't win the Derby, in four years after my old aunt dies?"* ' The old aunt, hearing that she was being post-obited, left her nephew a paltry £100.

One fashionable and engaging roué, who appears repeatedly in these pages, anyway went down with flying colours. 'I suspect', wrote Emily Eden in 1832, 'dear Alvanley is after all little better than a swindler. He writes beautiful letters . . . and he says he feels he deserves all the misery he is suffering, which misery consists in sitting in an arm-chair from breakfast till dinner-time cracking jokes without ceasing. He has taught his servant to come into the room and ask what time his Lordship would like the carriage, and what orders he has for his groom, because he thinks it sounds cheerful, though he has neither carriage nor horses. But it looks better.'

'My vig,' declared Mr. Jorrocks as he landed at Boulogne, 'there's Thompson! He owes us a hundred pounds.' 'You old fool!' replied Thompson on being unexpectedly accosted by his creditor, 'you forget where you are; if I could pay you your little bill, do you suppose I would be here?' 'When we read that a nobleman has left for the Continent,' wrote Thackeray in *Vanity Fair*, 'we respect the victim in the vastness of his ruin.' 'Leaving for the Continent' and 'rusticating over the water', like Surtees's Captain Coper, meant flight from creditors, with the King's Bench Prison and the workhouse, commonly called the Bastille, as the only alternatives. Boulogne was the last refuge of many of England's bankrupt roués. There they gathered, and there they had a pack of foxhounds. 'We lived like fighting-cocks . . .', declared Thompson, 'such a rollicking set of dogs! could hunt all day, race maggots and drink claret all night.' Respectable visitors to Boulogne who had the misfortune to fall among these exiles noted how each one of them always declared his intention to return very shortly to England. Few ever did. One of the exceptions was Jack Mytton who, after a spell in the Hôtel d'Angleterre as the long-suffering natives of Boulogne called their debtors' prison, came back only to die miserably in the King's Bench.

IX

The Family Travels Post

In the English countryside 'gentry' and 'carriage folk' were almost synonymous terms, and so continued up to Edwardian times. But to qualify, your carriage had to be enclosed — it had to have a fixed head. 'How the man who drives his close carriage', wrote Howitt, 'looks down upon him who only drives his barouche or phaeton; how both contemn the poor occupier of a gig. I have heard of a gentleman of large fortune who, for some years after his residence in a particular neighbourhood, did not set up his close carriage, but afterwards feeling it more agreeable to do so, was astonished to find himself called upon by a host of carriage-keeping people, who did not seem previously aware of his existence; and rightly deeming the calls to be made upon his carriage, rather than himself, sent round his empty carriage to deliver cards in return.'

Howitt's story will not surprise those old enough to recall the social customs at the beginning of Edward VII's reign, when it was permissible to send your empty carriage to represent you at a funeral. This was doubtless a relic of the old custom of a dead man's carriage being included in the funeral procession. When Coke of Norfolk (Lord Leicester) died his coffin was followed by his own carriage and four with shuttered windows.

A gentleman's equipage — the carriage, the horses and the coachman, with one or more footmen — was very personal to its owner. The livery of the servants and the colours of the horses and the coachwork, all probably traditional in his family, were distinctive and at once recognizable from a distance.[1] Moreover, as a form of personal representation the equipage had the in-

[1] So great was the pride that people took in their carriages that when they went to Brighton or some other fashionable watering-place they inclined to leave their carriages behind because the sea air harmed the varnish.

estimable value of lending itself to display; it invited ostentation which, in our period, as we have seen, was very much the fashion. The rich vied with each other in the magnificence of their horses, the sparkle of their harness, the immaculate liveries of their servants, and the numbers of their footmen. But the horses mattered most. Early in the nineteenth century Dr. Bathurst, the Bishop of Norwich, drove four roan horses in his coach or carriage, probably because roan was traditional in his family. But as roan was not sufficiently episcopal for great occasions he used sometimes to borrow from the Gurneys of Earlham their four blacks which so well became a great Quaker family.

With such a wealth of prestige attaching to a gentleman's carriage the coachman, in great families, was a man of immense consequence. 'On the sobriety, steady conduct, and respectable appearance of this important servant,' *The Complete Servant* tells us, 'depend the exterior appearance of the family with which he resides. Every genuine Coachman has his characteristic costume. His flaxen curls or wig, his low cocked hat, his plush breeches, and his benjamin surtout, his clothes being also well brushed, and the lace and buttons in a state of high polish.' In big establishments there was an under coachman who, the same authority tells us, also drove a coach, 'which is always the second best, and is driven by him at night; whereas the best coach and the best horses, are driven by the Head Coachman by day. . . . He is sometimes required to ride as postillion, or as courier, when the family travel *post*.'

The opportunities for display which an equipage provided were not limited to merely multiplying horses and attendant footmen. Indeed, there was hardly any limit to what the stables of the very great could lay on, especially under the threat of competition from another noble house. Describing Doncaster races in 1827 Creevey wrote: 'You must know our steward, the Duke of Devonshire, started the first day with his coach and six and *twelve* outriders, and old Billy Fitzwilliam,[1] had just the same; but the next day old Billy appeared with *two* coaches and six, and *sixteen* outriders, and has kept the thing up ever since.' Such magnificence was, of course, pure ostentation, but the teams of six and the galaxies of outriders did not greatly exceed what in fact, not many years before, these great men would

[1] The 4th Earl Fitzwilliam.

normally have employed when travelling. On some roads, especially in winter, six horses were probably still required to draw a heavy coach, and the outriders, or couriers, had their uses on the road. In the more lawless days of the eighteenth century the outriders were a protective escort. Like the running footman, they were also useful as couriers. They rode ahead to arrange accommodation at inns, and to pay the tolls so that the toll-gates could be flung open on the approach of their master without wasting time. The outriders, like the postillions, who usually took the place of the coachman on the road (and always so if there were six horses), were drawn from among their employer's stablemen.

By the third decade of the nineteenth century the main roads were becoming, as well as safer (the last highwayman had been hanged years before), very much better. This was due to the work of two remarkable road engineers, Thomas Telford and John McAdam, and their pupils. Telford and McAdam had successfully demonstrated the practicability of constructing roads to meet the requirements of traffic as opposed to the turnpike-trust system of making wheels conform to the limitations imposed by very bad roads. The main roads were being realigned, hills were being flattened and valleys filled in, and, above all, the roads were being given solid all-weather surfaces. Better roads brought incalculable benefits to the whole country, but especially to the rural parts. Many of these benefits derived directly from the stimulus that better roads were giving to the posting and the coach services.

When the aristocracy and the gentry wanted to travel there were three courses open to them. They could travel in their own carriages drawn by their own horses, which few did, or they could travel post which meant either hiring horses from stage to stage to draw their carriages or hiring postchaises and horses, also from stage to stage. They could of course also travel by either the mail or the stage coaches but they never would if they could afford not to. In those days of privilege the very idea of a public vehicle was abhorrent. In the same way that rural society was divided into carriage folk and the rest, so it was into posting and coaching company, the dividing line being much the same in both cases.

There must have been few regular visitors to London who

had to come so far as the Grants of Rothiemurchus. Yet in spite of those 500 miles of often bad or indifferent road they used regularly to make the three weeks' journey in their own carriage drawn by their own horses, once or twice a year. In 1803 they set out from London in the old family berline drawn by four horses. Inside were J. P. Grant and his invalid wife on a couch, and two children. The lady's maid and the valet were outside. 'We travelled with our own horses ridden by two postillions in green jackets and jockey caps', wrote Elizabeth Grant. 'In the heavy post-chariot behind were the two nurses, the baby in a swinging cot, William . . . and a footman in charge of them. What it must have cost to have carried such a party from London to the Highlands! and how often we travelled that north road! Every good inn became a sort of home, every obliging landlord or landlady an old friend. . . . We travelled slowly, thirty miles a day on an average, starting late and stopping early, with a bait soon after noon, when we children dined.' In July 1804 they set out from London 'in a new carriage — a sociable[1] — with a cane body, a roof on four supports hung round with leather curtains, which we were continually letting down or tying up according to the weather, which we never managed to arrange in time for either wet or dry, and which . . . let in the rain'. On the return journey, in the autumn of 1805, the sociable was 'rather cold work in cold autumn weather. We had to drive unicorn, for one of the grey horses was gone; the other therefore had the honour of leading, a triangular style not then common.' By 1808 they had something better than the uncomfortable sociable, and the journey north started from their house in Hertfordshire. 'The servants all went north . . . by sea, excepting those in immediate attendance on ourselves. A new barouche landau[2] was started this season, which served for many a year, and was a great improvement upon either the old heavy close coach or the leather-curtained sociable.' In 1812 the journey was unusually slow with long rests at inns to save the horses which, on account of unsoundness or bad roads, could not go far in a day.

But this form of travel had its compensations, as the thirteen-

---

[1] A sociable was a low-hung angular carriage with two seats facing each other, but only the rear seat could be covered by the folding hood.

[2] The barouche-landau was a stately carriage, hung high on cee springs, with a double folding head which enabled it to be completely closed in case of need.

year-old Elizabeth discovered in 1810 when she made a journey from Oxford to London with her father in his less pretentious post-chariot:[1] 'The first disappointment . . . was the conveyance we travelled in. I was accustomed to the barouche and four, the liveried servants, and all the stir of such an equipage; my father's plain post-chaise, pair of horses, and only one man, made no sensation along the road, neither at the inns nor in the villages. No one stared at so plain a carriage, nor was there any bustle in the inn-yards on our changing horses.'

The gentry sometimes treated the countryside to far more impressive spectacles than the passage of the Grants' comparatively modest equipage between Inverness-shire and London. When the wealthy had two or more estates in different parts of the country they often divided their time between them, preferring one in the summer and another, where perhaps the hunting or shooting was better, in the winter. In the case of a big establishment these seasonal movements between mansions sometimes assumed almost the form of a small tribal migration and the character of a royal progress. This is how, in the closing years of the eighteenth century, John Archer travelled between Welford in Berkshire and his other home, Coopersale, in Essex: 'First, the coach and six horses, with two postilions, coachman, and three outriders; a postchaise and four post horses, phaeton and four followed by two grooms, a chaise marine with four horses carrying the numerous services of plate — this last was escorted by the under-butler, who had under his command three stout fellows; they formed part of the household, and all were armed with blunderbusses. Next followed the hunters with their cloths of scarlet trimmed with silver, and attended by the stud-groom and huntsman; each horse had a fox's brush tied to the front of the bridle. The rear was brought up by the pack of hounds, the whipper-in, the hack-horses, and the inferior stablemen. In the coach went the upper servants, in the chariot the eccentric master's wife . . . or . . . she accompanied Mr. Archer in the phaeton, he travelling in all weathers in that vehicle, wrapped up in a swan's-down coat.'

On ordinary journeys the well-to-do usually made use of the old-established posting services which were readily available

---

[1] A post-chariot was a small closed carriage built to seat only two persons. Latterly it had a rumble added at the rear to seat two servants.

from one end of the country to the other. Every town had at
least one posting house, an inn at which post horses and chaises
could be hired, and many a village inn kept one or two pairs of
horses and a chaise for the convenience of the neighbourhood.
The posting business was not only traditional in the innkeeper's
trade, but far the most important part of it, so much so that
some inns would refuse to take in travellers who were not in
need of horses. It both served private travellers and provided an
essential ancillary service for the mail and stage coaches, many
of whose passengers needed transport to carry them on from
where the coaches dropped them, to their destinations. With the
improvement in the roads and the consequent increase in
traffic the posting business was unprecedently prosperous. The
chief posting house, or head inn as they called it, of a large
town was a hive of constant activity with public coaches and
private chaises and travelling carriages arriving at all hours day
and night, expecting, and usually receiving, immediate service
in horses and chaises, food and drink. The big inns which, as we
shall see in the next chapter, combined the horsing of the
coaches with their posting business, were very efficiently
managed. Attached to the inn would be a large range of stabling
for perhaps 50 or 60 post horses and perhaps as many coach
horses. The yard was under a horsekeeper who, so far as posting
was concerned, was paid by the postboys,[1] of whom there would
be one to every four horses.

The postboy, who was seldom young and often a rather
decrepit old man, had usually started life, like the postboy in
Lavengro, in a gentleman's stables and come down in the world.
Such a one was Surtees's Benjamin Buckrout of the fast-
declining Lord Hill hotel and posting house, 'an antediluvian
postboy . . . the last of twelve who had driven from that door —
whose geographical knowledge was said to be great. Buckrout
was an illustration of the truth of the old saying, that nobody
ever saw a dead postboy, for if he had been anything else he
would have been dead long since. As it was there was little left
of him but his chin and his hands, save what people might
conjecture was in his jacket and boots.' As postboys had to be
very active, hard-riding men, Benjamin Buckrout can hardly

---

[1] At the Epping Place posting house five postboys paid the horsekeeper eighteen
pence a week each.

XI   *The Red Lion, Paddington, Corner of Harrow Road*: This rural scene, painted late in the eighteenth century, lay within half a mile of the Tyburn turnpike, close to where the Marble Arch now stands.

XII *The Swan with Two Necks*: Commonly known as The Necks, this London inn was justly famous as the headquarters of William Chaplin, the greatest of the coachmasters.

have been typical, though his dress certainly was: 'scrumpy red jacket, with blue glass buttons and tarnished silver lace at the black cotton velvet collar and cuffs; questionable breeches, with seedy boots'. As we may see from contemporary prints, the postboy wore very short top boots (with spurs), a very short coloured jacket with tarnished lace and a tall beaver hat. Being a postillion, always riding the near-side horse of a pair, he also wore, strapped to his right leg, an iron guard to protect it from the off-side horse, or hand-poster. He also carried a very short knotty whip.

The postchaise was technically a chariot, a small closed carriage hung on cee springs and built to carry two passengers. It was almost invariably painted yellow and therefore known, in the jargon of the road, as a 'yellow bounder' (as opposed to the 'bounder' which was a gentleman's carriage). It was drawn normally by one pair of horses, but if the roads were very bad or the distance great two pairs and two postboys would be used. The post horses had to be a good deal better than their ramshackle chaise, for the reputation of a posting house depended more on the quality of its horses than anything else. With the improvement in the roads and faster travel the wretched animals of earlier years no longer sufficed. 'Up to the end of the last century', wrote Nimrod, 'the post-horse was, except in a few instances, an object of commiseration with travellers. With galled sides and sore shoulders, and scarcely a sound limb, he would not go without the lash or spur, whereas he now comes out of his stable in high condition, and runs his ten miles' stage in an hour.'

The patrons of the posting business required both good horses and prompt service. By the second decade of the nineteenth century speed had become the key-note of everything to do with the road. This insistence on speed gave the country the admirable posting and coaching services which excited the envy of all foreign visitors. A rule of the big posting houses was that at least two postboys had to be ready, booted and spurred and with their horses harnessed, from eight in the morning till seven in the evening, waiting for the traditional cry 'Horses on!' 'My inn', wrote Prince Pückler-Muskau, 'is as usual a post-house. I therefore told my servant to call for "horses" instantly. In less than a minute they were harnessed before the door, and in

K

fifteen, driving like the wind.' At night, however, the service was less good; some ten minutes or so had to be wasted before a sleeping postboy could be roused and the change horses brought out.

The posting houses served three kinds of travellers. First there were those who, preferring to ride, wanted saddle horses to hire from one posting house to another. They had to have two horses, and a postboy to bring the horses back at the end of the stage. There were few long-distance travellers who preferred to ride. Among them was Ralph Lambton who, representing his native County Durham in Parliament, for some years rode all the way to and from London, hiring horses from stage to stage, but always in his own saddle.

The postmaster's most valuable customers were the wealthy gentry who customarily travelled in their private carriages. Their own horses usually took them as far as the first posting house out from home. There they sent their horses back, and hired post horses from stage to stage for the rest of their journey. On the main roads there was seldom more than ten or twelve miles between posting houses. Private carriages being heavier than a postchaise, and speed mattering much, these travellers usually required two pairs of horses and two postboys. To be sure of not being held up by lack of horses they often booked their requirements ahead. At times this was a very necessary precaution. When Louis XVIII landed at Yarmouth in 1807 he was prevented from reaching Woodbridge the first night, as he had intended, by lack of post horses. For the same reason, the envoy sent down from London to welcome him on behalf of the government did not reach Yarmouth till long after he had landed.

Although sometimes there were not enough horses to meet all demands, the posting services seem to have been efficient, 'Our own horses took us to Woodford', wrote one of the Gurneys describing a journey from London to Earlham in 1822, 'and there four posters were "clapped on" in a very few minutes, at the sound of "Horses on" from the ostler of the inn. Then the two post-boys, in high white beaver hats, blue jackets, red waistcoats, white neckcloths, short white corduroy breeches, and bright top-boots, started off at a smart trot, which was continued the whole stage up and down hill, often stopping for a moment for a post-boy to dismount and put on a drag. . . . I remember my astonishment as a child at seeing my father pay away so many gold pieces as the post-boys came up to the window for their fare at the end of each stage.' Posting was expensive.

The less well-to-do — mostly those who had no carriage strong enough to risk the hazards of a long journey — travelled in postchaises hired from stage to stage. Usually one pair of horses sufficed, but if the roads were bad, as most of the by-roads were, or hilly, or there was great haste, two pairs would be hired. The aristocracy considered it so far below their dignity to travel in a postchaise instead of their own carriage that they never did so if they could possibly avoid it. When Lord Stormont, posting north to Scotland in hired chaises, decided to call upon the Duke of Northumberland on the way, he did not realize till he arrived how ill his conveyance became the grandeur of Alnwick, nor did he relish the Duke's discovery of his postchaise discreetly hidden away out of sight of the castle.

Postchaises, unlike private carriages, generally travelled at the gallop.[1] To the danger of this, on a bad road, was added the risk a postboy often took of not pulling up to put a drag or shoe on a wheel before going down a steep hill. The chaises being very light the dangers were not great, but the discomfort considerable. As Dr. Johnson remarked, a postchaise jolted many an intimacy to death. But for some people speed mattered more than comfort. The Duke of Cleveland, better known as Lord Darlington, always ordered his postboys to 'drive like the wind'. It is therefore not surprising to learn that the working life of a post horse was very short.

Travelling by postchaise was open to an objection which had much to do with people preferring to travel in their own carriages. This was the inconvenience of having to transfer your luggage from one chaise to another at the end of every stage. Another was that you could not have your servants with you unless you hired a second chaise for them.

Servants had always been rather a problem on the road. To the gentry life without personal attendants ever at hand was unthinkable, but when travelling it was not easy to have them

---

[1] The traditional postboy 'jog' was the jog-trot of the homeward bound postboy.

always at beck and call. It was no trouble if you were as rich as Lord and Lady Holland whom Greville saw arrive at Pans- hanger 'in a coach-and-four and a chaise-and-pair, — two footmen, a page, and two maids'. For lesser mortals when travelling post the custom had been for their servants to follow them on horseback, mounted on hired post horses, keeping up as best they could. Not altogether surprisingly, with the lady's maid presumably riding pillion behind the valet, to say nothing of neither being hardened to horseback, they seldom arrived at their destination till hours later. The inconvenience to which this put their master and mistress led to the placing of a dickey, or rumble, to seat two servants, on the back of gentlemen's travel- ling carriages. But there remained inconveniences for which there was no cure, such as Emily Eden's 'fussy lady's maid and valet who dispute every inch of the imperial[1] and expect tea, beer, feather beds, etc., at every bad inn on the road'.

The cost of hiring a pair of post horses varied from 1s. to 1s. 6d. a mile. Two pairs and two postboys cost twice as much. To the cost of hire had to be added 3d. a mile to the postboy with whom, if you were travelling in your own carriage, it was not safe to quarrel; if displeased he might stop at some lonely spot, unharness his horses and ride away leaving his patron stranded. Posting, being very expensive, gave scope for wild extravagance. The eccentric Lady Sarah Robinson once took such fright, as was her wont, at her husband's[2] having a head- ache that she summoned to their house in Lincolnshire a doctor from Norfolk and two more from London, each of whom was required to travel with four post horses. As the headache soon disappeared messengers were sent out to turn the doctors back, but the bill for posters alone amounted to no less than 250 guineas.

In the early part of our period posting would have made pleasanter travelling had the roadside inns been less unreliable. Donne, writing in the middle of the nineteenth century and looking back nostalgically to the days of his youth when England was famous for the excellence of its inns, tells us that 'indifferent roads and uneasy carriages, riding post, and dread

---

[1] The imperial was a travelling trunk made to fit on to the top of a travelling carriage.

[2] The future Lord Goderich who, for a few weeks in 1827, was a very ineffective Prime Minister.

of highwaymen, darkness or the inclemency of the seasons, led, as by a direct consequence, to the construction of excellent inns in our island'. That was not so. The good inns Donne recalled remained very rare until travelling became easy, and that was not till after the close of the eighteenth century.

Few men of culture and gentle birth knew the inns of England as well as John Byng who, between 1781 and 1794, spent several weeks a year travelling in the country on horseback. And none knew better how to guard against the discomforts of the average country inn. He always took a servant with him, partly to give himself consequence, thus ensuring a little extra attention, but chiefly to send on ahead 'to prepare for me, & my horses, proper accommodations at night. This is the true use of servants on the road, tho but selldom what their masters require of them; trusting to the waiter, and chambermaid for dirty glasses, and ill made beds, and confiding the care of their horses to drunken, roguish, hostlers; & whilst their own genteel followers are regaling themselves in a genteel parlour, the horses are neither clean'd, nor fed. As for my sheets I allways take them with me, knowing that next to a certainty, 5 sheets must be dirty, and 3 damp, out of number ten: these with a very few other necessaries, travell behind my servant; as for my night cap, great coat, and such other etceteras, they travell behind my own person, in & upon, a small cloakbag.'

At Oxford, in 1781, he reached the conclusion that 'the imposition in travelling is abominable; the innkeepers are insolent, the hostlers are sulky, the chambermaids are pert, and the waiters are impertinent; the meat is tough, the wine is foul, the beer is hard, the sheets are wet, the linnen dirty, and the knives are never cleaned!! Every home is better than this!'

A visit to the Crown at Ringwood started fairly well — 'I was well waited upon' — but he did not like having to sup off grey mullet — 'he is strong, and oily, . . . nor would any dressing, (even from a receipt of Mr Walton's,) render him palatable' — but he had a terrible night. 'Of all the beds I ever lay in, that of last night was the very worst, for there could not be more then fifty feathers in the bolster, and pillow, or double that number in the feather-bed; so there I lay tossing, and tumbling all night, without any sleep, or place to lay my head upon, tho' I rowl'd all the bolster into one heap.'

At the Bull's Head, Manchester — 'Oh! what a dog hole is
Manchester' — the bill of fare was encouraging, but the dinner
was a sad disappointment. 'My dinner, (order'd magnifi-
cently) was a salmon-peal, — lamb chops, and peas:—
look to the product; peas were not to be had; the salmon, serv'd
to me, was too stale to be eaten; and the thick, raw, fry'd
chops swam in butter! "God sends meat; but the devil sends
cooks". — I could not eat; I try'd to drink of the port wine, but
could not; the bread was intolerable, and the cheese was in
remnants; — I said "Take away, I cannot eat!" '

One of Byng's fads, which irritated one of his companions,
was a dislike of being waited upon at meals. For this he seems
to have had some slight excuse. 'Instead of a nasty, dirty wench,'
he wrote, 'watching you all the time, picking her nails, blowing
her nose upon her apron, and then wiping the knives and glasses
with it; or spitting and blowing upon the plates. Surely . . .
there is nothing so comfortable for a small company as dumb
waiters; as for myself, I am uneasy when a fellow stands behind
me, watching me, running away with my plate, and winking at
his fellows.'

But he had one great advantage over most travellers: 'I am
never stung by bugs, or fleas; and when I enter a bed, I believe
that they all quit it.'

However, there were good inns, and sometimes Byng had
remarkably good meals at very modest prices, though he was
often reluctant to admit it. At the White Swan, Middleham, he
dined off boiled fowl, cold ham, Yorkshire pudding, gooseberry
pie, loin of mutton and cheesecakes. 'A better dinner, and
better dress'd, I never sat down to; but fear that the charge will
be *heavy*, — 1s. 6d. at least; We shall see.' He was agreeably
surprised. It cost him 1s. 3d. He did even better at the Spread
Eagle, Settle, and had to admit it was cheap. 'I had an early
dinner of beef steaks, lamb chops, pickled salmon, and tart;
and for supper last night, a trout, lamb chops, potted trout, and
tart; so that under the article *eating* I have not been over-
charged. (9 *pence* for each meal!).' But no matter where he was,
nor how well he fared, nothing could compare with the Sun at
Biggleswade where the admirable Mrs. Knight 'governs all in
quietness', and provided dishes much to his liking. Once when
far away in Yorkshire he entered in his diary: 'Biggleswade, —

after all — for my money, with its young rabbits, and silver eels.'

The Sun at Biggleswade was one of many good inns on the Great North Road where, Byng wrote in 1793, the traveller 'will find frequent, and good stops . . . and will never suffer the uncertainty of where, or how he is to lodge'. The reason for the North Road inns being so much better than most of those elsewhere was that more gentry and men of consequence used that road than any other. The inns in the industrial towns seem to have been amongst the worst in England. We have seen how Byng suffered in Manchester. He fared no better in Birmingham, Macclesfield, and Doncaster. Rochdale was as bad: 'Oh! What a Wapping ale-house; and what a *Wapping* landlady!' The Roe Buck at Newcastle-under-Lyme seems to have been one of the worst — 'Travellers beware The Roe Buck in Newcastle'. But it was much the same wherever industry prospered, and Byng clearly saw the reason: 'The upstart man of riches known no better: the inns therefore are bad, dear, and presumptuous; but on roads where gentlemen travell, and scold, there will be *a reform*.'

He proved to be right. When the superior stage coaches of the early nineteenth century began to attract good-class passengers the coachmasters quickly found that they could not fill their coaches unless they fed and lodged their passengers at comfortable inns. This led to a marked improvement in inns throughout the country. Thus, eventually, did the coaches greatly benefit those who travelled post.

X

Swell Dragsmen

UNTIL late in the eighteenth century the mails were carried, under an ancient relay or posting system, by postboys, some with light carts but most of them mounted on horses or cobs which they changed at inns conveniently spaced along the main roads. These inns were called post-houses and their landlords, the postmasters, had both to mount the postboys and distribute the mail in their districts. They were also licensed to hire out horses to the public which, by law, none but a postmaster might do. With the abolition of this archaic monopoly in 1780, everyone was free to establish a posting business, with the result that the posting services described in the previous chapter became freely available in every district throughout the kingdom. The business naturally remained almost wholly in the hands of inn-keepers whose houses were now called posting houses. The benefit to the public was considerable but, as we have seen, the cost of hiring horses was too high, anyhow over long distances, except for the wealthy.

When the poor had to travel they used the old-fashioned stage waggons, drawn by four, six, or even eight horses, which were chiefly used for the carriage of goods. They never moved out of a walk and were in charge of a carter who usually walked beside his team. Such was the rude conveyance in which Little Nell travelled, 'comfortably bestowed among the softer packages. . . . What a soothing, luxurious, drowsy way of travelling, to lie inside that slowly-moving mountain, listening to the tinkling of the horses' bells, the occasional smacking of the carter's whip, the smooth rolling of the great broad wheels, the rattle of the harness . . . all made pleasantly indistinct by the thick awning, which seemed made for lazy listening under, till one fell asleep!' The stage waggon remained the only public conveyance suitable for the poor until the coming of the railways.

Meanwhile, travel for the middle classes had become very much easier. For some considerable time privately-owned stage coaches for passengers had been running on the main roads. They were primitive, uncomfortable, and slow. 'Walking; — or riding, on a tolerable horse, are delights to me,' wrote John Byng in 1787, 'but box'd up in a stinking coach, dependent on the hours and guidance of others, submitting to miserable associates, and obliged to hear their nonsense, is great wretchedness! However, the vulgarity of women is, at all times, better than the brutality of men: two women were my companions, and harmless enough — tho one eternally threaten'd to be sick.'

With the improvement of the roads under the turnpike trusts, stage coaches became faster, and outstripped the postboys with the mails. This led to their being much used for carrying letters, which was illegal but very difficult to stop, especially as letters could easily be disguised as parcels which the stages were allowed to carry. The serious inroads this abuse made into Post Office revenue, and the inefficiency of the postboy system — the postboys were mostly illiterate and dishonest, as well as defenceless against highwaymen — gave John Palmer the idea of the mail coach, with an armed guard, which would carry four inside passengers whose fares would pay for the carriage of the mails. Thus, in 1784, did the famous mail coach come into being. Better built, better horsed, and better manned than the stage coaches, it quickly became popular with the travelling public and before many years had passed all the principal towns in the country were being regularly served by Post Office coaches carrying passengers and mail. At times the mail coaches carried passengers only, and on such occasions speed was not so important and considerable indulgence was permitted. 'Had a delightfully jolly party', wrote the young Peter Hawker, describing a journey on the Exeter mail in 1811, 'and, not being post day, the mail stopped whenever we saw game, and during the journey I killed 4 partridges. When it was too dark to shoot, our party mounted the roof, and sang choruses (while I joined them and drove), and in which the guard and coachman took a very able part.' Such leisurely travelling did not last long.

In the second decade of the nineteenth century the efficiency of the mail coach services and the great improvement in the roads, on which Telford and McAdam were now at work, had combined to make travelling so fast, comfortable, and safe that there were more people wanting to travel than the Post Office could carry. Private enterprise stepped in and established stage coach services which for speed and comfort no other country could approach. In their short life of no more than twenty-five years or so, from about 1820 to 1845, they became the admiration of the world. Unlike the posting services, which were essentially rural, the stage coaches were urban enterprises, but the benefits they brought to the countryside, not the least of which was the daily thrill for many a village of seeing the coach go by, were so great that they merit some attention in our present context.

An aspiring coach proprietor, or coachmaster, wanting to 'get into harness', had first to choose his ground, as the coaching world called the road. It would, if possible, be one of the new macadamized roads radiating from London, where he would make his headquarters and from which his coaches would 'work'. The road over which a coach worked was divided into three parts, the upper ground nearest home, the lower ground furthest away, and the middle ground in between. That is why we still talk of going up to London and down to the country. The coachmaster's headquarters would have to be a large inn, which he might lease or buy, because nohow else could he provide the accommodation required for his passengers — bedrooms, kitchens, coffee-room, bar, etc. — and sufficient stabling for his horses. The placing of a coach on the road involved at least two and often several vehicles according to the length of the ground; the formula was one coach for every hundred miles of ground, which allowed for spares. Each coach of the fleet would bear the same name. Thus the Shrewsbury *Wonder*, the first long-distance fast coach of the new era, started in 1825, was not the name of a single vehicle but of a service between London and Shrewsbury.

A coachmaster never owned his coaches. He hired them from coach builders who built them to his specifications and 'miled' them to him; they charged him $2\frac{1}{2}d$. or $3d$. a double mile, that is to say out and back, and for this they also kept the

coaches in repair. Painted on the door panels of the coaches and
their hind boots would be the names of the coachmaster, and of
the 'yard' or inn out of which he worked, the terminal points of
his ground, and the name of the coach. The horsing of the
coaches was seldom done by the coachmaster himself, except
on the first stage out from his headquarters and the last stage in;
over the rest of the ground it would nearly always be done by
horse contractors. This was a worrying side of the business, and
the manning of the coaches with coachmen and guards was
hardly less so. On top of all that, the coachmaster had to have a
considerable headquarters organization, with a large inn to run,
a big range of stables to keep filled with sound horses, a corps of
stablemen, and numbers of clerks to run the booking and administrative offices.

It needed a man of marked ability to make a success of a
system so dependent on the integrity and competence of contractors and servants who were seldom under their employer's
eye, and who had endless opportunities for robbing his pocket
and ruining his reputation. Any weakness in his organization
was an encouragement to a competitor to try to drive him off
his ground with an 'opposition' coach at cut rates. But even if
all went well he was not free from this risk. Success sometimes
encouraged competitors more than weakness. Even the famous
Wonder was at one time challenged by an opposition, the *Nimrod*.
Sherman, the proprietor of the *Wonder*, retaliated by running a
second coach immediately ahead of the *Nimrod*. All three
coaches raced each other and sometimes reached the Peacock,
Islington, simultaneously two hours ahead of time. In the end the
Wonder prevailed but it cost Sherman £1,500 to do it. It was not
easy to make such a business pay, 'to make tongue and buckle
meet', with the result that most of the trade passed into the hands
of a small group of exceptionally able men. The greatest of these
was William Chaplin who, by the 'thirties, was working out of
five London yards, the best known being the Spread Eagle
in Gracechurch Street and the Swan with Two Necks (with
stables both above and below ground) in Lad Lane, Gresham
Street. He also horsed half the London mails on the first stage
out and the last in. His immense organization included 1,300
horses, 60 coaches, and 2,000 employees. Then there was
Sherman with his famous Bull and Mouth yard, so conveniently

opposite the General Post Office for a great horser of mails. There were also big men in the country, like Moses Pickwick of Bath into one of whose coaches Sam Weller, bewildered by the name on the door panels, bundled his master at the White Horse Cellar in Piccadilly.

The great London yards had to be centrally situated, where land was dear and rents high. The consequent need to economize space gave the terminal coaching inns a conventional form. Bedrooms for passengers were built over the stables surrounding the yard, and usually the only access to them was along an outside open gallery. Again to economize space, it was usual to build over the entrance to the yard which was consequently almost invariably an archway.

These great yards were constantly in the state of turmoil described by Dickens in his account of the departure of the Pickwickians from the Golden Cross (where the Nelson monument now stands). To the scores of passengers leaving and joining the coaches, coming and going night and day, to their many friends welcoming them or seeing them off, to those who thronged the coach office to book seats ahead, to the numbers of porters loaded with luggage, and the scores of horsekeepers, ostlers, and waiters, were added a swarm of pedlars, and an almost permanent crowd of sightseers. Next to a foxhunt, thought Cobbett, the finest sight in England was a stage coach, arriving or starting, and most Londoners thought there was nothing better. So they gathered outside the yard, many with experienced appraising eyes, to see perhaps some famous coach from a remote part of the kingdom come clattering down the street, smothered in dirt but dead on time, and the great man on the box gathering his tired team to swing them into the yard as smartly as if they were just setting out; or, perhaps better still, some other famous coach, with the horses' coats gleaming and the coachwork and harness all aglitter, coming out through the archway with the ostlers, carrying the quarter-cloths they had just whipped off the prancing team, running at the horses' heads to see them safely into the street.

From both Dickens and Surtees it is clear that the chief trouble of the passengers was the pestering horde of pedlars who thronged the coach yards. At the Bricklayers' Arms where the Dover coaches started, they were assailed, according to Surtees, 'with the usual persecution from the tribe of Israel, in the shape of a hundred *merchants*, proclaiming the virtues of their wares; one with black-lead pencils, twelve a shilling . . . another with a good pocket knife, "twelve blades and a saw, Sir"; a third, with a tame squirrel and a piping bullfinch, that could whistle God Save the King and the White Cockade — to be *given* for an old coat. "Buy a silver guard chain for your vatch, Sir!" cried a dark-eyed urchin, mounting the forewheel . . . "buy a pocket book, memorandum book!" whined another. "Sponge cheap, sponge! take a piece, Sir — take a piece." "Patent leather straps". Barcelona nuts. Slippers', and so on. But at last the great moment came. The coachman mounted the box, gathered his reins and at 'All right!' from the guard, off the coach went, 'amidst a loud flourish from the guard's horn', to quote *Nicholas Nickleby*, 'and the calm approval of all the judges of coaches and coach-horses congregated at the Peacock, but more especially of the helpers, who stood, with the cloths over their arms, watching the coach till it disappeared, and then lounged admiringly stablewards bestowing various gruff encomiums on the beauty of the turn-out'.

London was ringed with important coaching centres, one stage out from the capital, where the coachmasters' teams were changed and stabled while awaiting in-coming coaches. The most important of these centres was Hounslow, at the junction of the Exeter, Bath and Gloucester roads, with stabling for about 2,500 horses. Another important centre, for the northern traffic, was Barnet, but there were similar establishments on every main road leading out of London. These were the points at which the horse contractors took over the out-going coaches, and handed over the in-coming ones.

Most of these contractors were innkeepers with a posting business. They usually had plenty of stabling, and they knew how to buy horses. Moreover, they liked horsing coaches because of the trade it brought to their houses; but at that point their interests conflicted with those of the coachmasters. The longer it took to change horses the better for the bar and the worse for the coachmasters to whom speed, in order to counter the fierce competition of the mails, was essential. Another trouble was the contractor's favouring the posting side of his business for which he kept his best horses. Nevertheless, the horsing of the coaches, both mail and stage, remained almost wholly in the hands of the posting houses. The rest of it was in the hands of the gentry who, passionately interested in everything to do with the horse, were attracted by the efficiency and the resultant prestige of the new stages. Some, like Thackeray's Sir Pitt Crawley, horsed coaches to make money, at which they usually failed, as Sir Pitt did, through underfeeding and buying cheap; but others did so out of love of horses and pride in their work. Amongst the latter were a future Duke of Beaufort, Lord Chesterfield, and Count d'Orsay. Before long a number of them became professional or semi-professional coachmen, and very competent some of them were. The famous Brighton *Age* was for some years regularly worked by Sir St. Vincent Cotton whom bankruptcy had driven to the box where he acquitted himself with distinction.

No one seems to have computed the number of horses engaged in the coach business, but it must have been enormous. The wastage was very heavy — some horses did not survive what Nimrod called the seasoning — and ample provision had to be made for spares and horses at rest. The average life of a horse in a slow coach, a cheap night coach such as Tony Weller worked out of the Bull in Whitechapel, was six years, but in the fast coaches, which are all we are concerned with, it was only three years. William Chaplin sold and replaced a third of his 1,300 horses every year. Speed killed coach horses as it did posters. At, say, 8 miles an hour in a slow coach a horse could work every day of the year, but in a fast coach, at 10 miles an hour, he had to be rested every fifth day although he seldom worked more than one hour in twenty-four. The formula for horsing fast coaches was one horse for every mile of ground, but in summer, when the going was better, not so many were required.

It was from the compelling need for speed that most of the coachmaster's worries sprung. It demanded good horses and their constant replacement with new, but if the business was to pay they had to be bought cheap. This could only be done by putting up with faults that were not tolerated in private service. Hard mouths did not matter, nor did blindness which was very common among coach horses; but the slang phrase for a thoroughly bad team, 'three blind 'uns and a bolter', was not meant literally. Jibbers, although they were often good horses, were not much liked because they frightened the passengers; bolters, which were usually cared for by the rest of the team, were acceptable, and a kicker was all right as a near side leader where he was easy to punish and could not damage the coach. Tolerance of such faults enabled the coachmasters and the contractors to horse the coaches very cheaply, especially from private stables which were thankful to be rid of their misfits at almost any price.

But there was much more in horsing a coach than buying well-bred horses and stuffing them with corn and beans. If a coach was to run comfortably the horses had to be properly matched so that they worked together. The wheelers, besides having to be strong enough to hold a three ton coach on a hill, had to be of equal stride for if they were not the coach might rock dangerously. Leaders, which had lighter work and could not easily imperil a coach, were often unsound horses. The horsing of coaches would have been easier if leaders and wheelers had been interchangeable, but they seldom were.

It is astonishing that, horsed as they were, the stage coaches were so remarkably efficient. This was chiefly due to the excellence of the coachmen or dragsmen, as they called themselves. In the previous century, when any horse was considered good enough for a coach, no coachman was thought too bad to drive it. Uncouth, foul-mouthed hard-drinkers, the eighteenth-century coachmen loitered at inns as long as they chose and sought to make up for lost time (not that that mattered greatly to them) by mercilessly flogging their horses with the barbarous 'short tommy'. At the end of their last stage they invaded the inn to collect tips from the passengers — 'kicking the passengers' they called it — whom they freely insulted if the tips fell short of their expectations.

Coachmasters had been quick to realize that they could not compete with the mails for passengers unless they employed a very different type of coachman. The better roads, the placing of coaches on springs, the great improvement in the horses, the employment of a guard (copied from the mails), and the interest of the gentry in the horsing and driving of coaches, combined to attract the type of man that was required. It was soon found that the better the coachman, especially in regard to manners and the punctuality of his coach, the more passengers he attracted — the better the coach filled.

No man could rise to the box[1] seat of one of the fast long-distance coaches until he had proved his ability to keep time without distressing his horses. To achieve that he had to be a very good man for his task was made difficult by many factors beyond his control. First, there was the uncertainty of the horses which changed at every stage — every ten to fifteen miles. Then, what he could make of each team depended on how they were harnessed by the horsekeepers (the saying was that a team well put together was already half driven). Then there was the uncertainty of the stops on the road, to pick up both passengers and parcels, the latter an important source of coach revenue. Finally, there were the hazards of the weather: especially fog, snow, and, worst of all, floods. On these uncertainties depended the reputation of every coachman. He could not call himself a 'swell dragsman' until he had shown that he could 'drive any brute that could be harnessed, and could get any load through a country at almost any pace and in all weathers, by night or day'. Finally, he had to keep to his timetable without a horse sweating.

A coachman usually drove about fifty miles a day but there were men like Thoroughgood of the Norwich *Times* who covered his 112 miles of ground to or from London daily for two years without a day off. The fortunate men were those who 'drove double', taking a coach out in the morning and waiting at an inn for another which they brought in later in the day, for they always slept at home; so sometimes did those who drove till they met the 'other half', an in-coming coach, which they brought home. They were paid small wages, only eighteen to twenty shillings a week, because they were expected to do well out of tips, as indeed many of them did. Although the customary tip for a passenger to give the coachman was only a shilling for thirty miles and two shillings for a longer distance, many gave more, especially the inside passengers, and certainly the privileged sportsman who shared the box with the coachman and was perhaps allowed to drive, or 'waggon it', for a stage. An

---

[1] According to *The Servant's Guide* of 1830, the box was originally the hamper or box in which, in the early days of family coaches, provisions were carried. It made a convenient seat for the coachman and, on private carriages, was covered with the hamper cloth or, as it was later called, hammer cloth.

important perquisite of coachmen working out of London was the fares of passengers taken up, on the first stage out, beyond the 'stones', the sets or cobbles of the streets.[1] The coachman was also allowed to keep and share with his guard the 'short shillings', the fares of passengers travelling only a short distance. These concessions sprang from the coachmasters' endless struggle to stop 'shouldering' or the 'swallowing' of fares, the illicit pocketing of fares which lasted on public vehicles until the invention of the bell punch.

As time went on and superior coachmen and horses gave the stage coaches a reputation they had never before enjoyed, the wealthier gentry gradually became reconciled to travelling in a public vehicle and were generous to efficient and well-mannered coachmen. The box seat of one of the smarter coaches carrying plenty of these 'good cloth' passengers might be worth as much as £400 a year, a considerable income for men of lowly origin, as most coachmen were. But many of them were remarkably good men and the complete opposite of their predecessors. They had become 'swell dragsmen' with a smart appearance and polished manners, and they drank no more than the occasional glass of sherry pressed on them by a passenger. Most of them had discarded the traditional many-caped benjamin for a smart frock coat, and the old-fashioned beaver hat for a 'lily shallow' or a white caster. The swell dragsman, according to Lord William Lennox, 'was a well-dressed, natty-looking fellow, decked out in a neat dark brown coat, white hat, corduroy breeches, well polished boots, cloth leggings, and a splendid pair of double-sewn buckskin gloves'. They were often to be seen in the London theatres 'with a nice piece of muslin by their side'.

But good manners and an immaculate appearance did not suffice to make a successful coachman. None of the great men of the road would have been where they were, and become popular heroes, but for their skill on the road. The regret of the admiring crowds they drew to the great London coachyards was that they never saw their heroes at work beyond the stones. The many London admirers of Jack Hale of the *Defiance* would have given much to see him go down Henley Hill in a hard frost without a chain on the wheel, or James Witherington take the

---

[1] There is still a Stones End Street in the Borough.

fully loaded Worcester coach down Broadway Hill without a wheel tied. It needed, as we shall see, exceptional men to do these things without great risk to their passengers.

The aristocracy and gentry used to entertain these great men in their servants' halls, and vie with each other for the privilege of sharing the box seat with them. The inevitable consequence was that some of these men got shockingly spoilt. Some were like Leigh Hunt's coachman: 'His tenderness to descending old ladies is particular. He touches his hat to Mrs. Smith. He gives "the young woman" a ride; and lends her his box-coat in the rain.' Others reserved their good manners for their more distinguished passengers, and behaved odiously to their fellow servants. George Borrow, looking back on his service in the yard of a great coaching inn, where he had witnessed the arrogance of some of the coachmen, declared, 'I, who have ever been an enemy to insolence, cruelty and tyranny, loathe their memory.' When, as a weary pedestrian, he one day boarded a passing coach and, finding himself the only passenger, was about to seat himself on the box, the coachman turned him back with the words: 'No, no, keep behind — the box is for lords, or gentlemen at least.' But behaviour of that kind was not peculiar to coachmen. The inside passengers, and also the innkeepers, shared the coachman's contempt for the inferior outside passengers, other than the privileged one who shared the box seat, and sometimes refused to sit at table with them. De Quincey mentions outsiders, as they were called, having to take their meals in the kitchen of an inn.

The reputation of a coach depended a good deal on its guard who, although no longer armed, was still called the shooter. His first care was the way-bill — the passengers and their fares, their luggage, and the important parcels business. Out on the road he had to tie a hind wheel at the top of a steep hill, with chain or skid-pan, and untie it at the bottom. He could never be without his horn or, as some of them preferred, a bugle. The coach horn was three feet long, the traditional 'yard of tin',[1] and was an essential part of the guard's equipment, for without it no coach could keep time. It was sounded at the inns to summon the passengers, on the stones to clear the

---

[1] So unwieldy an instrument as the so-called coach horn now seen in the show ring could never have been used on a coach. Its provenance appears to be unknown.

traffic, and on the open road to warn waggoners, drovers, and shepherds to clear the way, and the pikemen to man their gates. In fog it had to be blown continuously to avoid collisions. Its most useful function was to give warning to the horsekeepers at the changes to lead out the fresh horses and to the inn servants to have food and drink ready for the passengers. Not only was the guard seldom at rest but, unlike the coachman, he had to accompany the coach throughout its journey which might mean forty-eight hours or more of continuous duty. His pay was usually only ten shillings a week, but he could do well out of tips and the perquisites he shared with the coachman.

The only real advantage the stages had over the mails was that they travelled by day, whereas the mails nearly always started in the evening or later. As speed and punctuality mattered more than anything else to passengers the coachmaster's life was a relentless pursuit of both. So successful were some of the proprietors that the best of the coaches captured much of the mails' passenger traffic. To achieve speed and punctuality a coach had to be as well served by the horsekeepers at the changes as it was by its coachman and guard. It usually took about three minutes to change a team, but at big coaching centres like Hounslow, where immense pride was taken in the work and a spirit of rivalry fired the horsekeepers, it might be done in under a minute. It was the speed of the changes which astonished foreign admirers of the English stage coach more than anything else. 'Why do the English', asked Von Raumer in 1835, 'take hardly two minutes to change horses, and the Prussians at least five times as much? It is only the ennui, hence arising, that drives the travellers to have recourse to coffee, beer, brandy, sausages, and such other palliatives.' It is surprising that he did not complain of the heavy demands which English insistence on speed made on the endurance of passengers. Only twenty-five minutes, and sometimes less, were allowed for a meal and, towards the end of the coaching age, on the two days' journey between London and Edinburgh there were only three stops for meals.

The speed of a coach naturally depended on the road. Ten miles an hour, including stops, was the average speed of the fast coaches, but in hilly country nine might be unusually good going. Contrary to what sporting artists (the great James

Pollard excepted) would have us believe, coaches very seldom galloped. Good trotting ground is what the coachmen demanded, and it was what Telford and McAdam were giving them. Even on very good roads galloping would have been too great a strain for horses, coaches, and passengers to be endured for long. Nor was there much to be gained by galloping, not more than three miles an hour against which had to be set the subsequent slow trot of exhausted horses. Sometimes a coachman would spring his team, as galloping was called, to carry a heavy coach up a short steep hill, or at the bottom of a hill to gain impetus to carry him up the next. Hump-backed bridges and snowdrifts might also be taken at the gallop. There were, however, two or three short straight stretches of exceptionally good road along which a coachman would regularly spring his team. One was over Hartford Bridge Flats; a more famous one, on the same Exeter road, between Hounslow and Staines, was known as 'the galloping ground of the western coaches'.

'Journeys', said Quilp, 'are very perilous — especially outside the coach. Wheels come off, horses take fright, coachmen drive too fast, coaches overturn. I always go to chapel before I start on journeys.' All these things did happen to coaches but they were not frequent and coach-travel was not considered particularly perilous. There were of course reckless drivers, but the most frequent causes of accidents were bad loading and errors of judgement. 'Coaches', said Tony Weller, 'is like guns — they requires to be loaded with wery great care, afore they go off.' A badly loaded coach, like one with badly matched wheelers, could easily start rolling, and then a stone in the road might suffice to turn it over. In hilly country the speed of a coach depended a great deal on the judgement of the coachman. An experienced man who knew his ground well could judge, taking into careful consideration the weight of his load, when it was safe to go down a hill without wasting time on stopping to tie and untie a wheel.[1] A lesser man, perhaps behind time, might risk it, with the possible result that half way down the coach overpowered the wheelers and turned

[1] Brakes were not invented till late in the coaching age, but they were little used because it was feared that they would spoil wheelers accustomed to holding a heavy coach on a hill.

over. On the other hand, tying a wheel was the surest way of upsetting a top-heavy coach. A man required great experience before he could become a swell dragsman.

Vicious horses seldom caused accidents. They were usually harnessed with steady ones which helped to control them. Even a team of four dangerous horses was no great peril because it was highly unlikely that they would all go wrong at the same time. Accidents were most common on the middle ground because it was more often covered at night. Under cover of darkness horse contractors could get away with horses and harness they dared not show in daytime. Bad harness could be a very great danger; nothing worse could happen to a coach than for a rein to break, for if it did the coachman was bound to lose control of his team. At night, too, a bad coachman could get drunk with comparative impunity. But, drunk or sober, a coachman could not look over the harnessing of his team at night as he could by day, so that the carelessness of horsekeepers could easily pass undetected.

It was not the hazards of coach-travel but the expense that set a strict limit to the passenger traffic. On the fast day coaches the fare was 4d. to 5d. a mile inside, and 2d. to 3d. outside which, with tips to coachman, guard and porters to add, confined travelling to those who had to travel. Travelling for pleasure had to await the arrival of railways. Yet at these fares, which were approximately half what the mails charged, it was not easy to make a coach pay. It carried only four inside passengers and was limited by law to eight to twelve, according to current legislation,[1] outside, and seldom was a coach fully loaded. Even if it were empty, what was called a 'crazy woman', it had to run in order to maintain the service. The root of the difficulty of making a fast coach pay lay in the heavy wastage of horseflesh. Although the slower coaches charged lower fares they were usually profitable, partly because they were allowed to carry more passengers, but chiefly because the working life of the horses was so much longer, fewer spares were needed and the horses seldom had to be rested. For this reason the big coachmasters ran slow coaches as a hedge against the financial risk of their smart fast ones, but the latter were the ones in

[1] With every pikeman eager for the rewards offered to informers, the law was easily enforced.

which they took pride, and on which their reputations depended.

From the passengers' point of view the difference between slow and fast coaches was not limited to the difference in speed. On the road, particularly at the inns, there was a wealth of social snobbery. The aristocracy, travelling post in their own carriages, received the utmost deference and consideration; nothing that contributed to their comfort was too much trouble. Next came those who travelled in hired postchaises who mostly had full pockets. The passengers off a smart fast coach could usually count on reasonable attention, especially if the dragsman was one of the great men of the road. But for those who could afford nothing better than a slow coach, usually travelling at night, anything was good enough.

'The old True Blue Independent', wrote Surtees, 'did not profess to travel or trail above eight miles an hour, and this it only accomplished under favourable circumstances, such as light loads, good roads, and stout steeds, instead of the top-heavy cargo that now ploughed along the woolly turnpike after the weak, jaded horses, that seemed hardly able to keep their legs against the keen careering wind. . . . Then the coach refreshments, or want of refreshments rather; the turning out at all hours to breakfast, dine, or sup, just as the coach reached the house of a proprietor "wot ors'd it," and the cool incivility of every body about the place. Any thing was good enough for a coach passenger.'

When Surtees wrote that, in *Ask Mamma* in the second half of the nineteenth century, he was recalling coach travel at its worst, in a slow coach at the end of the coaching era, in about 1845. By that time the coaching inns had fallen into decay, for the coaches both made and ruined, or nearly ruined, the English inn. When, in the early years of the nineteenth century, the stage coaches began to compete with the mails, their proprietors quickly found that their passengers expected a good deal more than speed and punctuality. In choosing the inns at which their coaches inned at night, as they called it, and to a less extent the inns at which they changed horses and where meals were to be had, the coachmasters had to make sure that their passengers were certain of good accommodation, good food and drink, and willing service. The mails were no less insistent on the need for their passengers to be properly cared for where-

ever they stopped. If an inn failed to provide the services required it lost the custom of the coaches, which might well spell
its ruin. This was the making of the English inns which were
just as much the envy of foreigners as the coaches themselves.

In English inns 'everything is far better and more abundant
than on the Continent', wrote Pückler-Muskau in 1826. 'At
every inn on the road', wrote Count Pecchio a year later,
'breakfast, dinner, or supper, is always ready, a fire is burning
in every room, and water always boiling for tea or coffee. Soft
feather-beds, with a fire blazing up the chimney, invite to
repose; and the tables are covered with newspapers, for the
amusement of the passengers.' At about the same time an
American, Washington Irving, 'admired, for the hundredth
time, that picture of convenience, neatness, and broad, honest
enjoyment, the kitchen of an English inn', and also the 'trim
housemaids . . . hurrying backwards and forwards under the
directions of a fresh bustling landlady'.

The difference between these descriptions of English inns
and those of John Byng in the latter part of the previous
century is a measure of the astonishing improvement which
the coaches had achieved. But when, in the late 'thirties, the
coaches, bowing to the insistence of the public for still greater
speed, began travelling all through the night, and seldom stopping for a meal, and then but for a few minutes, the roadside
inn began to matter less and quickly fell into decay. 'The quicker
rate of travelling,' wrote Macaulay, 'the less important is it
that there should be numerous agreeable resting-places for
travellers. . . . At present . . . a traveller seldom interrupts his
journey merely for the sake of rest and refreshment. The consequence is that hundreds of excellent inns have fallen into
decay.'

But in our period the inns were still good and a coach journey
a pleasanter experience than when everything was sacrificed to
speed. There are few better descriptions of such a journey than
Thomas Hughes's account of Tom Brown's ride to Rugby on
the fast Leicester *Tally-ho!*, working out of the Peacock,
Islington: 'The coachman calls out "Let 'em go" and the ostlers
fly back, drawing the cloths from their glossy loins, and away
we go.' Out on the road 'there was the music of the rattling
harness, and the ring of the horses' feet on the hard road, and

the glare of the two bright lamps through the steaming hoar frost, over the leaders' ears, into the darkness; and the cheery toot of the guard's horn, to warn some drowsy pikeman or the ostler at the next change. . . . Then the break of dawn and the sunrise, where can they ever be seen in perfection but from a coach roof? You want motion and change and music to see them in their glory . . . good silent music . . . the accompaniment of work and getting over the ground. . . . The coach pulls up at a little road-side inn with huge stables behind. There is a bright fire gleaming through the red curtains of the bar window, and the door is open. The coachman catches his whip into a double thong, and throws it to the ostler; the steam of the horses rises straight up into the air. He has put them along over the last two miles, and is two minutes before his time.'

Charles Dickens, whose knowledge and understanding of everything to do with the road and the coaches he loved so dearly were unrivalled, makes clear in his account of Tom Pinch's setting out from Salisbury in the 'swaggering, rakish, dissipated, London coach', how much to him the music of a fast coach meant. 'The four grays skimmed along as if they liked it quite as well as Tom did; the bugle was in as high spirits as the grays; the coachman chimed in sometimes with his voice; the wheels hummed cheerfully in unison; the brass-work on the harness was an orchestra of little bells; and thus, as they went clinking, jingling, rattling, smoothly on, the whole concern, from the buckles of the leaders' coupling reins, to the handle of the hind boot, was one great instrument of music.'

The new fast coaches did much to brighten the lives of simple country people. By keeping them in closer touch with the outside world, by giving them seemingly immediate news of all that was happening in London, they broke in upon the old feeling of rural isolation. But perhaps their greatest service to the countryman was to provide a daily spectacle which never palled, and with which the smartest equipage of the aristocracy could not compare. 'A stage coach', wrote Washington Irving, 'carries animation always with it, and puts the world in motion as it whirls along. The horn sounded at the entrance of a village produces a general bustle.' 'How proud we felt', wrote Thomas Jeans, 'as everyone we met stopped to admire the perfection of our turnout! When pretty faces peeped out at all the windows,

and when every one we passed, from the squire in the gig with
the high-stepping mare to the market gardener in his humble
donkey-cart, gave evident tokens of admiration of our splendid
team. It was beautiful to see the well-matched horses step
together, and perform their work as if they loved it. How skil-
fully old Weller holds them in hand! How cautiously he tacks at
ugly corners; how cleverly he makes play at the end of the
descent, and dashes at a gallop over the bridge in the bottom,
to help us up the stiff hill on the other side before us. . . . What
excitement we cause! The cobbler drops his last, the tailor
abandons his goose, and rushes to the door in time to give a nod
of approbation as we go by, as though he were satisfied that all
was right.' When, in the 'forties, the railways drove the coaches
off the roads, rural England suffered a grievous loss.

XI

Joe Manton and Peter Hawker

IN the first half of the eighteenth century the usual methods of
taking game were hawking and netting. Netting, which generally outlived hawking, lasted well into the second half of the
century. Nimrod described how it was done by a north-country
squire. 'He took the field', he wrote, 'with his two mounted
keepers, in their green jackets and gold-laced hats, accompanied
by a leash of setters, himself riding in the rear, whilst the dogs
were at work. When they came upon a covey and dropped,
the keepers advanced with the net, and at once secured their
prize, the dogs lying as though they were dead.' The great
merit of this system was that all the young birds could be set
free, only the old pair being killed, to the great benefit of the
shoot. This advantage was lost when the sporting flint-lock gun
was introduced in the same century, by the end of which
shooting had become a fashionable and popular sport.

'In the shooting season', wrote Emily Eden in 1826, 'they
only travel on Sundays.' Shooting had by then become a ruling
passion of the gentry. Of a shooting party at Ashridge in 1823 it
was recorded that 'the sports of the field on the three days of the
Duke of York's sojourning were never before equalled. The
Duke of Wellington's double-barrel gun brought down everything before it.' In the three days the eight guns, it was said,
fired 1,971 shots and killed 1,088 head of game. Had the party
been less eminent the chronicler's tribute to the marksmanship
would probably have been less extravagant. Nevertheless,
shooting had come to play so great a part in social life that big
bags were not unusual, and there were many excellent shots.[1]

---

[1] In 1828 Lord Chandos, at Wooton, killed 1,349 head of game, mostly pheasants
and hares, in the course of four days' shooting, but with ten to fifteen guns out a
day. *Annals of Sporting* gives the number of shots fired as 2,919.

Shooting had suddenly become fashionable largely through the brilliant work of an eminent gunmaker. With the invention of the flint-lock and hammer principle in the eighteenth century, and its application to the double-barrelled gun, the production of a gun sufficiently light in weight for general use had at last become possible, and the art of shooting flying common practice. But it was not till the early years of the nineteenth century that the most famous of all English gunmakers, Joseph Manton,[1] so perfected the flint-lock that the sportsman was provided with a gun which was so light and such a pleasure to handle that men who till then had shown little interest in shooting took to it with enthusiasm. 'I have shot with very many guns of London makers of repute', wrote Christopher Idle many years later, 'and found little difference — none, however, in the present day in my opinion are superior to Joe Manton, and few equal to him. Every part of Joe Manton's guns was equally good in point of quality and workmanship. Strength, combined with neatness and the highest possible finish; hence the extraordinary durability of his guns, and the good external appearance which they maintain even to the very last.'

Flint and steel were very soon replaced by the percussion system of ignition. The most popular form of this was a damp-proof copper cap charged with fulminate in the invention of which Joe Manton and one of his customers, the no less famous Colonel Peter Hawker,[2] played a part. Nevertheless, Peter Hawker, according to Anthony Trollope, 'seems to have retained a sneaking preference for flint and steel up to his dying day'. Nor was he alone in this. The extraordinary way in which the comparatively primitive flint-lock held its own against the detonator or percussion gun[3] was largely due to its association

[1] Joseph Manton was born in about 1766 and carried on business in Davies Street until 1825 when he moved to Hanover Square. He died in 1835. He was a close friend of Peter Hawker, a valued customer, who records in his diary in 1817: 'Received a detonating gun (No. 8111), value 100 guineas, presented to me by Mr. Joseph Manton.' This was only one of his many Manton guns.

[2] Peter Hawker, the author of *Instructions to Young Sportsmen*, was born in 1786. In 1801 he was gazetted to the 1st Royal Dragoons, but transferred to the 14th Light Dragoons in 1803. He was severely wounded at Talavera and invalided out of the service, but later was appointed to the North Hampshire Militia of which he became lieutenant-colonel in 1821. He lived at Longparish House, Hants. He was, to use his own words, 'shooting and music mad'. He died in 1853.

[3] Until far into the nineteenth century it was usual for writers of instructive books on shooting to assume that their readers still used flint-locks. It was not easy

with the man who perfected it. So greatly was he esteemed that the name Joe Manton virtually became a synonym for a shot gun. But the shot gun was still a muzzle-loader, and so remained, with all the limitations that placed on the sportsman and his bag, to say nothing of its dangers, until the middle of the century.

So long as he used a muzzle-loader the shooter had to encumber himself with various accessories; first the ramrod, which was attached to the gun, then a powder flask, a shot belt or pouch, a box of caps,[1] wads and spare gun nipples with a nipple key. The powder flask, which originally had been no more than a cow horn plugged at its tip, carried a device for measuring the charge. The shot belt or pouch was similarly equipped with an adjustable charger. The wads were cut at home with a punch to fit the calibre of the gun, from paper, pasteboard, or an old hat.

Guns were mostly of smaller but more varied calibres than those used today, ranging from 22 to 12 bores, but we seldom hear of anything larger than a 14 bore until the middle of the century. With guns varying a great deal in calibre and weight, and with both shot (No. 7. was recommended for general use)[2] and powder wholly under the control of the shooter, there was no standard charge, so the load was apt to vary considerably according to the taste and whims of the sportsman. As it would be tedious to pursue so technical a subject as the proper loading of muzzle-loaders it will suffice to quote from what Col. Hawker and another authority wrote about it. 'Much as may be said on this *important head,*' wrote the Colonel, 'I shall attempt to explain it by one simple example: for instance, to load a single gun of six, or double gun of seven, eight, or nine pounds weight, take a steel charger, which holds

to switch from a flint-lock to a detonator. 'As a detonator goes so very much quicker than a flint,' wrote Hawker, 'it becomes necessary, in firing one, to avoid shooting *too* forward . . . IF YOU HAVE A DETONATOR make only HALF the allowance; that is, where you would fire SIX inches before a bird with a flint, fire only THREE INCHES with a DETONATOR.' Hawker, as late as 1848, had the two systems combined in a duck gun. 'My detonator', he wrote, 'missed fire, or I should have got 20 birds. I fired after them, flying, with the flint barrel, and got 5 brent geese.'

   [1] Or flints for a flint-lock. The best flints, 'the most transparent of the common black flints', came of course from Brandon whose flint industry dates from prehistoric times. Quality was important. 'At eight good shots my gun mist fire,' wrote Colonel Thornton in 1786, 'though I put in five different flints.'

   [2] 'No. 7.', wrote Hawker, 'is best for everything, unless you take a duck gun.'

precisely one ounce and a half of shot, fill it brim full of powder, from which first prime,[1] and then put the remainder into the barrel: to this add the same measure *bumper* full of shot, and then regulate the tops of your flasks and belts accordingly.'

That tells us only half the story of how to load a gun. For the other half we can turn to Hawker's not very lucid contemporary John Mayer: 'In charging, the powder should not be rammed too hard, but only pressed close, and the wadding placed over it just tight enough to keep it from mixing with the shot, which should not be rammed down with that force used by some persons, as it is this practice which causes a heavy recoil. The use of ramming the shot is not to increase its force, but to keep it in a compact body. The wadding must be well fitted into the bore of the piece, and be carefully rammed, that it may not move or let out the charge. . . . When the gun has been much shook, in passing over the land, it will be necessary to examine the state of the charge and priming before attempting to fire.' Moreover, after every twenty shots the gun had to be cleaned.

This elaborate procedure placed a considerable burden on the gamekeeper going out with a party of guns armed with muzzle-loaders. These are John Mayer's directions to 'a keeper going a shooting with gentlemen', written as late as 1828: 'The guns being perfectly clean and new flinted, the flasks filled with powder properly dried, the steel chargers with shot, and a sufficient quantity of wadding, wrapped up in clean paper, for each gentleman, shut in between the hammer and pan; take a very large belt, and flask filled to replenish with, a joint cleaning-rod, tow, oil, lock-brush, which may have a little stone-brimstone dropped into the end, to rub the faces of the hammers with; flints, screw-driver, and aqua laudanum, to apply if a bite should take place. Put two small gins into the shooting canteens, to set where you find a head of game knocked down by vermin.' In addition, as we shall see, he had to carry restoratives for shattered nerves.

The shooter himself also went out loaded with cares. To the inconvenience of having to carry so much ancillary equipment, of the need to reload so laboriously after every shot, and to make sure that rough going did not disturb the charge, was

---

[1] Priming powder, of course, was only required for flint-locks.

added the difficulty of keeping everything dry in wet or foggy weather. The copper cap of the percussion gun did much to remedy this last trouble but it did not reduce the quite considerable hazards attaching to the use of muzzle-loaders. Injuries, varying from the loss of a finger or two to loss of life, were frequent.

Then, just as much as now, most shooting accidents were due to careless handling of guns, and failure to take elementary precautions, but the muzzle-loader was a far more dangerous weapon than the modern hammerless breech-loader. It was not difficult to discharge it accidentally in loading, especially if a spark remained in a barrel from a previous shot. To minimize the effects of this the ramrod was usually held only with one finger and the thumb, the butt of the gun resting on the ground and the muzzle pointing away from the sportsman and not at anyone else. The double-barrelled gun was particularly dangerous and fell into added disfavour when Charles James Fox was injured by the explosion of his. It was easy, when reloading, accidentally to put two charges into one barrel which on being fired would surely burst; but the commonest accident was from the vibration of the ramrod in one barrel causing the explosion of the charge in the other when the latter had been foolishly left at full-cock. When the percussion gun was introduced an added danger came from overcharging the cap with fulminate, which could cause a violent explosion. Any one of these accidents might of itself cause serious injury, but it might also cause a still more serious one by exploding the powder flask. This common and very dangerous accident could be caused even by too violent a spring-catch on the flask. Hawker adds final words of caution 'relative to powder horns in the *field*:— If you should have fired one barrel, and, while in the act of reloading it, other game should be sprung, *beware* of firing the other barrel until you have *either put the flask in your pocket*, or *thrown it on the ground*. I could name several, who, through a neglect of doing this, have been severely wounded by blowing up their flasks.'

Faulty guns, either badly designed or of inferior workmanship, were another cause of accidents. Most muzzle-loaders were dangerously light at the breech, seemingly in order to save weight, for when the breech-loader was introduced the few ounces saved on the ramrod were used to strengthen the breech-ends of the barrels. Possibly in our period, but certainly in the middle of the century, dishonest gunmakers imposed their inferior, and often very dangerous, guns on the public, especially on 'young gentlemen about to leave for India', by fraudulently engraving on their locks and barrels the names of eminent makers which were unhesitatingly accepted as a guarantee of first-class workmanship.

It is not surprising to find that the nervousness which every shooter has to overcome when he first handles a loaded gun was very much more pronounced in the days of muzzle-loaders. 'The first object, in acquiring the use of the gun,' wrote John Mayer, 'is to get the better of any trepidation or apprehension at the moment of discharge. . . . If you feel to flinch, take a sandwich and a glass of brandy.' But there seem to have been occasions in the field so shattering as to reduce a whole party of guns to nervous prostration. For this, too, Mayer's remedy was brandy and a sandwich. 'Do not forget', he wrote in his 'Directions for a Gamekeeper', 'the sandwich-case, and flask of brandy, to hand to the gentlemen, when their nerves get a little affected. Assist them in reloading, during which time let them stand as still as possible, till they get quite cool and collected. The trembling being quite off, proceed very deliberately.'

The methods of finding and killing game were, like shotguns, undergoing marked changes. Up to the end of the eighteenth century shooting was a sport for the individual rather than for parties of sportsmen; like deer-stalking, it derived much of its charm from its demanding self-reliance, endurance, and woodcraft. 'The creative and sustaining principle of genuine sport,' wrote Anthony Trollope in the middle of the century, 'is to be found in the laborious uncertainty of rambling for hours over forest and moorland without knowing what wild bird or animal may rise or spring up before us. A woodcock or snipe, three or four brace of partridges or pheasants, half a dozen hares or rabbits, a couple of teal or wild-duck, picked up in a wild walk of this kind, outweigh, in our estimation, the value of a hundred pheasants or hares massacred in a battue.' His contemporary William Lennox looked back nostalgically at the simpler ways of his youth. 'We own', he wrote, 'that early hours, a sufficient quantity of birds, the old-fashioned flint and steel gun, a staunch brace of pointers, a first-rate retriever,[1] on a fine autumn morning, was the height of enjoyment.'

But it would be wrong to suppose that shooting over dogs necessarily entailed considerable power of endurance as its advocates so often claimed. There was, for example, Lord Grantley whose method of shooting partridges is recorded by his kinsman, Grantley Berkeley. 'He would enter the field', he wrote, 'and stationing himself under the first tree, umbrella as well as gun in hand, in case there should be no shelter from the sun or rain, there he kept his place till his pointers had beaten the ground. If there was game, he went up to the point; if not, he proceeded to the next field, and did the same thing.' Moreover, it was very usual to go shooting on horseback.

In the eighteenth century there had been no other way to shoot than that described by Trollope and Lennox, and everyone was, of course, free to go on shooting like that if he wanted to, as he still is — though, alas, not often over dogs. It was not a form of shooting that satisfied the new social needs of the bigger country houses where large parties of guests were now being entertained. It was impossible to send out solitary prowling guns without their both interfering with each other and leaving much ground uncovered. Moreover, shooting over dogs, although it long continued to be practised, was getting more difficult; as the result of enclosure rough common land, so suitable for pointers and setters, had been greatly reduced, and the seed-drill had made arable less suitable for them because it encouraged birds to run. As the result of more shooting birds had become wilder. Partridges, still the principal game bird of the South, could not be shot over dogs after the first two or three weeks of September even in the long stubbies of those days, in spite of the use of paper kites to make them lie, and it was much the same with grouse. Pheasants were comparatively scarce[2] and found mostly in woodlands where walking them up

---

[1] Most good retrievers were what were then called Newfoundlands. In 1814 Peter Hawker described his 'favourite Newfoundland dog' as 'of the real St. John's breed, quite black, with a long head, very fine action, and something of the otter skin, and not the curly-haired heavy brute that so often and so commonly disgraces the name of the Newfoundland dog'. W. B. Daniel, writing in 1802 about shooting dogs, mentions only setters, pointers, and spaniels, which suggests that retrievers did not come into use till later.

[2] Peter Hawker's diary shows how scarce wild pheasants were, anyway in his native Hampshire. Between 1802 and 1853 he killed to his own gun 7,035 par-

XIII   *The Carriage and Horses of Smith Barry Esquire*: This picture of a gentleman's travelling carriage shows the dickey or rumble for the lady's maid and valet, and the iron rack on the roof to hold the imperial.

XIV *Pheasant Shooting*: Pheasants were comparatively rare until, early in the nineteenth century, rearing became general. That and the introduction of driving combined to make them a popular game bird.

with spaniels served only to drive them off the ground without
being shot at. In his *Rural Sports* Daniel mentions one way of
overcoming the difficulty of shooting pheasants over dogs in
woodlands. *'Pointers'*, he wrote, 'have been tried to be used in
woods with *bells* upon their collars, but the contrivance has ill
answered the intention.' Nevertheless, for a time it was widely
practised.

The need to provide sport for more guns over a longer
period — in short, to turn to better account the game on the
ground — led to the introduction of driving game to the guns,
a continental practice which brought with it its foreign name.
At first the word *battue* was applied to the driving of any game
with beaters but later, when pheasant shooting became more
general, it came to mean essentially what was later called a
covert shoot.

It was the introduction of driving, especially the beating out
of woodlands to the guns, that taught our ancestors that the
pheasant was a much more sporting bird than they had ever
suspected. While the outlying pheasant marked by pointers or
setters, or pushed out of a hedgerow by spaniels, presented,
compared with the partridge, too easy a target to be sporting,
the killing of a high driven pheasant was found to demand
considerable skill. It was also found that the successful driving
of game, whether partridges, grouse, or pheasants, was far less
easy than it appeared; the demands it made on the experience,
judgement, and organization of a host and his keepers added
greatly to the interest of a day's driving or covert shooting.
It was also found that, when driving, fewer birds were wounded
and not gathered — a bird coming head on was usually either
killed outright or clean missed. It was also found, especially
with grouse and partridges, that driving lowered the percentage
of young birds killed. To the elderly an added advantage of
driving was that although it demanded greater skill it required
less energy and endurance, especially in bad weather.

Thus did shooting develop and become more popular than
ever before; but with this went an increasing demand for
large bags which the prevailing spirit of competition, especially

tridges but only 575 pheasants. By 1819–20 rearing was yielding big bags; that
season at Woburn they killed 1,375 pheasants in seven days' shooting. Hawker's
personal bag for the same season was 2 pheasants against 216 partridges.

between landowners, greatly encouraged. Good keepering, particularly the control of vermin and poachers, became more important, but new methods had to be devised for increasing the head of game. Before the end of the eighteenth century the Duke of Richmond was importing partridge eggs from France for hatching in Sussex, and it is improbable that others were not doing the same for long after that.

In 1787 John Byng wrote of a visit to Blenheim that 'in various parts of the park are clusters of faggots around a coop, where are hatch'd and rear'd such quantities of pheasants that I almost trod upon them in the grass'. The Duke of Marlborough seems to have been much ahead of his times for, in spite of the hand-rearing of pheasants being comparatively easy and the surest way of increasing the head of game on most shoots, it did not become general until well into the nineteenth century. By then it had become common practice also to turn down pheasants which, like bag-foxes, could be bought in Leadenhall Market.[1] As the true value of the pheasant as a sporting bird came to be widely recognized, owners of shoots wisely took to forbidding the shooting of hens, sometimes to the ill-concealed annoyance of their guests. It may have been this unpopular restriction that prompted Sir Robert Peel to complain to his wife from Apethorpe, where he had been shooting with Lord Westmorland, that 'the shooting was exceedingly bad. The attempt of the whole day was to prevent us from killing the very little game there was to kill.'

Shooting's new-found popularity, the demands made on gamekeepers by their masters for more and more birds, and the resultant destruction of foxes on an unprecedented scale, brought foxhunters and shooters into conflict. Then, as now, there were plenty of public-spirited shooting men who demonstrated the practicability of having both game and foxes in plenty in the same woodlands, as did the many landowners who were fond of both shooting and hunting. Nevertheless, there were very few gamekeepers who could be persuaded that this was so, or that the disturbance of game coverts by fox-hounds did no harm. Thus sometimes arose the mutual antipathy of foxhunters and shooting men which for the next hundred years

---

[1] Jack Mytton once paid a single bill of £1,500 from a London dealer for pheasants and foxes.

and more was apt to provoke bitter discord in districts where the two sports came into unnecessary conflict.

The introduction of the driving of game excited much criticism. Its foreign origin, the very name *battue*, the alleged cruelty of forcing birds to fly over the guns, and the diminished physical exertion it required combined to create a strong prejudice against it. The urban middle classes, always eager to seize any opportunity to criticize a field sport, and the more narrow-minded foxhunters, joined in decrying this new method of shooting. But it was not until the advent of the hand-rearing of pheasants and the resultant big bags that the critics began denouncing covert-shooting as a cruel and barbarous sport, a cold-blooded massacre of tame birds. It is probable that at that time there was considerable justification for this charge, because keepers and their masters may well not have yet learnt the art of bringing hand-reared pheasants to the guns as wild and strong on the wing as they should be. Colour is lent to this supposition by Colonel John Cook who, writing in about 1825, relates how, hearing of a *'grande batuë'*, he 'enquired of the landlord of the inn *who* had bagged the most game: "I know nothing about that, Sir", said he, "but *the men who beat for the Gentlemen killed one hundred and twenty head*".' The birds knocked over by beaters can only have been immature hand-reared pheasants, and if this sort of thing was not unusual, as may well have been the case with hand-rearing not yet fully understood and the proper presentation of the birds to the guns yet to be mastered, there was good ground for criticism. From the complaints of game dealers that driven birds reached them badly mangled, it looks also as though guns had not yet learnt to leave low birds alone, which would certainly have lent point to the charge of cruelty and bad sportsmanship. It cannot be doubted that in its early days the covert shoot fell far below the high standards that were demanded later in the century and which still obtain.

In a chapter headed 'Shooting or Slaughtering' in *Plain or Ringlets?*, Surtees put the countryman's case against driving: 'It is hardly possible to imagine that one and the same amusement can be followed in such ways as to look like two distinct pursuits, as in the case of shooting and battueing. In one case a man goes out with his dogs and gun ... goes just as fancy prompts him, or his dog inclines to his game; if he gets his two or three brace of birds, well and good, if not, he gets healthy exercise, and the birds are there for another day.' But with the battue, he continues, 'there is little or no exercise, while there is great preparation, trouble and expense. . . . The exercise and the pleasure a man has in watching the working of his dogs, is quite as great as sending the poor birds neck and crop over. If, as is said of coursing, you are mad for a moment, and starved for an hour; so with the battue, you exterminate in a day what should serve you for a year.

'We never heard but one utilitarian reason attempted to be given for the battue, which was, that to lessen the quantity of game and to kill it for the surrounding district, the *battue* is infinitely the better way than to potter after game thinly spread over a wide extent, whereby a man would not be able to kill half so much; but that is rather an argument for not having so much game than for reducing it in that way.' Elsewhere he comes out more strongly against the covert shoot. His Squire Trevanion had 'no desire to see his name in the country papers with so many hundred head of game attached to it. Down with battues! say we.'

Later in the century another good sportsman, Lord William Lennox, objected to the battue on the same ground as Surtees: 'It is all very well to have two or three guns and a loader,[1] and fire away until your shoulder is black and blue, but it is not to be compared to a quiet walk with a good double-barrelled Westley Richards, a brace of steady pointers, and a retriever, with a bag at the end of the day of twenty or five-and-twenty brace.' But public criticism was aimed principally at the size of the bags. Anthony Trollope regarded 'such records with pain and aversion', and declared they were 'not sport'. Parson Jack Russell, another good countryman, condemned 'the gormandising battue-shooter'.

One undeniable objection to driving and the covert shoot was that it made dangerous shots more dangerous. The Duke of Wellington, who was very fond of pheasant shooting, appears, from contemporary records, to have been a particularly dangerous shot, and his victims were not always the beaters. 'The Duke', wrote Lady Cowper in 1823, 'has been unlucky at

---

[1] Then, as now, some owners of shoots, Lord Berkeley for example, would not permit the use of more than one gun.

Wherstead. He peppered Lord Granville's face with nine shot.
. . . These Battu's are dangerous things.'

In spite of all the criticism the covert shoot and the driving
of grouse and partridges rose steadily in favour among shooting
men, and before many years had passed they had become common practice. At the same time experience had taught the need,
and how, to avoid the blunders of the early days that had rightly
attracted criticism. With the new form of shooting thus purged
it would have been the height of folly to have abandoned it. It
made shooting both more skilful and more merciful. 'There is
more downright sport in tumbling from the sky one high fast-
flying pheasant (though you fail at five others)', wrote Sir
Ralph Payne-Gallwey many years later, '. . . than there is in
slaying a score in succession, without a miss, that fly slowly away
as they rise in front of your toes or your dog's nose as you march
forward. With the first method the game has fair play and a
chance of escape; with the second it has none to speak of.'

In the first half of the nineteenth century every form of
shooting had some very unattractive features. One of the worst
was the pride men took in long shots. 'The constant succession
of long shots', wrote Peter Hawker of a day's shooting in 1819,
'that my favourite old Joe Manton barrels continued bringing
down, surpassed anything I had before done, or seen, in my
whole career of shooting.' More usually he mentions a long shot
as an excuse for one of his rare misses. Thus the foregoing
extract from his diary is preceded by the following unfortunate
entry: 'Misses: 4 very long shots, 2 of which were struck and
feathered.' And again, 'I popped away twice, but too far to kill.'
One would like to think that Peter Hawker, whose *Diary*
reveals deplorable weaknesses of character besides bad sportsmanship, was the exception in taking such long shots, but
evidence is lacking.

Another prevalent vice was competitive shooting. 'As the
present race shoot only for book,' wrote Lennox, 'they care not
how they fill the game-cart; hares are blown up within a few
yards, pheasants are mutilated at a short distance, and partridges are hardly allowed to rise before the contents of an
unerring weapon lays them dead.' The notoriously evil consequences of competitive shooting were aggravated by betting.
This was inevitable, for not only was betting much in fashion

but the most popular summer amusement of the shooting man was trap-pigeon shooting of which wagering was a big attraction.

Owing to game having a high market value it was very necessary to keep a careful tally of the bag throughout the day, which the head keeper did on a notching stick he carried for the purpose. A tally was also often kept of what each gun shot and of the number of shots he fired;[1] this encouraged betting and in so doing led to unseemly disputes when two or more guns fired simultaneously at the same bird. Each gun was often accompanied by a marker to record on a notching stick what he killed.[2] When the markers took to betting among themselves on each gun's performance, and rigging the scores, the results of competitive shooting were seen at their worst.

Peter Hawker, to his credit, was much opposed to competitive shooting, and this may in part have accounted for his dislike of shooting parties. 'I had some very fair game shooting,' he wrote of a visit to Norfolk in 1813, 'though with parties (as is the unpleasant custom of this county and Suffolk), I kept no account of what I killed, which I seldom do on such days. Though I have never yet been beat by anyone in any country that I have ever yet seen, still this style of shooting leads to a jealousy that I detest; and as I consider more than two guns a party for fun and society, and not a party for sport, I reckon all the game shot as much a general concern as a fox when killed by a pack of hounds, though I certainly killed far more than anyone else.'

That was a very proper attitude, but probably a rare one in those days. Less in tune with modern ideas of good sportsmanship is the following entry in Hawker's diary years later: 'The birds would not let us get into the same field with them. Determined to "serve them out", I loaded "Big Joe" with Eley, started at five in the evening in the cart, and was in again

---

[1] The gamebooks of the day included columns headed: 'No. of shots had'; 'No. of shots killed'; and 'No. of shots missed'.

[2] The marker's principal duty, however, was to mark down birds that had been flushed. 'Always be sure to tell a young marker', wrote Hawker, 'that he must *carry his eye well forward* when a covey of birds begin to skim in their flight, and consider, that as they may continue doing so for a field or two, he cannot safely say that he *has marked them down* till he has *seen them* stop and *flap their wings*, which all game must do, before they can alight on the ground.' The remarkable bags Hawker made when shooting alone were only made possible by his very free use of markers of whom he would take out several at a time, each 'judiciously placed'.

by half-past six, with 10 first-rate young partridges. Nothing like a duck gun from a horse and cart on the road to fill a bag, when all popgunning becomes a wild-goose chase.' In pleasant but humble contrast is the amusement of a shooting party at Lord Hertford's Sudbourne when the Duke of Wellington 'detected' Sir Henry Cooke shooting a sitting rabbit.

At the beginning of the century there seem to have been only two generally practicable methods of shooting game (as opposed to wildfowl with which we are not concerned): over dogs and driving. As we have seen, shooting over dogs was not suitable for the entertainment of a party of guns and conditions were becoming less favourable for it. On the other hand, driving was not always practicable or even desirable, especially early in the season. These circumstances led to the introduction of a third method, walking in line, to us the most familiar and simplest of all organized methods of shooting. In those days it was a little complicated by the need, so long as guns were muzzle-loaders, for each of the party to have two guns and a loader. We owe to William Lennox this account of the customary procedure at the beginning of a day's walking which shows that shooting was taken very seriously and well organized: The guest arrived to find the head keeper surrounded by his under keepers 'and a host of rustics engaged to act as beaters . . . each keeper, loader and beater has a number in his hat. The list of the sportsmen is read over. No. 1. is, say, the host; as his name and number are pronounced, the men, — a keeper, loader, boy with ammunition, and five or six beaters marked No. 1. — fall out and join him, and so on to every "gunner". When all have passed muster, you are placed in the line by the head-keeper, the men having strict injunctions to keep all day with their *numbered* master.'

Guests expected a great deal of their hosts in those days. Probably on account of the difficulties of travel and the limitations they placed on impedimenta, guests were sometimes provided with guns and dogs, but they did not expect to have to bring their own powder and shot. They also did very well out of the game. Besides giving a guest all the game he wanted for himself, a shooting host also gave him what he wanted for his friends, and his servants packed it up and sent it off; and guests did not hesitate to ask for more than had been given

them, which was probably often excusable because, the sale of
game being prohibited by law, the disposal of a large bag was
not always easy.

Before the end of the eighteenth century shooting men had
begun to visit the north of England, Wales and particularly
Scotland for grouse-shooting and deer-stalking, and very soon
an annual migration to the North in time for 'the Twelfth'
became a social habit. This was not wholly due to the sporting
attractions of the Highlands. Sir Walter Scott's works did a
great deal to popularize Scotland for tourists as well as sportsmen. With the publication of *The Lady of the Lake* the Trossachs
became thronged with English visitors. 'The Salisburys', wrote
Sir Frederick Lamb in 1829, 'have been touring about these
wretched Scotch lakes to avoid, I suppose, the expence of being
at Hatfield for such Inns, Horses, roads and climate could be
endured with no other object by any body who had ever seen
anything else.' Great as were the discomforts of touring in
Scotland they were more than outweighed by the magnificence
of the scenery and the irresistible charm of the Scots, and very
soon no part of the Highlands was secure from the disturbance of
game by 'some romantic London tourist'.

The lairds were not slow to take advantage of the new and
welcome source of income which the growing popularity of their
country with the sporting English gentry provided. They began
improving their moors by killing vermin and ceasing to curb
their shepherds' zeal in burning the heather. So great was the
demand for moors and deer ground that almost anything became lettable, and the sporting writers of the day were at
constant pains to emphasize the foolishness of renting shooting
in Scotland without first inspecting it. 'Let us urge the southern
sportsmen', wrote Lennox, 'to be very cautious before he engages
a moor, or he will find to his cost, as a friend of ours did, that
there were more keepers and gillies to provide for than birds to
kill.'

The reactions of the lairds to this annual immigration of
English, travelling by road or by sea (with their carriages lashed
to the deck), emerges from Elizabeth Grant's account of life in
the Highlands at this time. In 1804 the Sassenachs were not
thought much of, or anyway at Rothiemurchus where the many
English 'making hotels of the houses of the Highland proprie-

tors . . . in general . . . were hardly agreeable enough to be remembered'. Four years later, however, the approach of the shooting season required a visit to Edinburgh dressmakers, 'and we went to silk mercers, linen-drapers, haberdashers, etc.' In 1816 the English, instead of staying with their Scottish friends, were leasing farm houses and, we learn elsewhere, finding them very uncomfortable; but what with dinners and dances, 'a merrier shooting season was never passed'. Ten years later the Grants had to leave Doune because 'the house was to be left in a proper state to be let furnished with the shootings, a new and profitable scheme for making money out of the bare moors in the Highlands'. In this same year, 1826, a Wiltshire squire, William Scrope, was stalking at Bruar and collecting material for a book which was to enrich Scottish literature and remain till today the standard work on deer-stalking.

XII

The Poaching War

THE unhappy but short-lived consequences that flowed from the invention of the threshing-machine paled before the long-drawn misery that the invention of the flint-lock gun brought to rural England. For more than half a century much of the countryside was wracked by a bitter war, costly in human life and happiness, provoked by the sporting gun having given to wild game an importance it had not known before. There is no greater proof of the stability of the social structure of the English countryside than its having survived unscathed a merciless struggle in which an infinitesimal privileged minority fought to retain an exclusive right to what the whole of the rest of the community were convinced was a gift from God to be enjoyed by all.

'The great business of life, in the country,' wrote Cobbett, 'appertains, in some way or other, to the *game* . . . and, as to the anger, the satisfaction, the scolding, the commendation, the chagrin, the exultation, the envy, the emulation, when are there any of these in the country, unconnected with *the* game?' That, one of the very few understatements that ever came from Cobbett's uncurbed and venomous pen, was written in 1825. It would have been equally true over half a century before that.

Under an Act of 1671 the killing of game was prohibited, in general terms, to all except owners of land worth £100 a year,[1] lessees of land worth £150 a year, the eldest sons of esquires or of persons of higher degree, and the owners of franchises. A curious anomaly was that if an esquire or a person of higher degree had not the necessary qualifications to kill game, his

---

[1] *The Black Book* of 1831 pertinently noted that fifty times more property was required to enable a person to kill a partridge than to vote for a knight of the shire or, as someone else pointed out, to qualify him as a juror to kill a man.

eldest son was not debarred from doing so. Another was that although a lord of a manor might grant the right to kill game to his gamekeeper, he might not do so to his younger sons. This led to younger sons sometimes engaging themselves as keepers in order to secure the right to shoot. Thus owners of only a few acres could not enjoy the game their fields harboured, and which destroyed their crops, unless they could persuade a qualified neighbour to shoot it for them. In practice qualified neighbours usually treated the small man's game as if it were their own, to be shot and disposed of as they chose. The small man had his remedy in an action for trespass, but it was one he seldom dared to use.

The sale of game was altogether prohibited, and any un-qualified person found in possession of it was liable to a fine of £5 per head of game. Rabbits, woodcock, snipe, quails, and landrails, however, although they had the legal status of game so far as shooting was concerned, might be sold. The occupier of land might kill the rabbits on it, but the law forbade him to lift a finger against the hares which, in those days of few rabbits and many hares, did far greater damage. The penalty for taking or wilfully destroying pheasant and partridge eggs was £1 for each egg. No unqualified person might own a sporting dog, including greyhound and lurcher (farmers sometimes got round this restriction by cutting off a lurcher's tail and passing him off as a sheepdog), nor might he take with him any sort of dog when he was accompanying a qualified friend out shooting. A servant might 'beat bushes etc. for his master', and so might a stockbroker, attorney, surgeon, 'or other inferior person' if invited to do so by a qualified sportsman, but they might not take part in the actual killing of game. Such, in brief outline, was the penal code which sought to preserve for the privileged few the game of the countryside.

An early advocate for the reform of the Game Laws pointed out in *The Farmer's Magazine* of 1800 that as they stood they failed altogether in their object. 'In fact, since all these laws', he wrote, 'instead of preserving the game for the rightful owner, have been fabricated in the genuine spirit of a grasping monopoly, the present property in the game is completely vested in the hands of the nocturnal poacher, who has, in most manors, even the *undisputed* possession: Indeed it is a necessary consequence of all unjust laws, to create the very thing they are intended to prevent.'

With the killing of game so closely restricted and its sale prohibited, game could legally come to the table only as a gift from the few the law permitted to shoot it. This gave it a high prestige value which greatly enhanced its price in the black market. In the shooting season no dinner party with any pretensions to smartness was complete without a game course. None was more aware of this than the *nouveaux riches* whose inability to acquire game legally was matched by their determination to appear as if they could. They got it with what came to be called the silver gun, by paying for it. 'A waddling fat fellow', wrote Cobbett, 'that does not know how to prime and load, will in this way, beat the best shot in the country.' The same silver gun placed game on the menu of every good eating-house in London.

These were the circumstances in which the farming community became resentfully opposed to shooting, and poaching first became a serious menace to rural peace.

The bitter hostility of farmers to game preservation, for bitter it soon became, was not entirely due to the unjust and discriminating Game Laws. A contributory cause was the value which their landlords attached to hedgerows as covert for game. Many landlords forbade the cutting and trimming of hedges more than once in seven years; some went so far as to prohibit them altogether. At the same time that the hedgerow was finding increasing favour with the landlord it was falling into greater disrepute with his tenants. To begin with the hedgerows of the Enclosure Acts had been too small to interfere with agriculture; they occupied little ground and were too low to shade crops. As they grew to maturity, spreading far out at the base and towering high above the crops, farmers began to resent having to pay rent for so large an area of unproductive and often harmful land. When, with the new craze for shooting and game preservation, they were required to leave the hedges alone in the interests of the hares[1] that ate their crops but which

---

[1] On many shoots, perhaps on most, rabbits were, or soon became, the perquisite of the keeper with whom a tenant often could not afford to quarrel. It was not until the passing of the Ground Game Act of 1882 that occupiers of land were given the right to shoot both rabbits and hares.

they might not kill, their resentment became bitter, and many a poacher found stout allies among them.

One of the first to realize that the unjust Game Laws were defeating their own ends by antagonizing the farmers and encouraging the poachers was Joseph Chitty who, in 1770, wrote: 'Those vagabonds are rather encouraged than prevented by the present Laws: For if the Farmers who live upon the lands, and visit their fields every day, are not allowed to sport themselves, or to be game-keepers of their own farms, or licensed to kill Game upon them, for their own use; they will either destroy the Game out of resentment, or allow the poacher to do it for them; neither will their servants prevent, or inform against a Poacher, who can perhaps afford to make them a small present, which most of them would accept of, rather than a share of a large fine, accompanied with the detested name of an informer. . . . Many farmers have told me . . . that they would allow their Dogs to destroy every Hare, and every Bird in the breeding time, which is certainly in their power. . . . Others have acknowledged that they often had entertained Poachers in their houses, and in return for the hospitality, have had a Hare, or a brace of Birds, to send to a friend in town.' Joseph Chitty, it was clear, saw that the surest way to protect game was to secure the good will of the farmers by granting them some right to the game on their land. But nobody liked the idea of 'a new legion of Nimrods . . . in the farmers and their sons'. It took over sixty years for Chitty's view to win sufficient support to secure the abolition of the archaic restrictions on the killing of game.

In the meanwhile the trend was markedly away from any relaxation of the restrictions. As shooting gained in popularity so did the demand for more repressive legislation. As prices in the black market rose so did poaching increase. Clearly game must be given greater protection than the laws of Charles II afforded, and during the reign of George III thirty-two new Game Laws were passed.

Landowners endeavoured to curb the poachers by employing more keepers and watchers, which forced the poachers to confine their raids to hours of darkness. This was countered by the passing of an Act in 1770 under which anyone convicted of poaching between sunset and sunrise was to be punished with imprisonment up to six months; for a second offence the punishment was doubled with a public whipping added. This had little deterrent effect and two years later William Taplin, following Chitty's example, began advocating the relaxation of restrictions. 'Till the present Act is repealed', he wrote, 'there will be almost double the Quantity killed yearly, more than there would be were there no restraint, and every Person had an unlimited power to kill. . . . It is most certain if there were more Shooters, there would be more Birds. . . . I have in the Sporting Season, visited many Farmers, and never saw one that could not take me into his Pantry, and produce a Hare or more, and two or three Brace of Birds.' Taplin also perceived that the worst of all poachers were the gamekeepers themselves. Those who, he truly said, 'are known by all but their Employers to be the greatest Poachers, are the *pretended Preservers* Deputies, called game-keepers. . . . The extensive Game Trade that is carried on by these plush-coated, black-capp'd Gentry with the Road Waggoners, would, to those unacquainted with it, surpass Belief.' He knew of one waggoner who had bought in a small Hampshire inn as many as twenty-one hares at a time from a gamekeeper for half-a-crown apiece and sold them for 3*s*. 6*d*. each to a London poulterer. So long as keepers were paid only £20 a year, more keepers meant less game.

The blind confidence of the landowners in the integrity of their servants seems to have continued, for in 1802 W. B. Daniel, writing in much the same sense as Taplin, said that game poached by keepers 'readily finds its way to market, through the medium of the *Coachmen* and *Guards* to *Mail* and other coaches; (the *Higlers*[1] generally deal with the Poachers themselves.) The Gentlemen, in conjunction with the *Porters* of the different inns where they arrive at, carry on almost a *public traffic* in this article of Game, and at prices which render it astonishing how *purchasers* are to be met with, viz. *four* and *five* shillings (and sometimes as high as *eight*,) a brace for *Partridges*; *twelve* to *sixteen* for Pheasants, and from *five* to *seven shillings and six pence* for a Hare.'

Before the end of the previous century rising prices and the employment of more keepers and watchers had combined to bring about an alarming change in the poaching business. Poachers had begun forming themselves into gangs, the better

[1] Higglers were dealers who travelled round the country, from farm to farm, buying poultry and eggs.

to deal with the keepers, and were taking much greater risks. In 1781 a gang, eleven strong, raided the Duke of Cumberland's coverts in Windsor Park, and shot two keepers, but, on running out of ammunition, were pursued and taken by the Duke's servants armed with cutlasses. A few years later, in 1795, in an affray in the Bishop of Winchester's park at Farnham Castle, one of his servants was killed, but his keeper 'then fired his remaining barrel, which was loaded with ball, and killed one of them'. Gangs such as these were becoming a terror to the countryside and leading to grave disturbances of the peace. In 1800 Parliament sought to stop them by passing an Act by which if two or more persons were found poaching together they were to be treated as rogues and vagabonds and punished with hard labour; for a second offence they were to be treated as incorrigible rogues, imprisoned and whipped, or alternatively they could be made to serve in the army or navy. The severer penalties, far from achieving their object, only encouraged resistance to arrest and the formation of bigger and more determined gangs. So in 1803 Parliament passed the Ellenborough Act by which anyone who offered armed resistance to lawful arrest was to be hanged as a felon. This terrible Act seems to have served its purpose, but only for a time.

The control of poaching was made especially difficult by the conviction of most country people that there was nothing morally wrong in it. 'It is utterly impossible to teach the common people', wrote Sydney Smith, 'to respect property in animals bred the possessor knows not where — which he cannot recognise by any mark, which may leave him the next moment, which are kept, not for his profit, but for his amusement. . . . It is in vain to increase the severity of the protecting laws. They make the case weaker, instead of stronger; and are more resisted and worse executed, exactly in proportion as they are contrary to public opinion.' 'The same man who would respect an orchard, a garden, or a hen-roost', he wrote on another occasion, 'scarcely thinks he is committing any fault at all in invading the game covers of his richer neighbour.' In consequence no one had 'the slightest shame at violating a law which everybody feels to be absurd and unjust'. Moreover, they would protest, it was contrary to the teaching of Holy Writ. 'A wonderful lot of working men', said an old labourer, dictating his autobiography to Eleanor Eden, 'don't believe as there's any harm in poaching. We never read that in the Testament, nor yet in the Bible. We always read there, that the wild birds is sent for the poor man as well as the quality.'

That attitude of mind, which still sometimes persists, has always ensured to the habitual poacher more sympathy than a common thief would be accorded. Among the educated the poacher has often also enjoyed the respect that love of sport commands. 'Some are incorrigible poachers', wrote Howitt, 'from the love of the pursuit of wild creatures, of strolling about in solitary glens and woods, of night-watching, and adventure.' The man who insists on indulging his love of sport, and of wandering at will over the countryside, in defiance of the law, is often regarded by those who know him least as a romantic and engaging character. Alas, he usually, but not always, proves to be the least estimable character in the parish, the ne'er-do-well of the village who has taken to poaching in preference to honest toil, and who spends his money in the pub rather than on the home. Moreover, poaching has unfortunately far too often led to a career of crime extending far beyond the illicit killing of game.

Only by bearing this in mind can we understand the bitterness with which poachers were execrated a century and a half ago. Surtees described them as 'the very scum and scourings of the country, men whose least crime is that of poaching'. Surtees, though eminently fair-minded and not a shooting man, was a squire and therefore his testimony is suspect. But Sydney Smith, who railed against the injustice of the Game Laws and the selfishness of the gentry, confirmed every word that Surtees wrote. The poacher, he wrote, 'proceeds from one infringement of law and property to another, till he becomes a thoroughly bad and corrupted member of society'.

Nevertheless, the greatest disservice poaching did the country was the corrupting of so many honest men. It was too easy and too profitable. 'What we say in regard to poaching', declared Eleanor Eden's friend, 'is this: "Poachers' money, it ain't worth fourpence a bushel; it comes light and it goes light." ' But he had one friend who turned it to good account. With a stool as the only bit of furniture in their house and nothing but straw to lie on, this man and his wife decided to invest all the

XV *Before the Magistrates* : This picture reflects the popular, but usually erroneous, belief that, because the magistrates were often the owners of the stolen game, poachers seldom got a fair trial.

XVI   *The Quorn at Quenby in 1823:* Many of the noted foxhunters in this picture could remember Hugo Meynell who made the Quorn hounds famous and in so doing transformed foxhunting into the most exhilarating of all field sports.

cash they had, four pennies, in poaching. He bought 'four-penn'orth of wire, and set off a-poaching, and he done very well. He soon laid £5 on one side, for fear he might get ketched, and in a few years he had got £40 worth of household goods in his house.' Another observer, of a slightly earlier period, noted that 'where wastes and commons are most extensive, there I have perceived the Cottagers are the most wretched and worthless . . . for cottagers of this description the game is preserved, and by them destroyed; they are mostly beneath the law and out of reach of detection; and while they can earn four or five shillings, and sometimes more, in a night, by poaching they will not be satisfied with 10*d.*, or 1*s.* a day for honest labour.' 'The village poacher', wrote W. H. Hudson, 'as a rule is an idle, dissolute fellow.'

The conclusion that the habitual country poachers were nearly always drawn from the lowest ranks of village life is inescapable. Many of them, corrupted by easy money, had become, as Sydney Smith said, 'thoroughly bad and corrupted members of society'. Closely associated with them, and perhaps often the major partners in their trade, were many desperate men from London and other towns, mostly fugitives from justice, who had been attracted into poaching by the large profits it yielded and the comparative security of life in the open country from the arm of the law. Thus, through the creation of a black market for game by archaic and absurdly restrictive laws, had poaching become the refuge and main support of a large part of the criminal classes.

When the Napoleonic wars ended and rural England was plunged into the misery of an acute agricultural depression, with half the farm workers dependent on parish relief on which it was often impossible for married men to live, the savage Ellenborough Act began to lose some of its terrors. For many a labourer poaching became the only means of keeping alive a starving family. Poachers multiplied, and the gangs became more desperate. In the early days of 1816 one of Lord Fitzhardinge's keepers was 'killed by a gang of miscreants, who', according to a contemporary chronicler, 'with blackened faces, and armed with guns, had taken an oath, administered by one of them . . . not to 'peach on each other. Scarcely ever did any criminal trial excite more interest. . . . Eleven young men . . . led on, in the unlawful pursuit of game, to the destruction of human life, and consequently making their own lives dependent on the decision of a court of justice, could not fail to create an interest of the highest degree in the feelings of the public.' All were found guilty, but only two were hanged. In the same year poaching convictions more than doubled.

Clearly an even greater deterrent was required than the Ellenborough Act. Therefore in 1817 Parliament passed an Act, almost without debate, under which anyone poaching at night with no more than a net was to be transported for seven years even if he were unarmed. From the moment of the passing of that Act the long-drawn poaching war assumed a bitterness it had never known before. This was because, as we saw in an earlier chapter, transportation, for no matter how short a term, was virtually a life sentence because return from Australia was impossible for all but a very few. It was the terror of transportation, the parting for ever from wife and children and all that made a hard life endurable, that drove the poacher to risk his life by resisting arrest. 'The preposterous punishment of transportation', wrote Sydney Smith, 'makes him desperate, not timid. Single poachers are gathered into large companies, for their mutual protection; and go out, not only with the intention of taking game, but of defending that they take with their lives.' It was a theme to which he returned a few months later: 'If the question concerned the payment of five pounds, a poacher would hardly risk his life rather than be taken; but when he is to go to Botany Bay for seven years, he summons together his brother poachers — they get brave from rum, numbers, and despair — and a bloody battle ensues.'

In the poacher's eyes the gallows were only slightly more terrible than transportation. This explains the fierce resentment the new Act provoked, but it only partly explains the tragic tale of murders and hangings that followed. These were largely due to the enforcement of the Game Laws depending on the corrupting influence of informers. Not only was the informer offered a substantial reward but he was also 'entitled to it, even though he should have been an accomplice, and will, by *turning evidence, escape* all *penalties*'. Now that poachers had been forced to work in gangs, so great an inducement to treachery as escape from gallows or transportation added immeasurably to the fierce resentment the new Act provoked. Its 'first and most palpable effect', wrote someone in 1818, 'has naturally been an exaltation of all the savage and desperate features in the poacher's character. . . . A marauder may hesitate perhaps at killing his fellow-man, when the alternative is only six months' imprisonment in the county gaol; but when the alternative is to overcome the keeper, or to be torn from his family and connections, and sent to hard labour at the Antipodes, we cannot be much surprised that murders and midnight combats have considerably increased this season.'

At about the same time a Bath newspaper quoted an anonymous letter, which was being circulated amongst local landowners, reading: 'We have lately heard and seen that there is an act passed, and whatever poacher is caught destroying the game, is to be transported for seven years — *This is English Liberty.*'

'Now, we do swear to each other, that the first of our company that this law is inflicted on, that there shall not one gentleman's seat in our country escape the rage of fire. We are nine in number, and we will burn every gentleman's house of note. The first that impeaches shall be shot. We have sworn not to impeach.'

In spite of the terrible penalties attaching to poaching, the acuteness of the distress in many districts was such that some men had to poach to keep alive. Cobbett tells of a young Surrey labourer who, asked how he managed to live on the half-crown dole he got from the parish for breaking stones, replied: 'I poach: it is better to be hanged than starved to death.' The extent of the poaching by humble village labourers in defiance of the terrible Game Laws is a measure of the miseries in which so much of rural England was sunk. Despite the laws and everyone being a potential informer, distress and the easy money sometimes set more than half a village poaching. One of the Bow Street runners, who from time to time were summoned into the country to deal with particularly desperate gangs, related how the whole of one village, including the constable, were poachers. 'Within four months', he added, 'there have been twenty-two transported that I have been at the taking of, and through one man turning evidence in each case, and without that they could not have been identified; the game-keepers could not, or would not, identify them. . . . The gangs are connected together at different public houses, just like a club at a public house; they are all sworn together. If the keeper took one of them, they would go and attack him for doing so.'

The repression of poaching was made very difficult by public opinion being so much on the side of the poachers and the consequent reluctance of village constables to interfere. The village mentioned by the Bow Street runner, where the constable himself was a poacher, was not exceptional. After a burglary and a murder in an Essex village the constable called in outside helpers who found and took the murderer. Before the man was tried and hanged the constable was heard to say to him: 'Good God, Tom, is this you? If I had known it, you would have been the last man I should have taken.' The murderer and the constable had been in the habit of poaching together. The story was afterwards used in general condemnation of the rural police.

No useful purpose would be served by cataloguing here the many affrays in which keepers or poachers were killed or the hangings that ensued. Poaching and gallows alike were too familiar to Englishmen of every class to be of more than local interest. 'There is hardly now a jail-delivery in which some gamekeeper has not murdered a poacher,' wrote Sydney Smith, 'or some poacher a gamekeeper.' At the Lent Assizes at Winchester in 1821, however, something happened which deeply shocked the usually insensitive public opinion of the day. Among the prisoners who were tried at these assizes were two young poachers. One, James Turner, aged 28, was accused of assisting to kill one of Thomas Assheton Smith's gamekeepers at Tidworth; the other, Charles Smith, aged 27 years, was accused only of shooting at a keeper employed by Lord Palmerston at Broadlands. Both young men were sentenced to death and were hanged together on the same gallows. The eminence of the two squires involved, the one a great landowner and the other the Secretary at War, was enough to excite more than usual interest in a double execution which otherwise might have escaped notice. Certain very unpleasant facts about the two trials quickly became widely known. These were, first, that of the sixteen prisoners condemned to death at those assizes these two poachers were the only ones to be hanged;[1]

---

[1] Smith, who had only shot at, and not killed, a keeper, was of course condemned to death under the Ellenborough Act of 1803.

second, the jurors had recommended both young men to mercy; third, in passing sentence Mr. Justice Burrough observed, to quote Cobbett, that 'it became necessary in these cases, that the extreme sentence of the law should be inflicted, to deter others, as resistance to gamekeepers had now arrived at an alarming height, and many lives had been lost.'

The public found it very disturbing that the only two prisoners chosen to die from among the sixteen condemned to death should be poachers, 'those who had been endeavouring to get at the hares, pheasants or partridges' of two great landowners. The suspicion this circumstance provoked appeared to be confirmed by the words attributed to the judge. The lives of gamekeepers, employed to protect the game of the rich, were evidently more sacred than those of men less valuably employed. Cobbett was not alone in denouncing these hangings as 'for the preservation of the *game* . . . for the preservation of the *sports* of that aristocracy'. The suspicion that poachers were not always given a fair trial was further confirmed by an utterance, at about the same time, at the Salisbury Assizes, of Sir Allan Park — 'that most able and excellent judge', as Peter Hawker called him. After fining two men £5 each, one for having a snare in his possession, and the other a pheasant, he assured the jury that he would always punish the crime of poaching 'whenever he could do so, because he was convinced it led to enormities of the darkest hue, and frequently to an ignominious death at the gallows'.

The dicta of the two judges certainly reflected the less veiled sentiments of the magistrates. It is beyond question that then, and for long years afterwards, the gentry considered poaching a particularly heinous crime which must be punished with the utmost severity that the law permitted. The charge brought against local magistrates engaged in suppression of the Swing Riots in later years, of singling out the poachers for trial rather than less obnoxious rioters, was never proved; in fairness to the magistrates it must be remembered that poachers were, as we have seen, usually drawn from the dregs of rural society and poaching was seldom their only crime. Nevertheless, there were many to applaud the words which, one day in 1828, fell on the shocked and resentful ears of the Commons from the lips of Henry Brougham: 'There is not a worse constituted tribunal on the face of the earth,' he declared, 'not even that of the Turkish Cadi, than that at which summary convictions on the Game Laws constantly takes place; I mean a bench or a brace of sporting Justices. I am far from saying that, on such subjects, they are actioned by corrupt motives; but they are undoubtedly instigated by their abhorrence of that . . . *fera naturae*, a poacher.'

The repugnance in which game preservers were held did not derive wholly from the misery which the Game Laws introduced into country life, nor was it confined to the lower orders who were the principal, but not the only, victims of the unjust laws. The absurd restrictions imposed on the killing of game by the archaic laws ranged on the side of the poachers all those who did not have the necessary territorial qualification. As Sydney Smith said, 'An Englishman may possess a million of money in funds, or merchandise — may be the *Baring* or the *Hope* of Europe . . . and yet be without the power of smiting a single partridge, though invited by the owner of the game to participate in his amusement. It is idle to say that the difficulty may be got over, by purchasing land: the question is, upon what principle of justice can the existence of the difficulty be defended?'

Less easy to bear than this injustice was the daily spectacle of those who were qualified under the Act of 1671 openly raiding other people's game with complete impunity. Many of the gentry, indeed, were habitual poachers and beyond the reach of the law. Peter Hawker was one of the worst. Reference was made in the last chapter to the Exeter mail, on which he was travelling, stopping for him to shoot whenever he saw game from the road. This, a not uncommon practice of 'qualified' travellers, was made possible by a strange legal anomaly. Game was not private property and consequently a landowner had no remedy against a qualified intruder — one entitled to kill game — who raided his preserves, other than an action at law for trespass, but he could not succeed in such an action unless the trespasser had previously been warned off. Thus we read that 'it is now no uncommon practice for persons who have the exterior, and perhaps the fortunes of gentlemen, as they are travelling from place to place, to shoot over manors where they have no property, and from which, as strangers, they cannot have been warned'.

Thus was Peter Hawker able to shoot his way down to Exeter. But he had not far to go beyond the neighbourhood of his own Hampshire estate to shoot other people's game with impunity which, as we read in his diary, was his habit. This is from his account of a raid on his neighbour Lord Portsmouth's coverts: 'Having heard that his gang of myrmidons . . . were watching to warn me off Lord Portsmouth's land, and to follow me where-ever they dared, I got some men with guns and pistols to draw their attention to different parts while we attacked their grand preserve; everything was arranged agreeably to a military plan . . . which answered so well that we got two hours' glut of their pheasants before the gang came up to warn us off; to my own share I bagged 28 pheasants (including 2 white ones), 3 par-tridges and 1 hare.'

In 1812 Hawker set out for the north to shoot his first grouse. In due course, after passing through Bowes, he arrived, late in October, at the Spital Inn[1] kept by one Kitty Lockey, who also horsed the mail. 'Never was there a more admirable situation', wrote Hawker in his diary, 'than this public-house. It stands in the very best part of the moor . . . and being an isolated place, the grouse are as likely to be found close to the house as anywhere farther.' Next morning he set out with his dog, accom-panied by Kitty Lockey, and shot a grouse. Hawker's enthusiasm for the Spital Inn is more than understandable, for in the whole of the kingdom there was no place better suited to the unprincipled colonel than this disreputable inn. 'Spittle, near Bowes, in Yorkshire,' wrote someone in *The Annals of Sporting* a few years later, 'may be regarded as a sort of general rendezvous for those sportsmen who either do not choose to ask, or are unable to obtain, permission to range more private and par-ticular domains. At this place, there is a great extent of moor, which is claimed by a number of proprietors, who possess no paramount right, and therefore are unable to prevent a general unsolicited range, which uniformly takes place. At the same time, the mountains . . . being surrounded by excellent pre-serves scarcely ever fail to abound in game. Spittle is also a general resort for dog-dealers and *dog-stealers*; and the sports-

[1] The New Spital Inn, now called the Bowes Moor Hotel, on the Scotch Corner–Penrith road, was built in 1773-4 on the site of a hospital founded in the twelfth century.

man, who visits this neighbourhood unprovided with this very essential assistant in the chase, may be accommodated exactly according to his means, or the price he is willing to give.'

Landowners naturally did not rely wholly on the terrors of the law to protect their game. The worse poaching became the more they reinforced their keepers. Lord Berkeley, for example, employed eight head keepers, twenty under keepers and thirty night watchmen, and no doubt when a raid was expected he called in many more, from farm and garden, to help. Less estimable characters than Lord Berkeley relied principally on a free use of the barbarous man trap and spring gun. The man trap, an immense toothless gin, was, by comparison with the spring gun, almost humane; it might maim a man for life, but it was unlikely to kill him. The spring gun, on the other hand, was customarily loaded with ball or shot, and could, and sometimes did, kill the innocent man, woman, or child who had the misfortune to stumble over the trip wire that fired it, or whose dog did the same. The spring gun served chiefly to em-bitter the poachers and make them more desperate. In 1805 Lord Suffield's keepers came up with a Norfolk gang 'just after one of the party had been wounded by a spring gun — when in the hopes of rescuing their wounded comrade, they fired on the keepers and wounded four men. A desperate battle then followed; his Lordship's men fighting with their sticks, and the poachers with their guns. Three poachers were taken and the rest ran away.'

The invariable answer to those who criticized the use of these barbarous engines was that as there were always warning notices, wherever they had been set, anyone they maimed or killed had only himself to blame. Mr. Justice Holroyd was reported as having said that 'the trespasser who has had a notice of guns being set in the wood is the real voluntary agent who pulls the trigger'. Mr. Justice Best is on record as having declared that 'if an owner of a close cannot set spring guns, he cannot put glass bottles or spikes on the top of a wall'. But he was doubtful about their use for the protection of game. He considered them 'as lawfully applicable to the protection of every species of property against unlawful trespassers. But even if they might not lawfully be used for the protection of game, I for one should be extremely glad to adopt such measures, if they were found sufficient for that purpose.' As the victims of spring guns and man traps were as often innocent people — sometimes game-keepers or even their masters — as poachers, Parliament at last decided that they must be abolished. Under an Act passed in 1827 their use became illegal.

The intensification of the war against poaching and the in-creasing ferocity of the Game Laws naturally affected the methods employed by the poachers to take game. The days had long passed when it was easy to take pheasants at night by snatching them off their roosts, or shooting them down. Guns could only be used by a gang powerful enough to defy any force the local keepers could put into the field against them. When forces were likely to be evenly matched part of the gang would, by firing guns and pistols, decoy the keepers away from where the rest had planned to make their bag, as Hawker had done when he raided Lord Portsmouth's coverts. But for the most part poaching was done as silently and unobtrusively as possible, preferably with nets or snares. Four of five men skilled in the use of snares could clear two or three coverts of pheasants in a few hours. Having set their snares, perhaps two or three hundred of them (which experienced men can do in a very short time), they would go to the other end of the covert and walk it in line towards the snares where they were sure of finding a good bag. When hand-rearing led to regular feeding at fixed places, the taking of pheasants with snares or nets became very much easier.

Partridges required more skill than pheasants. Horse-hair nooses pegged to the ground where the coveys jugged at night was a favourite device of the solitary village poacher. We also hear of poachers using a setter with a small lantern on his head; when the dog came to a stop the poachers would draw their net up to him and over the covey. These old-fashioned methods were ill-suited to the changed conditions. The gangs seldom dared to use dogs, which attracted attention, and, with penalties so severe, much bigger bags were needed to make the risk worth while. One of their methods was to disturb the coveys at dusk, mark carefully where they dropped, and draw the net over them after dark. Another, but less rewarding, method was to walk the fields in line at dawn when the birds would lie very close, and fling a heavy stick into the coveys as they rose. An experienced man expected to take a brace or two of birds at each throw.

Hares were easily taken with nets. After blocking the hares' runs or meuses, as they called them, through the hedgerows, the poachers would set nets across the gateways and drive the hares into them. Some poachers used a small terrier, closely muzzled to prevent him barking, to range the fields for them.

The grouse, a very profitable bird, especially if it could be got on to the market in time for a rich man's dinner party on the Twelfth, did not lend itself, because of its habits and the rough-ness of the moor, to capture by conventional poaching methods. That grouse usually had to be shot, and that silence and secrecy were therefore impossible, did not present an intractable prob-lem to the desperate gangs of miners who harried the Yorkshire moors. 'The mode adopted by the lead-miners of procuring grouse,' wrote a correspondent of *The Annals of Sporting* in 1822, 'is with the dog and fowling-piece; the *net*, so effective in the destruction of the *partridge*, being . . . quite out of the question. The poachers frequently sally forth in such bodies as to bid defiance to the united strength of the *watchers* in any particular district. . . . They generally commence *their* season a week prior to the 12th. August, and send horse-loads of grouse to different large towns, to the watering-places, and particularly to *Harro-gate*; at which last place, the grouse are frequently sold for as much as *ten shillings a brace*.'

But the Yorkshire miners operated all through the season, and, in cold weather, were able even to supply London. 'During the whole of the season', continued the same corres-pondent, 'grouse are regularly conveyed by the stage coaches to all the large towns, and particularly to *Manchester* and *Liverpool*. For this purpose there are certain days appointed, when quanti-ties of these birds are brought to particular houses by the road-side, at which the coachman and guards call, and this unlawful traffic is continued with as much regularity, if not with as much publicity, as the authorized dealings in any other species of marketable commodity. Abundance of game is thus conveyed from Yorkshire and the northern parts of England to places situated at a distance, or more to the southward; and when the weather becomes cold, and the game will keep, immense quantities are brought from *Scotland*.'

There was one form of poaching which caused heavy losses of game but which, owing to most farmers and nearly all farm hands being hostile to game preservation, was almost impossible to detect. This was the theft of game eggs which was carried on exclusively by village people. 'Even young women go a-egging,' said Eleanor Eden's old poacher, 'I've known a young woman to make £5 a week by pheasants' eggs. She could get more nor a hundred eggs a week. I myself once got sixty in a night and a day, and I made sixty shillings on 'em then and there.' There was no easier way of getting even with an unpopular squire than by destroying nests and taking eggs. A villager, just out of Winchester gaol, confessed to Peter Hawker that he had 'in the spring destroyed above a hundred partridges' nests, and another man had feasted on above 200 partridges' eggs, besides destroying others, and all this they confessed was done to spite the lord of the manor, who is universally disliked'.

Poaching could not have been carried on in the face of so many difficulties and on so large a scale without assured facilities for getting it to market, which usually meant Leadenhall Market, and for selling it at high prices. Leadenhall Market was supplied through two channels. The more important was the coachmen and guards of the mail and stage coaches — hence the greater prevalence of poaching on the main trunk roads. 'Almost any poulterer, waiter or book-keeper of the different coach and waggon inns', wrote Daniel at the beginning of the century, 'can give ample information where game of any kind can be procured with one hand provided money is carried in the other.' The innkeepers on the main roads, who of necessity had to keep on good terms with the coaches, provided a ready market for anything the local poachers had to offer.

The other source of supply, especially from districts off the coach routes, was the higglers, who travelled round the country buying poultry and eggs. In the season they probably handled game more readily than their legitimate trade, for it was more profitable. In 1802 it was recorded that two of these higglers 'in *two* seasons shared upwards of *fifteen hundred* pounds (after deducting all expenses) for Game purchased at very inferior prices from the *Poachers*, who caught it in the country, by forwarding and selling it to the London Poulterers, who again supply the taverns, coffee-houses, & where it is a regular article in the bill of fare'. The higglers arranged with the poachers where game was to be left, to be picked up on their rounds. They fed the London market from as far afield as Scotland, forwarding the game in the same packages as their poultry. As the result of hot competition from the coaches the higglers found it necessary to associate themselves more closely with poachers. In 1812 Daniel wrote that the illicit game trade had become so profitable 'that there now exists in several Places, an *Association* of *Poachers*, and the *Abettors* of them, who are ready to advance Money, for the Purpose of paying Penalties, or otherwise assisting any of the suffering *Brethren*'. The higglers were also doing a good trade with dishonest gamekeepers who, once in their clutches, found escape very difficult, for, as Daniel said, 'the Gamekeeper (after having sold them one Partridge) is placed, with *these Purveyors* of Game, in the same predicament as a Revenue-Officer after having once touched a bribe from a Smuggler; both are completely in the power of the *buyer* and *briber*, and must proceed, under the dread of being reported to their different employers if they hesitate or refuse'.

Leadenhall Market, besides being the centre of the trade in dead and live pheasants, was also that of the trade in the eggs of both partridges and pheasants of which, with the growing popularity of shooting and the clamorous demand for bigger bags, game preservers, to their own undoing, were avid buyers. Many a landowner stocked his shoot with birds and eggs stolen from his own ground. The prices game eggs fetched in London in 1822 reflects the comparative scarcity of pheasants and the abundance of partridges. Pheasant eggs were 8s. a dozen against 2s. for partridge eggs.

Parliament sought to curb the illicit game trade, which was carried on as freely as if the laws against it did not exist, by making the purchase of game also illegal, and subject to the same penalties as its sale, but, of course, to no effect. The trade was quite unaffected. Sydney Smith saw the futility of all such legislation and was convinced, as William Taplin had been in the previous century, that the remedy was to legalize the sale of game. 'The foundation on which the propriety of allowing this partly rests', he wrote, 'is the impossibility of preventing it. There exists, and has sprung up since the Game Laws, an enormous mass of wealth, which has nothing to do with land. Do the country gentlemen imagine, that it is in the power of human laws to deprive the Three-per-cents of pheasants? — that there is upon earth, air, or sea, a single flavour (cost what crime it may to procure it), that mercantile opulence will not procure? Increase the difficulty, and you enlist vanity on the side of luxury; and make that be sought for as a display of wealth, which was before valued only for the gratification of appetite. The law may multiply penalties by reams. Squires may fret and justices commit, and gamekeepers and poachers continue their nocturnal wars. There must be game on Lord Mayor's day, do what you will. You may multiply the crimes by which it is procured; but nothing can arrest its inevitable progress from the wood of the esquire to the spit of the citizen.'

The humble countryman's deep conviction that there was morally nothing wrong in stealing the rich man's game natur-ally influenced the attitude of the higglers and poulterers. Respectable London tradesmen who would never have wittingly touched stolen goods felt no pang of conscience in regularly dealing in game. In 1823 a Committee of the House of Com-mons on the Game Laws reported that no poulterer could afford not to deal in game because if he did not he would lose all his regular customers for poultry. It was also virtually impossible to prosecute a poulterer for he had only to report an unpopular customer, a higgler with whom he had quarrelled, a keeper who had let him down, or even one of his competitors, for some breach of the Game Laws to secure the informer's reward, a part of the fine, and the acquittal of himself.

No one who bought or sold game was ever safe from black-mail. One Christmas the ingenious wife of a well-known Penrith poacher called on the townspeople her husband was in the habit of supplying with game, and told them that he had been caught and fined, but if each of them would contribute 5s. he would be able to pay the fine 'without his being under the necessity of informing against them'. The story that her husband had been caught was a lie.

The report of the Commons Committee emphasized the immense scale of this illicit traffic. One of the smaller London poulterers, asked the quantity of game he handled a year, answered 'perhaps 10,000 head; mine is a limited trade . . . I only supply private families'. Asked whether he could obtain a thousand pheasants a week if he had an order for them, he said he could get 10,000 a week if he wanted to, and he explained how he would set about it. 'I should, of course, request the persons with whom I am in the habit of dealing, to use their influence to bring me what they could by a certain day; I should speak to the dealers and the mail-guards, and coachmen, to produce a quantity; and I should send to my own connections in one or two manors where I have the privilege of selling for those gentlemen. . . . Being but a petty salesman, I sell a very small quantity; but I have had about 4,000 direct from one man'. *The Black Book* gives one explanation of this dealer's sinister reference to his 'privilege of selling' for certain gentlemen. After pointing out that 'the poor labourer, mason, or weaver, who imperilled his life, his limbs, and his health, in the covert attempt to catch a hare or partridge, could not possibly be adequate to support a commerce like this', with waggon loads of game pouring into London, the report continues: 'No, it was not done by poaching exactly; the *wholesale* dealers are the lawmakers themselves — those who had interdicted the traffic — NOBLE LORDS and MEN OF TITLE, who had condescended to supply the London poulterers and salesmen with game, on commission, as a means of augmenting their territorial revenues.'

The illicit sale or bartering of game by owners of shoots had long been carried on. A writer to *The Sporting Magazine* in 1804 inquired: 'What shall we say of those who send venison, hares, pheasants, partridges, and all other game to their poulterer in London, to receive an equivalent in poultry and fish in winter, when they are in town. Though these sportsmen do not truck their commodities for money, they are nothing less than higlers, hucksters, dealers, and chapmen, in the proper sense of the words; for an exchange was never denied to be a sale, although it is affirmed to be no robbery?'

It is not surprising to learn that at times there was such a glut of game that the surplus was 'either thrown away or disposed of by Irish hawkers to the common people at very inferior prices'. In 1823 there was one of these gluts, with pheasants retailing at 7s. a brace, and partridges at not more than half-a-crown. But the normal prices are not easy to determine. In 1817 the poacher had got 7s. a brace for pheasants, for which the London poulterer paid 15s. and the consumer two guineas. It is improbable that such high prices returned after the slump of 1823, but they were attractive enough for poaching to continue to flourish and expand.

Parliament was at last beginning to find that the Game Laws, far from checking poaching, were in fact encouraging it by their very severity. So strong had public hatred of these laws become, so convinced was everyone that they were absurd and unjust, such odium attached to anyone who aided their enforcement, that even common informers, 'too well aware of the coldness of pump and pond', were refusing to come forward. Juries, wiser and more humane than Parliament, were countering the savagery of the laws by refusing to convict. Thus were the Lords and Commons at last compelled at least to consider a new approach to the problem and a reform of the Game Laws. The proposals, which had been urged on Parliament for long years past, and which till now it would not even consider, were three: The abolition of the qualifications which restricted the killing of game to a privileged few; the making of game the property of the owner of the land on which it was found; and the legalizing of the sale and purchase of game.

These proposals were widely debated, in and out of Parliament, for many months during which hardly any objection to them was raised that does not today seem ridiculous. The general feeling was that such revolutionary measures would quickly result in the total destruction of game throughout the country, 'and if there is no game, there will be no country gentlemen'. To legalize the sale of game would inevitably provoke a price-cutting war between gentry and poachers without any certainty that the former would win. Lord Londonderry particularly disliked the idea because 'it would deprive the sportsman of his highest gratification — the pleasure of furnishing his friends with presents of game: nobody would care for a present which every body could give'.

Meanwhile, the dreadful war continued. In June 1829, when rural England was sunk in the misery that culminated in the Swing Riots, there were ninety-six prisoners for trial in Bedford gaol of whom, wrote Potter MacQueen to Lord Grey, 'seventy-six were able-bodied men in the prime of life, and chiefly of general good character, who were driven to crime by sheer want, and who would have been valuable subjects, had they been placed in a situation, where by the exercise of their health and strength they could have earned a subsistence. There were in this number eighteen poachers, awaiting trial for the capital offence of using arms in self-defence, when attacked by game-keepers; of these eighteen men, one only was not a parish pauper, he was the agent of the London poulterers, who, passing under the apparent vocation of a rat catcher, paid these poor creatures more in one night than they could obtain from the overseer for a whole week's labour.' These poachers included two brothers. One, aged twenty-eight, had a pregnant wife and two children, but could not get work; he was, he said, 'allowed 7s. a week for all; I was expected to work on the roads from light to dark, and to pay £3-3-0 a year for the hovel that sheltered us'. His brother, aged twenty-two and unmarried, received 6d. a day. Both were hanged.

At last, in 1831, when nearly one sixth of the total number of convictions in the country were for offences against the Game Laws, the archaic qualifications were abolished and the sale and purchase of game were made legal.

XIII

The Debt to Hugo Meynell

By pure coincidence, and in wholly unrelated circumstances, the period that saw the shooting of flying game become the most popular sport of the gentry witnessed also the rise of foxhunting to the status of a great national sport. While shooting was almost universally execrated, on account of its restriction to a privileged few by unjust and repressive laws, there was very little criticism of the rapid extension of foxhunting. This is surprising for there was a general belief that a law, no less unjust than those which protected the shooter, gave foxhunters the right of entry to any man's land, regardless of the harm they did. That this alleged right was little resented and that after the courts, early in the nineteenth century, had shown it had no legal sanction, it continued to be exercised by common consent are things no foreigner can understand or any Englishman explain. Whatever the reason, be it the countryman's latent love of the chase which the sight of a pack of hounds has always awakened, the dislike of the fox as a noxious animal, the democracy of the hunting field which knows no barrier of class or means, or the brightening of rural life by the splendid spectacle of the chase, or a combination of them all, without it foxhunting could never have become a great national sport.

The fox did not become a favourite beast of the chase until the middle of the eighteenth century. Until then the humble hare, coursed by farmers and hunted by squires with their private packs of harriers, had sufficed. The hare being very local in its habits, the squire's harriers seldom hunted much beyond the confines of his estate, but when a straight-running hare took them farther afield it did not displease the neighbouring farmers. Many of them coursed or hunted themselves, and those that did not enjoyed the sight of hounds on their land.

Thus when the squires turned their harriers into foxhounds and the new quarry set them ranging many miles from home, everywhere making as free with everybody's land as if it had been their own, there were few to mind, and none openly to resent, the exercise of a right that had the sanction of custom and also, so they thought, of law.

To catch their hare harriers required only good noses; speed mattered not at all. So the squires bred their hounds purely for nose. When they started using their harriers to hunt foxes they found themselves hampered by lack of speed. The only fox they could catch was one found early in the morning with his belly still full of undigested food. It was a waste of time to attempt to catch a fox found later in the day. So the early foxhounds used to meet at daybreak and find their fox by working up to him after finding the drag, or trail, he had left in the night. With excellent noses and no speed, they killed their fox by virtually walking him to death, unless, as usually happened, they ran him to ground and dug him out.

'It may be doubted', wrote Trollope many years later, 'whether men who now think that the cream of hunting is to be found only in a fast run of forty-five minutes, almost without a check, and with a kill in the open, would enjoy the sport as it existed even at the end of the last century. Hounds had not been trained to run with the speed which is now attained, nor had the profession of hunting produced men skilled in casting when the hounds themselves were at fault, as is done now. There was no great crowd, and the fox had a better chance when there were few or none to halloo to him. The hounds were obliged then to puzzle out their own quarry, or to give it up. Men were more patient than they now are, and the hounds were allowed to puzzle out their game. We hear more of the length of the days spent than we do of the rapidity of the pace, and we know that neither hounds nor horses can have gone very fast during those runs of many hours of which the accounts have reached us.'

When every pack of hounds was the private property of a squire, who probably owned also most of the land over which they hunted, the followers were limited to the few friends and neighbours he chose to invite to join him. These favoured few were enthusiasts who hunted out of pure love of the chase; their pleasure was watching hounds at work, not galloping across country. To such men the slowness of the hounds mattered as little as the earliness of the start. The slowness of the sport, the early start, to say nothing of the long, cold, and dreary hours of digging which ended most hunts, were an effective bar to foxhunting's becoming a popular sport.

It must have been apparent to many foxhunters that faster hounds would mean better sport — more foxes killed above ground and fewer hours with pick and spade — but so profound was the belief that speed could only be improved at the expense of nose that none would risk breeding for speed until the coming of the greatest man in the history of foxhunting. Hugo Meynell of Quorndon Hall, who hunted from 1753 to 1800 what was later the Quorn country, was the first master to attempt to breed fast hounds. He astonished his profoundly sceptical fellow masters by breeding a fast pack with first-rate noses and tremendous drive which showed sport such as no foxhunter had before enjoyed, and which quickly made Leicestershire famous. The example he had set, which others were quick to follow, made foxhunting the most exhilarating of all field sports.

It so happened that while Meynell and his close friend and associate the first Lord Yarborough, of Brocklesby, and their disciples were breeding faster foxhounds, England was becoming more enclosed. As we saw at the beginning of this book, the process of enclosure was costly and therefore slow. The immediate effect of an Enclosure Act was for each landowner to put a ring fence round his allotment, and as soon as he could he subdivided it into large fields of, say, 200 acres; as these fields improved under efficient management, notably by draining, they too were subdivided. It often took decades for finality to be reached. 'The richer land becomes,' wrote Surtees, 'whether by draining or other artificial means, and the larger crops it yields, the likelier it is to be subdivided; and there is little doubt that many of the large fields we still see, parts of common lands enclosed within the present century, will gradually become smaller and smaller as the land becomes richer and more valuable.'

That was going on over the greater part of England, much to the disgust of the old foxhunters. The more unenclosed the country the better hounds could be watched and the greater the pleasure of following them. 'The hedges', wrote Cobbett of a part of Hampshire, '. . . are more for boundary marks than for fences. Fine for hunting and coursing; no impediments; no gates to open; nothing to impede the dogs, the horses, or the view.' The new fences were a hindrance; they slowed hounds down and made them difficult to see and to follow. Foxhunters had objected to them from the early days of Enclosure Acts. The neighbourhood of Burford, wrote John Byng in 1781, 'formerly so noted for hunting, is now spoilt by enclosures'. Similarly he complained that Gloucestershire was spoilt for hunting by the new stone walls.

Some followers of hounds liked jumping fences, and even gates, but a great many did not. John Corbet, the great Warwickshire master, was said never to have jumped a fence in his life. Chute of the Vine used to dismount at a fence, seize his horse by the tail, and make him pull him through or over. Most followers of hounds pushed through; when compelled to jump they did so from a stand which was enough to make them reluctant. *The Sportsman's Directory* of 1828 counselled dismounting on coming to a big fence, for 'dashing at difficult leaps is only a proof of thoughtless hardihood'. Surtees said that 'real sportsmen take no pleasure in leaping . . . if there isn't a gap where they want to be over, why they make one'.

Nevertheless, but for enclosure foxhunting would never have become a popular sport. Faster hounds and more fences, which as time went on became less easy to push through or avoid, combined to make foxhunting more hazardous. This gave it a thrill which appealed to the great horse-loving public far more than the slow but more scientific hound-work of the past. An added source of pleasure was the need to be mounted on better-bred horses, both to gallop and to jump, to which Hugo Meynell's preference for thoroughbreds, which till then had seldom been seen in the hunting field, clearly pointed. With the coming of well-bred horses riders to hounds learnt, before the close of the nineteenth century, to gallop at their fences. To begin with, and for some years, 'flying leaping' was thought so dangerous that even bold riders made a practice, on coming to a big jump, especially a brook, of freeing their feet from the irons and crossing their stirrups over their horse's withers.

Other great changes followed. The needs of the increasing

number of people who wanted to hunt could not be satisfied by privately owned packs of hounds. A man could not hunt with them unless invited by the master who had many good reasons, notably the interests of the farmers, for being very sparing with his invitations. Most masters hunted when and where their whims or the weather dictated so that none but intimate neighbours knew where they would be. Private packs being small and widely separated, great parts of England were unhunted and out of reach of hounds. But all over the country there were people wanting to hunt regularly and conveniently from wherever they happened to live. Their requirements could only be met by larger packs hunting more country on regular days a week. This called for more hounds, horses, and servants, and bigger kennels and stables at greatly increased expense in both capital and revenue. Not many masters could afford it, and not all of those who could were prepared to do so at the cost of their old freedom to hunt their countries as they chose. Nevertheless, a considerable number did, thus creating what Trollope called the 'very English phase of hunting, . . . the phase in which the great lord undertook the enormous expense of hunting the country in a lordly style, for the amusement and recreation of all those who lived within reach of his magnificence, and defraying the whole expense of the establishment out of his own pocket'. Notable among these splendid masters were successive Dukes of Beaufort and Earls of Berkeley, J. J. Farquharson of Langton in Dorset, and Thomas Assheton Smith of Tidworth. The debt of fox-hunting to these public-spirited and unselfish men is profound, for it was they who provided the model of how hunts should be organized and managed in the interests of the public instead of in those of their masters. It was they who, by precept and example, ensured the success of the subscription system which was first established at this juncture and which was ultimately to become almost universal.

Some masters of private packs, who could not afford the larger establishment which the new needs demanded, decided, as Hugo Meynell had done in 1780 when his hounds became too expensive for him, to accept subscriptions and conform to the wishes of their subscribers in the way they hunted their country. Where there were large areas unhunted subscriptions were raised for the formation of new packs with, of course, the approval and consent of the landowners concerned. One great advantage of the subscription system was that the subscribers could both choose their master and get rid of him if he failed to show good sport, which, under the old system of private packs, had never been possible. Another advantage was that subscription packs hunted regular days a week and hunted their country fairly so that hounds were within reach of everyone in turn.

With so many people wanting to hunt it had become highly inconvenient for hounds to meet at daybreak. Happily the increased speed of hounds had both removed the need for early meets and made it practicable to have a good hunt at any hour of the day. Hounds began to meet at 10.30 or 11 o'clock, but this called for a radical change in hunting technique. The fox could no longer be found by dragging up to him because the scent had by then become cold. So hounds began drawing for him as they do today. The advantage of the new system was immense. Whereas the fox found at daybreak, with his belly still full, was too quickly killed by the fast hounds now in fashion, the fox found later in the day was much more difficult to catch and therefore more worth hunting. 'What chiefly contributes to make fox-hunting so very far superior to other sports', wrote John Cook, '*is the wildness of the animal you hunt, and the difficulty in catching him.*'

The new system of hunting gave a far better chance of long fast hunts which was what the new subscribers wanted, for most of them were much more interested in cross-country riding than in hunting. For its fullest enjoyment the new system required a different sort of country to the old, except that grass was always better than arable. In the past the rolling, unenclosed uplands of Salisbury Plain, broken only by scattered patches of gorse which harboured plenty of foxes, were accounted a fine sporting country. Under the new system, with foxhunters more interested in jumping fences than in hounds, an enclosed country was required, as unobstructed by woodlands as possible, carrying scent well, and the older its pastures the better. These needs were most fully met by the Shires — Leicestershire, Rutland, and Northamptonshire — where the pastures, unlike those elsewhere, had largely escaped the plough in the French wars. The pre-eminence of the Shires, to which Meynell's great reputation had first drawn attention, made Melton Mowbray the greatest of all foxhunting centres and the winter resort of many of the richest in the land. Solicitous though most of these rich people certainly were for the poor where their own homes lay, few of them appear to have been aware that Melton was the centre of one of the most depressed of all rural areas and that, for lack of food and fuel, the problem of survival was the daily obsession of half the Leicestershire countryside.

The change from the old style of hunting to the new was of course gradual, and for a time a man could often start a day's hunting with a private pack meeting at daybreak and complete it with a neighbouring subscription pack which hunted till dark. But the transition was not always easy. The impact on the countryside of many more men claiming, as foxhunters, the right to ride over other people's land, and the inevitable clash of interests between foxhunters, farmers, and shooting men are the subject of the following chapter. Suffice it here to say that most of the difficulties which foxhunting encountered in this period of transition were domestic in origin, stemming from the creation of subscription packs of which the proper management had yet to be mastered.

In the early days of subscription packs the hounds were nearly always the property of the master, and theoretically subscriptions were expected to cover the cost of hunting the country, any shortfall having to come out of the master's pocket. In practice this arrangement seldom worked out to everyone's satisfaction. Many people who had hunted for years at someone else's expense resented having to shoulder their share of the burden. Their parsimony would have mattered less had they not been much given to putting down their names at the beginning of the season for a larger sum than they intended to subscribe. Consequently a master who had started the season confident that all outgoings would be covered by subscriptions was apt to find himself faced with a very serious shortfall at the end of it. It was probably because subscriptions were expected to cover expenses and the master was only expected to see that the money was spent in the best interests of the subscribers that the master of a subscription pack was usually called its manager, and that he talked more often of managing instead of hunting his country. Subscription packs usually had regional names, taken from the country they hunted; private packs, on the other hand, were always known by the name of their master which often had been handed down from one generation to another. But where, as often happened, private packs became subscription packs, they sometimes retained their original names. Thus we see from their names today that the Grafton, Fernie, and Meynell, for example, were once privately owned. When, as sometimes happened, a pack reverted to private ownership, the master paying all expenses, as the Quorn did twice, it at once assumed the name of its master.[1]

The most valued right of subscribers was that of appointing the master. It was not a matter in which they had complete freedom of choice for it was useless to appoint someone unacceptable to the landowners who, if they did not like him, could close their coverts to the hunt, with or without dog-spears to make the closure effective. Landowners had been known to claim an exclusive right to choose the master of the hunt that drew their coverts but the right does not seem ever to have been established. There was, however, an occasion on which the local landowners successfully insisted on the retention of a master whom the subscribers wanted to dismiss. That was in 1831 when the Duke of Bedford and other landowners refused consent to the dismissal of Grantley Berkeley from the mastership of the Oakley. But, on the whole, there was very little trouble of this kind. Many landowners were keen fox-hunters and those who were not were usually content to let the hunt manage its own affairs.

While a master might prove satisfactory to his subscribers he, for his part, might find them unendurable, usually on account of their constant interference in his very exacting duties. When this happened the master could, as Sir Richard Sutton did with the Quorn in later years, sack his subscribers and hunt the country in his own way at his own expense. Indeed, subscribers' uninformed criticism, irresponsible interference, and niggardly subscriptions made many a master's life as much of a burden as it was to Surtees's Jovey Jessop who, 'not caring to be a servant, soon gave it up, and finding that a nominal subscription was in reality worse than none, resolved to hunt the next country he

---

[1] At one time the Quorn was known as Sir Harry Goodricke's Hounds, and at another Sir Richard Sutton's.

took at his own expense'. But nothing was worse for a hunt than a master who paid all the expenses because of the difficulty of replacing him; every potential master knew only too well the difficulty of getting money out of people who had enjoyed the luxury of hunting at someone else's expense. The Quorn's princely establishment cost Sir Harry Goodricke, who paid all expenses, £6,000 a year, but the most that could be raised by subscription for his less opulent successor was £2,500.

Nevertheless, in spite of the many difficulties with which the early subscription packs were faced, the subscription system was greatly to the advantage of foxhunting. 'Subscription packs', wrote Surtees, 'are productive of more energy and less cavilling than private packs; every man feels his interest at stake both summer and winter, and will look to things all the year round, instead of lounging carelessly out during the season, leaving the breeding and protection of foxes, the propitiation of farmers and other etceteras to the private owner of the hounds, who in all probability leaves it to the huntsman, who deputes it to the earth-stopper, who leaves it to an assistant who leaves it undone. A subscription pack makes every man put his shoulder to the wheel, not only to keep down expense but to promote sport, each subscriber feeling his own credit identified with the credit of the establishment.'

In spite of all these changes and the abandonment of so many old customs, the influence of the eighteenth-century foxhunters remained profound. Their whole-hearted devotion to the science of hunting, the Noble Science as it was called, to the exclusion of any thought for the riding and social aspects of the sport, which mattered so much to their descendants, resulted in their establishing principles which have remained fundamental. As exponents of how to catch a fox the great masters and huntsmen of those days have never been surpassed, but posterity's greatest debt to them sprang from their mastery of hound-breeding. The importance of Hugo Meynell's work in this field was nearly equalled by that of Lord Yarborough. Indeed, the latter had more lasting influence, for while Meynell's pack was lost to the Quorn when he died, Lord Yarborough's remained with his family at Brocklesby where the hound lists go back to 1746. So great was the prestige attaching to Meynell and Yarborough blood that it soon became predominant in the best kennels in the country, and produced great stallion hounds whose fame still endures. Nevertheless, mistakes were made as the result of the new emphasis on breeding for speed. The most serious one sprang from the widely-held belief that tongue was incompatible with speed. Consequently some kennels, notably the Belvoir and Bicester, began to suffer from the grievous fault of muteness. It was corrected by using the faultless Brocklesby blood.

With the deep interest in breeding went great care for puppies. History does not record any other hunt having gone to the lengths of the Windsor kennels of the Royal Buckhounds, where, at the taxpayers' expense, port was provided for the puppies. But most hunts kept a cow or two for theirs. The importance of good walks was fully appreciated. Meynell used to send his puppies as far as Sussex to be walked. A condition of the leases of Lord Berkeley's tenants was that they walked hound puppies for him. The Duke of Rutland sent puppies he could not place with his Belvoir tenants to his Derbyshire estates. John Cook was so convinced of the imperative need for good walks that he advised masters who could not count on them to give up breeding and buy unentered drafts from well-known kennels.

The prevailing belief in the value of bleeding as a protection against ailments extended to foxhound kennels, where it was customary to bleed puppies before cubhunting started. When, later in the century, bleeding began to go out of fashion Robert Vyner, an acknowledged authority on hounds, declared that 'To bleed about a fortnight before cub-hunting has a most salutory effect. . . . Never mind what the new-fangled say about not bleeding, I am sure it is a good system.'

An odd survival from the previous century was to take hounds cubhunting in the evening instead of the early morning. Scent was often very good on the evening dew but the practice had to be given up because, with scent often improving as light failed, young hounds were sometimes left out all night. Another curious survival, which probably had its origin in the old days when hounds hunted the first quarry that came to hand — deer, fox, or hare — was the entering of foxhounds to hare when they first came in from their walks. Many packs of course had started life as harriers (some, like the Beaufort, as staghounds), and up to the end of the eighteenth century there had been packs that hunted hare until Christmas and fox after it. Despite the insistence of such outstanding huntsmen as, for example, William Shaw of the Belvoir, that entering young hounds to hare made them better hunters and did not lead to riot, experience showed that it usually did, and the practice was dropped.

In spite of the vast attention given to hounds, in the early years of the century a pack could be bought for little more than a rich man would pay for a hunter. When John Warde, in 1825, sold his noted Craven hounds for £2,000 it was thought an astonishingly high price. As hounds were almost always the private property of the masters, who were frequently changing, it was not unusual for two or three packs of hounds to come up for sale at Tattersall's in the spring.

The public sale of whole packs was a product of the subscription system, and experience had not yet taught that hounds which performed brilliantly in one country might fail in another. In 1821 Squire Osbaldeston moved his famous Quorn pack from Leicestershire to Hampshire, taking with him the exceptional Tom Sebright as his first whip, and declaring that he would soon be the death of every fox in the country. But the great Quorn hounds were an utter failure. In fourteen weeks they killed only $3\frac{1}{2}$ brace of foxes. 'It is not enough', wrote Surtees, 'to bring into the field men, hounds, and horses of the best pretensions . . . unless all are pre-eminently qualified for the particular country in which their lot is cast.'

The fast runs which resulted from hounds bred for speed and better-bred horses had one distressing consequence. This was the appalling tale of dead and foundered horses which marred every great hunt. The riders, far from realizing how badly this reflected on them as horsemen, would sometimes boast of the number of horses they had ridden to death as a proof of their superior courage and endurance. This was largely caused by the sudden appearance in the hunting field of competitive riding, a grievous vice from which the sport has never since been wholly free. It mattered far more in those days because, clipping not yet having been introduced, every horse carried a heavy winter coat, and the worse bred the horse, and therefore the less his staying powers, the thicker his coat. When, early in the

nineteenth century, clipping was first introduced it was astonishingly slow to become general practice. Its introduction
was strongly resisted because it was thought that it would
shorten the horse's life and, still more absurd, that it caused
blindness. More excusably it was objected to on the ground that
it spoilt a horse's appearance. Even as late as 1846 Charles
Bindley (Harry Hieover) held 'a clipped horse a beastly sight'.
The only valid objection to it was that, the clipping machine not
having been invented, clipping a horse with scissors was slow
and very laborious. The vicar of Aldenham was therefore not
being altogether unreasonable when he refused to take Sunday
duty for William Capel, the vicar of Watford, because he was
busy clipping his horse. When at last the great value of clipping
became apparent, but before its general adoption in the middle
of the century, clipping enthusiasts, such as Surtees, started
shaving their horses with ordinary razors.

While some foxhunters mercilessly rode their horses to death,
others went to extraordinary lengths to spare them. History
records three singularly athletic foxhunters, in different parts of
England, who trained their horses to follow them over fences
and gates which they themselves jumped on foot.

There were two innovations that went a long way towards
saving horseflesh. The first of these was the cantering or covert
hack, usually a rather common horse that carried his master to
the meet at 12 miles or so an hour while a groom took his
master's hunter on at a quiet jog. At the meet the groom was
sent home with the covert hack. In Leicestershire, where everything was done on a far grander scale than elsewhere, a covert hack
had to be a much better type of horse for he was expected to carry
his master to the meet across country at about 20 miles an hour.

A far more valuable innovation was the second horse in the
field. It came into use late in the eighteenth century, but was
popularized in about 1800 by Lord Sefton who, weighing 20
stone and expecting to see the whole of a fast hunt, had out
with him two second or spare horses ridden by light-weight
grooms. He kept all three horses out all day and changed from
one to another, and back again, at frequent intervals. Other
heavy-weights soon followed his example but with only one
second horse. So great was the saving in horseflesh that light-
weights also adopted the practice. At first the second-horseman

followed closely on the heels of his master, but as this virtually doubled the size of the field and the damage to farmers' crops and fences, the practice had to be stopped. It then became customary for second-horsemen to follow in the wake of the hunt as they have done ever since.

There was much controversy over the proper care of horses. 'If the horse is distressed,' wrote Tom Smith of the Craven, 'have about two or three quarts of blood taken from him.' It was customary to bleed horses when they first came up from grass, a practice which Nimrod condemned as 'not only useless but improper'. But he, like many others, was also very much opposed to turning horses out in the summer, chiefly on the ground that it was foolish to allow them to lose the fine condition in which they ended the hunting season. Early in the century the loose box was introduced but there was a strong prejudice against it, and when, in 1830, Assheton Smith provided a loose box for every horse in his new stables at Tidworth he was much ahead of his times. The objection to loose boxes was that, to quote Nimrod, 'horses lying loose are apt to refuse to lie down in stalls, when removed to premises where boxes cannot be had'. As it was the fashion for hunting men to visit various packs in the course of a season, their horses were moved about a good deal which gave weight to a prejudice for which there was little real excuse.

The fashion for touring encouraged the hiring of hunters, a trade in which the great horse-dealer John Tilbury was pre-eminent. Tilbury, the designer and maker of the fashionable gig that bore his name, had had a remarkable career. 'When he first began', wrote the Druid, 'he had a little wheelwright's shop in Bryanston Street, Edgware Road, and let out buggy horses. From this humble spot, he went to South Street, the scene of his fine tilbury trade, and rising at last into all his glory in Mount Street, began to let out hunters.' Indeed Tilbury's yard in Mount Street became almost as fashionable a resort as Tatter-sall's. Some hunts mounted their staff exclusively on Tilbury hirelings, and he eventually had horses standing throughout the Midlands, especially in Melton and Northampton. He mounted such noted foxhunters as Nimrod and John Mytton, and most of the eminent foreigners who had begun to visit England annually for foxhunting.

A meet of hounds in those days was in all essentials not very different from today. The covert hacks greatly swelled the number of horses, and the grooms all wore livery. The horses were mostly cock-tails, and there were very few mares, which were not liked in the hunting field. Nearly all the field were men, who wore top hats and red coats, the former rather high and the latter with long skirts. The almost total absence of women was probably due to foxhunting having become more hazardous. Those that did hunt wore voluminous habits and hats trimmed with feathers. Few though they were, they do not seem to have been very welcome. John Cook considered them 'more in their element in the drawing-room or in Kensington Gardens than in the kennel or the field', and in later years Surtees gallantly complained that 'a man does not like riding before them, or leaving them in the lurch; and even if they do "go along", the whole field is kept in alarm lest an accident happen'.

The hunt servants, then usually called hound servants, wore top hats cubhunting but hunting caps afterwards. In the eighteenth century they carried a spare stirrup-leather round their horses' necks but at the turn of the century they took to wearing it over their shoulder. It was worn thus by all hunt servants. The huntsman usually carried a straight hunting horn, but some preferred a bugle, slung over the shoulder. Jem Hills, the first huntsman of the Heythrop, the son of an earth-stopper and a huntsman's daughter, carried a bugle on which he used to play 'Over the Hills and Far Away' before throwing his hounds into covert.

Many a hunt was ruined at the start by the deplorable lack of discipline among riders to hounds. Masters had yet to learn the difficult art of controlling a field for which, with so many jealous and competitive riders, there was never greater need. The trouble was that, to quote Nimrod, 'a slow man with hounds, how good soever his horsemanship, is little thought of these days'. The consequence was shocking overriding of hounds, especially when they had just found their fox, and it mattered most. 'The rush of the horsemen at starting is little less than awful', wrote Nimrod of Leicestershire. 'Many, many a day's sport', lamented Cook, 'is spoilt by the sole circumstance of hounds being overrode.' Overriding was naturally at its worst in the grass countries, especially in the Shires. On at least two occasions

Osbaldeston took the Quorn hounds home because of their being overridden. With the lack of discipline went a great deal of unnecessary damage to farmers' crops.

Apart from the unruly field, a good hunt in those days was much as it has always been. Preserved in contemporary literature are two splendid descriptions of a good hunt, both fictitious but none the worse for that. Sporting literature has little better to offer than Nimrod's stirring description, in *The Chace*, of a hunt from Ashby Pastures in 1826 when the Quorn, under the famous Squire, was at the height of its fame. In pleasant contrast is Surtees's account, at the beginning of *Handley Cross*, of a hunt with Michael Hardy's humble trencher-fed pack. As history only records good runs, contemporary chronicles give the impression that sport was far better then than in modern times. With a much smaller population, little traffic on the roads, and no railways, a fox was seldom headed and had a better chance. Long hunts were therefore more common. But, then as now, the best packs in the country would have bad seasons, when week would follow week without a good hunt. 'A real good run seldom occurs,' wrote Tom Smith, 'for to get one requires so many circumstances combined — first, a good fox, then a good find and a good scent, then a good country, good luck etc. The chances against it are innumerable.'

At the end of a hunt the procedure was markedly different from today owing to three customs which, happily for fox-hunting, were discontinued before the middle of the century. These were brushing, capping, and treeing.

Brushing was riding for the brush of the hunted fox to which the first man up at the death was by custom entitled. He helped himself to it by plunging into the pack, knife in hand, and cutting it off. In those days of ruthless competitive riding it was considered highly meritorious to secure the brush at the end of a good hunt. This led to unseemly wrangles when there were two or more riders trying to secure it, but what mattered much more was the crippling of hounds by hot-headed riders who, in their eagerness, would gallop their horses right into the pack. Brushing also encouraged the overriding of hounds and too often resulted in the coveted brush going to the man who least deserved it, for, as Trollope wrote, 'it unfortunately happens that he who rides foremost in most runs is generally where he ought not to be'. The practice was therefore stopped, and it became customary for the brush to be given by the master or his huntsman to anyone he chose out of the field. When Soapey Sponge fixed a brush in the flowing plumes of Lucy Glitters's hat he was less orthodox than his successful rival for the lady's favours, Facey Romford, who fastened it to the bridle of her horse.

Capping was making a collection from the field, usually half-a-crown a head, as a reward for the huntsman when he killed a fox. It was an old custom, going back to the days of Peter Beckford, which was beset with evils. The chief of these was the encouragement it gave to huntsmen to use bag-foxes which cost as many shillings to buy as the pounds a cap might yield. It also encouraged the chopping, heading and, when scent was bad, the mobbing of a hunted fox — the securing of blood at any price. It betrayed one noted huntsman, Tom Hill of the Surrey, into claiming that a fox that had been shot in front of his hounds had been killed by them. As capping so often corrupted good huntsmen and was ruinous to sport, it was dropped early in the nineteenth century.

Treeing the fox, a favourite subject of sporting artists, was hanging his dead body over the branch of a tree to be bayed by the hounds for a while before it was thrown to them. The intention, Beckford tells us, was 'to make the hounds more eager, and to let in the tail hounds'. By the end of the eighteenth century it was thought to serve no useful purpose but was continued, in the interests of the huntsman, in order to give time for the tail of the field to come up and contribute to the cap. When capping went out treeing went with it.

The dropping of these old customs was accompanied by other improvements in standards of sportsmanship. In Hugo Meynell's early days, when hounds were still very slow and most foxes were run to ground, the spade and pick were an essential part of the foxhunter's equipment. As hounds became fast and earth-stopping became customary, so many more foxes were killed above ground that it then came to be considered unsporting to dig out a hunted fox. 'Digging for a fox is only allowable', wrote John Cook early in the nineteenth century, 'when your hounds are in great want of blood; from experience I know it may be sometimes necessary, and on such occasions it cannot be considered unsportsmanlike.' Assheton Smith, like Delmé Radcliffe, very seldom dug, and in no circumstances would he dig a fox that had given him a good hunt.

In the old days, when many packs left much of their country unhunted and an unhunted no-man's-land often separated one hunt from another, there were few recognized boundaries to cause trouble between neighbours. When foxhunting became a popular sport and subscription packs multiplied so that there was hardly a part of the country left unhunted, hunt boundaries had to be carefully defined and strictly observed. At the start, however, the right of a hunt to pursue a hunted fox into a neighbouring country had been recognized by everyone, but it was subject to hounds being whipped off should they change on to a fresh fox after crossing the hunt boundary. This proviso sometimes led to trouble owing to its often being far from easy to determine whether hounds had changed or not. Invaders naturally tended to give themselves the benefit of any doubt, and the invaded, who would have done just the same, seldom took much notice.

Another unwritten law defined the procedure to be followed if a hunted fox got to ground in a neighbouring country. 'If you should . . . run a fox to ground in a neighbouring hunt,' wrote John Cook, 'according to the laws of foxhunting, it is not correct to dig him. If you run into a main earth, the best way will be to leave the place with as little delay as possible, to prevent any misrepresentation that might lead to a misunderstanding; for no people (I will not even except the riders of the present day) are so jealous of each other as masters of foxhounds. But if you should run your fox into a drain, or any hole that is not a regular fox-earth, it is then thought fair to bolt him in any way you can, except by digging; but on no account must you allow a spade to enter the ground. It may be your hunted fox, or it may not.' A few years later you might dig in a neighbouring country if the fox could be reached with a stick.

But whenever and wherever you ran to ground and did not dig, it was very necessary to take precautions to see that no one else dug out or trapped your fox after you had gone home. It was customary to pay a trusted man to watch the earth or drain till the fox had come safely out or, failing that, to see that no traps were set. There was just as ready a market for live foxes as there was for dead game.

P

XIV

Essex v. *Capel*

THE transformation of foxhunting into a national sport was carried through in the face of two serious handicaps, shortage of money and shortage of foxes. The first, arising from the parsimony of subscribers, was generally overcome by the affluence of those who wanted to become masters of hounds, either out of love of the sport or because of the prestige which attached to a mastership. The lack of foxes was a far more intractable problem.

Lack of foxes has usually been associated with hostility to foxhunting, but this was not the main source of the trouble in the period with which we are concerned. Traditionally the fox was a public enemy, and the law placed a price on his head. In the eighteenth century churchwardens were required by law to pay a reward for every fox killed in their parish. Either owing to the effectiveness of this law in reducing the fox population or through so many squires having taken to hunting the fox instead of the hare, by the end of the century the law had fallen into abeyance except in a few parishes where, well into the nineteenth century, the churchwardens continued to pay a reward, half-a-crown or five shillings, for every fox's head brought to them. When, early in that century, Parson Jack Russell first kept hounds in Devonshire, church bells would sometimes be rung 'in a jingling fashion, and with more than usual clamour. . . . It was the signal that a fox had been tracked to ground, or balled into a brake, and the bell summoned every man who possessed a pick-axe, a gun, or a terrier to hasten to the spot and lend a hand in destroying the noxious animal.'

The shortage of foxes certainly dated back far into the eighteenth century, as Peter Beckford makes clear, and a little later it forced Hugo Meynell temporarily to quit Leicestershire for Huntingdonshire. In 1804 John Cook had to give up the Thurlow because he found 'foxes and subscriptions damnably short'. Up to the end of the previous century, the shortage of foxes had not been due to antipathy to foxhunting among farmers and gamekeepers, their traditional enemies. Foxhunting had not yet become general, many farmers were ardent foxhunters and most of the others welcomed hounds on their land; and as regards gamekeepers, neither game preservation nor foxhunting had developed to the stage where their interests seriously clashed. The shortage of foxes was due to the unremitting efforts of country people generally all down the ages to destroy them as noxious animals. Thus when foxhunting became a popular sport, with packs of hounds increasing annually and no part of the country left unhunted, there were not enough foxes to go round. A serious aspect of the shortage was its reaction on finance. A succession of blank days inevitably drove subscribers to more fortunate neighbours.

Care was taken to make the best of such foxes as there were, and hounds were sometimes whipped off when they looked like catching one. The shortage had a marked effect on the duties of that half-mysterious, shadowy character, the earth-stopper. He was still required to go out in the middle of the night, before a day's hunting, to stop the earths to ensure that there were foxes still above ground the following morning and unable to get to ground when they were hunted. But in countries seriously short of foxes he was also required, the day before the hounds met, to stop any earth with a fox in it, if he could find one, so that when hounds arrived the following morning he could unstop and bolt the fox. This probably explains why contemporary pictures of meets of hounds so frequently and otherwise unaccountably include an earth-stopper, with his spade and his terrier.

The short-term solution to the problem of the often chronic lack of foxes was to buy and turn them down which, as Meynell found to his cost, was a sure way of antagonizing farmers. Nevertheless, in coming years it was widely practised and sometimes on a large scale. Most masters contented themselves with the crude *ad hoc* solution of the bag-fox, turned down as and when required to avoid the embarrassment of a blank day. There was no difficulty over supplies, which were so readily obtainable in Leadenhall Market that bagmen came to be called Leadenhallers. Important dealers outside the Market were M. Herring, described in the Post Office Directory as *Dealer in Foreign Birds and Beasts*, who also supplied carted deer to staghounds, and Hopkins of the Tottenham Court Road who was always to be found booking orders at Tattersall's on sale days.

The dealers got most of their supplies from the Continent, chiefly from France. Imported foxes were so badly treated in transit that they usually arrived in such a miserable condition as to fail altogether in their purpose, but unfortunately the reason for this was thought by the buyers to be lack of stamina. Robert Vyner complained of the increasing degeneracy of English foxes, 'mongrel-bred vermin . . . stained as they are by the introduction of French blood'. Osbaldeston, a pretty regular hunter of bagmen, always stipulated 'old English foxes, no damned French dunghills'.

The consequences of the growing prejudice against French foxes, and the insistence of buyers on English ones, were disastrous, for they created a strong market for the home-bred article. As Peter Beckford had written years before the importation of foxes from the Continent had begun, 'Gentlemen who buy foxes do great injury to foxhunting; for they encourage the robbing of neighbouring hunts: in which case, without doubt, the receiver is as bad as the thief. . . . I am told, that in some hunts it is the constant employment of one person to watch the earths at breeding time, to prevent the cubs from being stolen. . . . The price that some men pay for them, might well encourage the robbing of every hunt in the kingdom, their own not excepted. But you despise the *soi disant* gentleman who receives them, more than the poor thief who takes them.'

The position had become much more serious since Beckford's day for the shortage of foxes was more acute, the demand much greater, and there were exceptionally good facilities for obtaining them. Although the hunting of bagmen was considered unsportsmanlike, to say nothing of its ruinous effect on hounds, and was usually done surreptitiously, many masters were quite shameless about it. Jack Mytton always had bagmen in his kennels at Halston. George Templer of the South Devon normally had twenty on hand; but at least he was extremely economical in the way he used them. Not liking the expense of their replacement, he had evolved a remarkable technique for saving a hunted fox, be it wild or out of a bag. Amongst the chroniclers who witnessed his extraordinary procedure was Nimrod, who tells us that when hounds were getting close to their fox 'some of the field — among whom are two or three particularly *au fait* at this work — get forward and pick him up by his brush'.[1]

The facilities for obtaining English foxes had been greatly improved through the poaching of game having become so well organized. Gangs who were regularly raiding pheasant coverts at considerable risk of transportation or worse were naturally very ready to turn their hands to catching foxes, to which no penalties attached. The depredations of these gangs became a sore trial to many a master with a country well stocked with foxes. When Corbet had the Warwickshire he paid £40 a year blackmail to one such gang to keep them out of his coverts. Those who were short of foxes also suffered, for in real life there were dealers like Surtees's Mr. Diddler of Leadenhall Market, 'who by dint of stealing back as fast as he supplies, manages to carry on a very extensive business with a very small stock-in-trade'.

The troubles that flowed from the hunting of bagmen were manifold. First, as we have seen, it aggravated the shortage of wild foxes; then, as Beckford had pointed out years before and as every experienced master and huntsman knew, it was ruinous to good hounds; it also gave foxhunters a reputation for being bad sportsmen (as indeed many were); and finally it encouraged the destruction of foxes by farmers and gamekeepers who argued that if people wanted to hunt they could hunt a bag-fox as easily as a wild one.

Efforts to increase the natural fox population of the country were not, however, confined to merely turning down foxes. Hunts took to renting woodlands, and planting gorse coverts where steps could be taken to protect the foxes they were intended to harbour. Gorse was, indeed, in itself an effective protection to foxes against fox-stealers. In the Shires, where woodlands were scarce, gorse was extensively planted. Other

---

[1] Templer claimed to have one fox that had been turned down and recovered no less than 36 times.

It is possible that in later years Lord Lonsdale, who had the O.B.H. from 1842 to 1862, followed Templer's example, for we hear of him too recovering his bagmen alive.

protective measures were artificial earths — then called false earths — and stick heaps, both of which were much used.

The chief enemies of foxes were the farmers, not out of hostility to foxhunting but because foxes killed their poultry. Their tolerance of hounds on their land and the inevitable damage done to their crops and fences was beyond praise. They scorned men like Sydney Smith who, in 1821, wrote: 'Is there, upon earth, such a mockery of justice as an Act of Parliament, pretending to protect property, sending a poor hedge-breaker to gaol, and especially exempting from its operation the accusing and judging Squire, who, at the tail of the hounds, [has] that morning, perhaps, ruined as much wheat and seeds as would purchase fuel for a whole year for a whole village?'

From the beginning of foxhunting the dependence of the sport on the farmers, and the need to consider their interests, had been recognized. It was said that Hugo Meynell would wait only ten minutes at the covert-side for a duke but twenty for a farmer. 'You should . . . endeavour to gain the good-will of *the farmers*', wrote John Cook; 'if any respectable body of persons suffer from hunting it is them; and I think it is not only un-gentlemanly, but impolitic, to treat them in the field, or else-where, otherwise than with kindness and civility.'

Relations with farmers had been made more difficult by foxhunting having become a popular and fashionable sport. So long as foxhunting had remained in the hands of benevolent squires who were well known to every farmer in their district there had been no lack of good will on both sides. Farmers certainly sometimes killed foxes but they did it, in a foxhunting country, surreptitiously. With the passing of the sport into the hands of subscription packs, often with a master from outside the country, the personal touch was largely lost. The non-hunting farmers, always in the vast majority, took little interest in hunts whose masters and most of whose followers were un-known to them, and had no compunction in destroying every litter of cubs they could lay their hands on.

The entry into the hunting field of many more followers was naturally not popular with farmers, but it would have mattered less had not so many of them been ignorant townsmen who realized neither the damage they did nor that they hunted on sufferance. Nevertheless, farmers were extraordinarily tolerant. 'We must say, and greatly to their credit we say it,' wrote Surtees, 'that it really is astonishing the damage and inconvenience farmers put up with every year, and the extraordinary good grace with which they do it. . . . Nothing can be more annoying to the true sportsman than to see wanton or unnecessary mischief; crushing young quicksets for the sake of a leap, letting cattle escape for want of shutting a gate, or any of the numerous acts of omission or commission that all go to swell the catalogue of damage. . . . It is only the real sportsman, or person who takes part in the management of a country that can be fully sensible of the obligations foxhunters are under to farmers. In the first place, we are indebted to them for the existence of the animal we hunt; and their sufferance, nay, protection of it, is the more disinterested and meritorious, inasmuch as foxes cannot by any possibility do farmers any good, but, on the contrary, are almost certain to occasion them loss and inconvenience.'

These were the circumstances in which it at last became common practice to compensate farmers for the damage they suffered. 'How can you expect to have foxes', asked Ralph Lambton, the best-loved master of his day, 'if you don't pay for the mischief they do?' Besides paying poultry and other claims[1] for damage, some hunts endeavoured to limit the damage to crops by restricting the number of people who followed hounds. Hunting appointments were therefore not published, but the Old Berkeley (O.B.H.), which suffered from incursions of Londoners and hostile landowners, went so far as to forbid their subscribers to tell even personal friends where hounds were going to meet. Whenever there was secrecy about meets it led to difficulties. Even subscribers were sometimes left in doubt about when and where they could hunt, and it made the recruitment of new subscribers difficult. This led to the posting of hunting appointments on church doors, and on occasions, as when the Rev. John Lucy was vicar of Charlecote, to their announcement from the pulpit.

The growing popularity of shooting, already the favourite

---

[1] The paying of poultry claims did not become common practice until well into the nineteenth century; but as early as 1791 their payment, and their abuse, were not unusual. In that year John Byng, hearing of a miller who was 'fee'd to preserve [foxes], and could bring in a bill of their damages', commented: 'Then he never loses a fowl or a duck by illness, who is not thrown into the bill.'

sport of the gentry throughout the greater part of England, and the consequent importance attaching to game preservation, aggravated the problem of the fox supply. Although there were then, as there have always been, plenty of landowners who demonstrated on their own estates that it was perfectly practicable to have enough of both foxes and game to please everyone, most gamekeepers were vulpicides. No matter how keen a fox-preserver a landowner might be, it was not easy for him to make sure that his keepers were as conscientious as himself. Landowners interested only in shooting were not necessarily, or indeed usually, opposed to foxhunting. In many a hunting country social ostracism was, as it long remained, the penalty for the destruction of foxes, though apparently to a diminishing degree. Cook, writing in 1825, lamented the day 'when it was thought *dishonourable* to destroy foxes'.

In some parts of the country where shooting and foxhunting really clashed there was a marked social cleavage aggravated by a curious and persistent prejudice which attributed to fox-hunters unusually coarse and uncouth habits, a prejudice well exemplified in the future Lady Palmerston's description of Lady Euston as 'a nice bouncing milk-maid, married to a hunting brute, little better than his dogs'.[1] To Mrs. Arbuthnot Lord Clonmell was 'a drunken hunting squire and cant bear Henry (his son-in-law) because he does not drink or hunt'. This prejudice was a great annoyance to John Byng who wrote: 'I do experience (with peevishness sometimes) the plumpest opposition on the subjects of hunting, wine, &c, from those who never sported, and only drank water. Thus comes my desire of writing!'[2]

But even the eccentric William Beckford had sadly to admit, as he built an immense wall round Fonthill to keep out the local hounds and their followers, that in the countryside foxhunting was the key to popularity.

As we shall see, the hostility of some landowners to fox-hunting was bitter and relentless, but for the most part either

[1] This description of the future 5th Duke of Grafton was probably unfair for he was an intensely religious recluse.

[2] But even in those days there were those who regarded all blood sports as degrading. 'Eat as much game as you please,' wrote Lord Chesterfield to his godson, 'but I hope you will never kill any yourself; and, indeed, I think you are above any of these rustick, illiberal sports of guns, dogs and horses, which characterise our English Bumpkin Country Gentlemen.'

they hunted or, in the customary live-and-let-live spirit of the English countryside, they were well disposed towards it. Excusably enough this was not often the case with their game-keepers who, in the face of demands for ever greater bags, found it very convenient to blame disappointing results on the foxes. The custom on most shoots of treating rabbits as the keeper's perquisite was an added reason for the continuance of the latter's traditional antipathy to the fox. The good will of keepers was in large measure secured by introducing payments of rewards for litters of cubs reared and foxes found on a keeper's beat, as well as for earth-stopping, a necessary service for which hunts were greatly indebted to many a friendly keeper.

It was many years before the cumulative effect of these long overdue but well-merited concessions to farmers and game-keepers was reflected in the fox population of the country. In the end it not only ensured the continuance of foxhunting but, so profound was the success with which fox-killers were converted into fox-preservers, that by the second half of the century there was hardly a hunt that lacked foxes. There is nothing more surprising in the history of English field sports than the success that attended this seemingly impossible task, with nine-tenths or more of the countryside brought up to the killing of foxes and most of them standing to lose far more than they could gain from their preservation. It was indeed fortunate for foxhunting that in the period in which it was transformed into a popular and fashionable sport, a transformation that might well have been its ruin, its fortunes were presided over by some great masters of hounds.

Early in the nineteenth century foxhunting was faced with a crisis which at one juncture appeared to imperil its very survival. Although, as we have seen, the public antipathy to shooting as a sport, provoked by the Game Laws, did not extend to foxhunting in spite of the general belief that it was similarly protected by unjust laws, there were a number of landowners, and probably not a few farmers, who were not so complacent, and who bitterly resented not having the right to keep hounds off their land.

In 1793 *The Sporting Magazine* published the following letter from a farmer: 'The laws of the country hold out a reward, to be paid by the church-wardens of every parish for the destruction of a rapacious, noxious animal; and the sportsmen, on the other hand, have formed a resolution, to discharge or distress every tenant who shall have the audacity to "interrupt gentlemen's diversions", by destroying a litter of fox's cubs.' Enclosed with this letter was a copy of another sent by a 'Nobleman of considerable property' to his agent, dated December 1792. 'I must desire', began this second letter, 'that all those tenants who have shewn themselves friends of the several fox-hunts in your neighbouring countries; viz. Lord Spencers', the Duke of Rutland's, Mr. Meynell's, Lord Stamford's,[1] etc. may have the offer and refusal of their farms upon easy and moderate terms; and, on the other hand, that you will take care and make very particular enquiry into the conduct of those tenants who shall have shewn a contrary disposition by destroying foxes, or encouraging others to do so, or otherwise interrupting gentlemen's diversions . . . as it is my absolute determination, that such persons shall not be treated with in future by me, upon any terms or consideration whatever! . . . Landowners as well as farmers and labourers of every description, if they know their own interest, would perceive, that they owe much of their prosperity to those popular hunts, by the great influx of money that is annually brought into the country.'

'These Game Laws form a grievance to the cultivator of the soil', wrote an anonymous correspondent of *The Farmer's Magazine* in 1800, '. . . because his crops and fences are generally injured by men, with their horses and dogs, taking liberties utterly inconsistent with that security of property which ought to be held inviolable in all civilized countries.' The taking of these liberties was not in fact protected by any law, but it could and did shelter under an action tried by Sir John Popham, Chief Justice of the King's Bench, in the reign of James I. It was an action for trespass 'brought for hunting and breaking of hedges, and the case was, that a man started a fox in his own land, and his hounds pursued him into another man's lands, and it was holden that he may hunt and pursue him into any man's land, because a fox is a noysom creature to the Commonwealth'.[2]

---

[1] That is to say the Pytchley, Belvoir, Quorn, and Albrighton respectively.
[2] These words are taken from the judgment of Mr. Justice Boderidge in a similar action, *Millen* v. *Faudrye*, in the King's Bench in 1656.

Much more recently, in 1788, a similar action, *Gundry* v. *Feltham*, had been tried on pleadings in the King's Bench in which the plaintiff had admitted that hunting was the only way of killing a fox, and had lost his case. But Mr. Justice Buller, while finding that hunting was the only effective means of killing a fox, and that a man had the right to follow a fox on to the land of another, qualified his verdict with these words: 'This case does not determine that a person may unnecessarily trample down another person's hedges, or maliciously ride over his grounds: if he do more than is absolutely necessary, he cannot justify it.' It was some years before foxhunting had become sufficiently general, and sufficiently popular, to cause serious damage and thereby make for itself enough enemies for anyone to bother about the closing sentence in the above extract from Mr. Justice Buller's dictum. Sooner or later someone was bound to appeal to the courts to decide whether the master or huntsman who followed a fox on to another's land and took with him a hundred or so horsemen was in fact doing no more than was necessary to kill his fox.

There was probably no more unhappy hunt in the country than the O.B.H. The master was the Hon. and Rev. William Capel, vicar of Watford, a sporting character who perhaps did not allow his cure of souls to interfere unduly with his foxhunting, but appears nevertheless to have been a much-loved parson. Although he sometimes hunted hounds himself he usually left that to his huntsman, Tom Oldaker who, at the time with which we are concerned, must have been approaching the end of his thirty-two seasons carrying the horn of the O.B.H. Oldaker, painted twice by Ben Marshall, was one of the great personalities of the foxhunting world, of whom it was said that when scent failed he could 'guess a fox to death'.

With a good master and an exceptional huntsman the fortunes of the O.B.H. should have prospered. But circumstances were against them. As the reader will recall, their proximity to London and the hostility of the landowners forced them to keep their meets secret. The landowners might have been easier to handle had not their leader been the 5th Earl of Essex, the master's half-brother.[1] The brothers were bitter enemies. As Lord Essex had himself once kept a pack of hounds, either

[1] They were both sons of the 4th Earl.

harriers or staghounds, it is probable that his hostility to the O.B.H. sprang more from his dislike of his brother than from any distaste for foxhunting. The feud between the two resulted in a famous test case in which the foxhunter's traditional right to follow a hunted fox wherever he might lead him was first successfully challenged.

In June 1808 a meeting of 'Noblemen, Gentlemen and Farmers, and other proprietors and occupiers of land', presided over by Lord Essex, was held at the 'Abercorn Arms' in Stanmore to consider the most effectual means of preventing 'the very serious evils resulting from the practice of hunting with the Berkeley hounds in the vicinity of the Metropolis, and particularly in the neighbourhood of Edgware, Stanmore, Bushey, Pinner, Harrow and the adjacent parishes; a practice which for many years had been the subject of complaint, but which latterly had arisen to a height most alarming and intolerable'.

From the record of what took place at the meeting and of all that followed, it is clear that the instigators of the attack on the O.B.H. were fearful of attracting criticism and alienating public opinion by giving the impression that their action was directed against foxhunting generally. They were at pains to emphasize that they were assailing the O.B.H. only because, under local conditions, serious damage was unavoidable. It was unanimously resolved, we read, 'that on account of the value of the land so close to the Metropolis (scarcely an acre now left unenclosed) the practice of hunting (under these particular circumstances) is attended by injuries too serious to be tolerated. Because, from the vicinity of London . . . the hounds are attended by a multitude of horsemen (from one hundred to one hundred and fifty, being the average number in the field) the majority of whom are both ignorant and careless of what damage they do, and from whom it would be impossible to recover satisfaction for injuries sustained. . . .' The report of the meeting records specific grievances, mostly in the way of damage suffered, but one was that 'the subscribers to the Hunt are mostly Londoners with little or no landed property in the neighbourhood'.

'Because', concludes the report, '. . . a right has been assumed (as if authorised by law) to commit such trespasses, it is highly expedient that the question should be legally ascertained of the right of the people of this country to the peaceable enjoyment and protection of their property', and it was unanimously resolved 'That all legal means be used to put a stop to such unjust, unreasonable, and injurious trespass'.

Warnings to forbear from trespass, accompanied by printed copies of the resolutions passed at the meeting, were served by the aggrieved landowners on all regular followers of the O.B.H. These communications, we read, 'were treated with indignity, and were attributed *"to private pique and personal resentment"*. . . . The gauntlet of defiance was now thrown down, and the Berkeley Hunt . . . boldly stood forward in justification of themselves, upon the broad ground of RIGHT, and challenged the landowners and occupiers to join issue upon the question, "Whether their conduct was not sanctioned by law". . . . Such being the temper and such the undisguised sentiments of the Hunt, nothing remained for the Committee but . . . to discover the principal aggressors, and bring the matter . . . to a legal decision.'

The trouble came to a head on 1 April 1809, when the O.B.H. hunted a fox from Bricket Wood into Lord Essex's park at Cashiobury. William Capel, who was hunting hounds that day, followed them across the park, accompanied by the field, until he came to a locked gate over which he and one of his field, a Mr. Gosling, jumped. They then came to another gate through which a timber gig was passing. Standing by was one of Lord Essex's keepers who, after the waggon had passed, slammed the gate to and locked it so that Capel and Gosling could not pass. The latter got off his horse and tried to force the gate open. Failing to do so, he, encouraged by Capel, smashed the top rail of the adjoining fence to let the master get to his hounds; the field followed. By modern standards this was shocking behaviour — first, the trespass after having been warned off, and then the aggravation of the trespass by deliberately smashing the park fence. But in those days, when foxhunters believed they had a legal right to go where they liked in pursuit of a hunted fox, trespass meant nothing and the deliberate locking of the gate in the face of the master therefore appeared to be merely malicious and so unreasonable as fully to justify the smashing of the rail as the only way of getting to hounds.

Lord Essex brought an action for trespass against his brother.

It was hoped by Essex and his friends that the trial would be held in suburban Middlesex rather than their native Hertfordshire, 'where the general countenance given to foxhunting was expected to create certain prejudices' in favour of the defendant who was far more popular than his brother. They were disappointed. The case was tried before a special jury at the summer assizes at Hertford the same year. The judge was Lord Ellenborough,[1] of game law fame, now Chief Justice of the King's Bench.[2]

Mr. Harrison opened for the plaintiff: 'The Defendant', he said, 'broke and entered certain closes of the Plaintiff, and with hounds, dogs, and horses . . . trod down and destroyed the grass and herbage of the Plaintiff.'

To this declaration the defendant pleaded, explained Harrison, that the fox 'being a noxious animal, he hunted it with his dogs, hounds and horses; and then he states that hunting the fox . . . was the only way of pursuing and killing the fox. . . . To these Pleas there are Replications, which deny that hunting the fox was the only and the most effectual way of Killing and destroying it; and further state, that the trespasses were committed for the sport and diversion of the chace, and for the purpose of amusement and pleasure only.'

In his opening speech leading counsel for Lord Essex, Serjeant Shepherd, who was clearly apprehensive lest the jury should share the ordinary countryman's predilection for foxhunting, and mindful of the unpopularity of his client, was at pains to emphasize that the plaintiff had only been compelled to bring the action by exceptional circumstances. Someone had suggested that a verdict for the plaintiff would put an end to foxhunting. This, he assured the jury, would not be so, 'for in those parts of the country which are so inhabited, and are in such situations as to render the amusement a fit and proper amusement, no person would think of objecting to gentlemen hunting, whether they may have the right by Law to enjoy it or not. Therefore, no decision in this cause will, I am persuaded, affect any one hunt in any part of the Kingdom.'

---

[1] Lord Ellenborough had just bought, or was about to buy, J. P. Grant's house, Thorley Hall, near Bishop's Stortford.

[2] The author is indebted to the late W. Le Hardy, M.C., F.S.A., County Archivist of Hertfordshire, for finding him a copy of the very rare published account of the trial.

'They would infer by their plea', continued Serjeant Shepherd, 'that they are actuated only by the patriotic motive of destroying the noxious vermin that infest the lands of the farmer. . . . For these proprietors of the Berkeley Hunt to state that they have associated . . . for no other purpose than to rid the country . . . of the noxious animals that infest it, is a proposition so highly absurd, that one cannot help laughing at it . . . their Plea is ridiculous and absurd. . . . Is it possible you can believe, by any stretch of your imagination, that Clergymen are descending from their pulpits; Bankers neglecting their counting houses; Brewers running away from their breweries; tradesmen, clerks, and a variety of description of persons are all occasionally flocking from London, in order to confer upon the farmers of Herts the obligation of freeing the country from noxious animals. . . . Their object is only the amusement of following the fox, not caring three-farthings, except for the triumph of his brush, whether the fox is killed or not — the plea therefore is ridiculous.'

Serjeant Shepherd then proceeded to play on the traditional prejudice of the countryman against the townsman. 'Gentlemen,' he continued, 'the Berkeley Hunt consists of a considerable number of persons, and of that number there are very few indeed who have possessions, or even habitations in the county of Herts. Is it to be endured, that a set of gentlemen of any description whatever, living in the Metropolis . . . are to associate . . . in order to trespass upon the lands of this country and the next . . . and then, when they do damage, say that their object is to rid the country of foxes? . . . It is obvious that the gentlemen who compose [the Berkeley Hunt] have no other object than their own amusement. . . .

'In point of fact, the avowed object of these gentlemen is to *preserve* those noxious vermin. Lord Essex . . . had employed a man to take the most effectual modes of killing foxes, namely, by catching them in a trap, or by shooting them with a gun. . . . Mr. Capel did not like either of them, and he spoke to the man on the subject; but the man was steady, and he went on shooting wherever his bullets would reach, and catching wherever his traps would take. Mr. Capel then said to him, "I do not ask you not to destroy the foxes, but I'll tell you what I'll do; I'll send you a barrel of ale to drink success to the Berkeley Hunt." '

The first witness to be called was Lord Essex's steward who testified to shooting and trapping being the best means of killing foxes. Here Lord Ellenborough interposed that 'The question is, Whether this Hunt has been for the purpose of amusement, or of killing vermin? . . . Whether they hunt as *vermin killers* or as *sportsmen.*'

'Really it is a contention against all nature and conviction', continued the Chief Justice. 'Can it possibly be supposed that these gentlemen hunt for the mere purpose of killing vermin, and not for their diversion? . . . Why, even if the dogs might by Law be allowed to run in pursuit of the game, that could be no reason for saying, that any number of persons could be justified in riding over the lands, and breaking and destroying the fences in places where the dogs do not go through. . . .'

'The Defendant states in his Plea', resumed Lord Ellenborough, 'that the trespass was not committed for the purpose of the diversion and amusement of the chace merely, but as the only way and means of killing and destroying the fox. — Now, if you was to put it upon this question — Which was the principal motive? — Can any man of common sense hesitate in saying that the principal motive and inducement was not the killing of vermin, but the enjoyment of the sport and diversion of the chace? . . . These pleasures are to be taken, only, where there is the consent of those who are likely to be injured by them, but they must be necessarily subservient to the consent of others. . . . But even if an animal may be pursued with dogs, it does not follow that fifty or sixty persons have therefore a right to follow the dogs, and trespass on other people's lands. . . . The good of the public must be the *governing* motive — Then I would ask the jury this question: Was the good of the public, by the destruction of noxious animals, the *governing* motive of the Defendant? Why, the last Witness has expressly stated, that he rather wished to nourish and preserve these noxious animals than destroy them.'

In the face of this Serjeant Best threw in his hand: 'After what your Lordship has said, I will not occupy the time of your Lordship or the Jury with one word more.' The jury returned a verdict for the Plaintiff and, as he had asked for only nominal damages, these were assessed at one shilling.

No less than seven similar suits followed, by various plaintiffs, presumably landowners or farmers, against various defendants. Every defendant agreed to the same verdict and damages as in *Essex* v. *Capel*. These actions included one brought by Essex against Gosling, and another brought by one Hume against Tom Oldaker, the huntsman. In the latter case Lord Ellenborough made good what he evidently regarded as a serious omission on his part in *Essex* v. *Capel* by declaring, to quote the Druid, 'that damages might be recovered, not only for the mischief immediately occasioned by the defendant himself, but also for that done by the concourse of people who accompanied him'.

The results of the *Essex* v. *Capel* and *Hume* v. *Oldaker* trials were a nasty shock to foxhunters. Instead of their having an unassailable right to ride over other people's land, the landowner and the farmer now had an unassailable right to prevent their doing so. Almost overnight foxhunters had become common trespassers who could be warned off like anyone else. Privilege had vanished as suddenly as snow in summer, and heaven only knew what would happen to foxhunting.

In fact very little did happen. Lord Essex, of course, straightway warned the O.B.H. off his thousands of acres, and, eighteen months or so later, in the Midlands, Sir William Manners warned the Belvoir off his immense estate, extending over thirty-four parishes. A few opponents of foxhunting, who had hitherto remained silent because they had thought that protests would be futile, took courage and declared that they would not have hounds on their land. But their voices were very quickly stilled by popular opinion in the country being determinedly on the side of foxhunting.

Now that everyone had the right to warn hounds off, hardly a soul wanted to exercise it. An aggressive Warwickshire farmer reminded John Corbet of his new right, but a present of game sufficed to recover his good will. To the credit of landowners and farmers on the one hand and foxhunters on the other, the sport was so little affected by the revolutionary change in their relationship one to another, and so little store was set by the right to warn hounds off that its very existence came near to being forgotten. Years later, in 1878, in a case tried in the Queen's Bench, Lord Coleridge declared that it was at that time still 'popularly supposed that foxhunting may be exercised over the lands of any person without his consent, and even his

Q

will'. Foxhunting had not only survived the greatest crisis in its history but had emerged from it with added strength. So long as everyone believed that the law did not permit the prosecution of foxhunters for trespass half England, for all anyone could tell, might be secret enemies of the sport. Now, with all England given the power to stamp it out and making not the slightest use of that power, foxhunters had nothing to fear so long as they conducted themselves decently.

Why did rural England hold foxhunting — by no means a harmless sport — in such warm regard, why did it foster and nourish it at a time when it execrated shooting which did no direct harm to anyone? There is no simple answer to that question. No doubt the vicious Game Laws were part of the answer, but only a small one, as also was the explanation Cobbett gave. 'There is', he wrote, 'an important distinction to be made between *hunters* (including coursers) and *shooters*. The latter are, as far as relates to their exploits, a disagreeable class, compared with the former; and the reason of this is, their doings are almost wholly their own; while, in the case of the others, the achievements are the property of the dogs.' That raises the question why Cobbett's unreasoning hatred of shooting men did not also embrace foxhunters? Surely such a ranting Radical, so bitter a hater of squires, should have condemned with equal venom both of the favourite field sports of the gentry? He did not because as a good countryman and a democrat he perceived that the great merit of foxhunting, apart from the demands it made on courage, skill, and endurance, was its freedom from class distinction.

'The non-hunting world', wrote Trollope, 'is apt to think that hunting is confined to country gentlemen, farmers, and rich strangers; but any one . . . will find that there are in the crowd attorneys, country bankers, doctors, apothecaries . . . maltsters, millers, butchers, bakers, innkeepers, auctioneers, graziers, builders . . . stockbrokers, newspaper editors, artists, and sailors. . . . Beneath [the master] there is freedom and equality for all, with special honour only for the man who is known to be specially good at some portion of the day's work. . . . And this feeling of out-of-door equality has, we think, spread from the hunting-field through all the relations of country life. . . . That riding together on terms of equality of the lord and his tenant and his tradesmen has produced in English countries a community of interests and a freedom of feeling which exist nowhere else.'

Trollope might have added still humbler men to his catalogue of those to be met in the hunting field. There was the hairdresser who hunted with Ralph Lambton — 'no man ever turned out a horse with a finer mane and tail'; a pauper in receipt of out-door relief was a regular follower of the Pytchley, on a horse as aged and worn as his ragged coat; then there was the famous Oxford sweep who, like many an aristocrat, dearly loved to boast that he 'hunted with the Duke'. This was the man whom Trollope's contemporary, John Conyers, must have had in mind when he told a meeting of the Essex Hunt that foxhunting had 'this great and peculiar characteristic, that it equally contributes to the enjoyment of the rich and of the poor, of the exalted and of the lowly. No other country but England knows anything of a sport which allows a chimney-sweep or the lowest man of the community to ride by the side of a duke. The humblest man in the population, provided only he be decent and well-behaved, may ride by the side of a duke when both are in pursuit of the fox, but in what other country but dear old England could such a right be seen?'

But the love of foxhunting was not confined to those who rode to hounds. Foxhunting, wrote Howitt, in spite of his dislike of blood sports, 'is now the chief amusement of the true British sportsman; and a noble one it is. . . . A fine field of hunters in their scarlet coats, rushing over forest, heath, fence or stream, on noble steeds, and with a pack of beautiful dogs in full cry, is a very picturesque and animating spectacle.' This was the aspect of foxhunting that endeared it to the humblest villagers. They loved it for brightening their drab lives in the bleak winter months. Cobbett described the excitement preceding a meet of hounds in a Hampshire village in 1825, an 'anxiously looked-for event. I have seen no man, or boy, who did not talk about it. There had been a false report about it; the hounds did *not come*; and the anger of the disappointed people was very great. At last, however, the *authentic* intelligence came, and I left them all as happy as if all were young and all just going to be married.'

It was the devotion of all rural England, regardless of class and wealth, which enabled foxhunting to survive the crisis of *Essex* v. *Capel*. The great majority of countrymen were like the humble Mr. Petulengro who did not 'approve of any movements, religious or not, which have in aim to put down all life and manly sport in this here country'.

XV

Reform and Rail

THE reign of William IV was clouded by Georgian gloom. Nevertheless, in the new reign intense legislative activity and the frantic building of railways were laying the foundations for a happier era.

Some of the horrors of the Swing riots in the first winter of William's reign were repeated twelve months later, in the winter of 1831–32. The fury of the masses at the rejection of the Reform Bill affected town and country alike. While the industrial towns of the Midlands and the North were being harried by rioters preaching bloody revolution, while troops were saving Bristol from the flames, and cholera, for the first time in history, was ravaging England, ricks were once more ablaze but on a more terrible scale than in the previous winter, and the Home Office was forced to admit that the gallows had lost its terror for starving men. Meanwhile the gunsmiths were doing a thriving trade with the new political unions who were training their members in the use of arms. These were the circumstances in which Parliament was forced to yield, and the Reform Bill became law.

Democracy had triumphed, the middle classes, or a large part of them, had been emancipated and the political omnipotence of the aristocracy had been broken. But the immense prestige attaching to birth and acres, the awe which the way of life of the aristocracy inspired, and the respect in which most country squires were held, remained unbroken. The social structure of the countryside was therefore little affected, but not so the relationship of one class to another. In the face of the transference of much political power, the landed gentry had to take more account of the middle classes. While, on the one hand, the gentry became less aloof, on the other the middle classes, to whom the franchise and the Municipal Corporations Act of 1835 had brought increased self-respect, became more socially ambitious and found their aspirations less difficult to realize. Thus were the two brought closer together. The gap could never be wholly closed for, as Byng wrote in 1792, 'a man must be born and bred a country gentleman or a country labourer; for a citizen, and an artisan will never make one, or the other'.

The turning point in the chequered history of village economy was the passing of the Poor Law Act of 1834. It abolished the Speenhamland system of outdoor relief which, by introducing parish relief in aid of wages, had pauperized the labourers and had been abused by both them and the farmers. Unfortunately no steps were taken — perhaps because none was then administratively possible — to see that wages were raised, so that until they did rise, some years later, the distress of the rural poor became even more acute. In the same year, but before the passing of the Act, the Poor Law Commissioners recorded in their report the answers they had received to a question put to certain parishes asking whether their labourers could live on their wages without parish relief. Of the sixteen Essex parishes to which this question was put only four answered No, but only one gave an unqualified Yes. For the most part the labourers in the other parishes could live on their wages provided they and their families contented themselves with bread and potatoes, 'bread and coarse tea', or bread alone — and Essex was more fortunate than some counties.

Such were the people who later in the year found themselves denied out-door relief. The social consequences were disastrous. Mothers and children, often of the tenderest age, were forced into the fields under the notorious gang system, managed by ruthless contractors, thus introducing into the countryside some of the worst horrors of industrial life. Under the new system all able-bodied persons in need of parish relief were driven into the workhouse, the 'bastille' as they called it, where, in the interests of the public purse, they were deliberately made as miserable as possible. And how miserable they could be we know from *Oliver Twist*.

The Reform Bill and the Poor Law Act had been preceded by another measure of great import to village life. This was the Game Act of 1831 which abolished the archaic restrictions on the killing of game and made it subject merely to the taking out of a certificate, the forerunner of the modern game licence; the Act also legalized the buying and selling of game, but dealers had to be licensed. The Act did not, as its opponents had foretold, result in the extermination of game, nor did its promoters realize their expectation that it would abate poaching. This was in part due to the continuance of acute poverty among those from whom poachers sprang; it was more particularly due to most of the large poaching fraternity not knowing either a different way of life or a more rewarding source of livelihood. The legalizing of the sale of game did not materially increase the quantity of game coming on to the market because most of those who had wanted to sell their game in the past had, as we have seen, found ways of doing so in spite of the law. The dealers continued to encourage poaching because they preferred snared to shot game.

Not a few people denounced the new Act as an encouragement to poaching, and among them was Delmé Radcliffe who wrote: 'The last new Game Bill put the finishing stroke to the preservation of game, on petty principalities. The sheltering roof of one "licensed dealer in game" covers the whole multitude of crime committed by all the gangs of poachers in the vicinity. Previous to this enactment, some shew of concealment was necessary; some little delicacy was requisite in the disposal of the booty; but now all obstacles are removed, by a safe and sure asylum for the spoil; a premium is offered to successful theft; the perpetrator has only to escape detection in actual commission. It is well known that these dealers consider game, which is shot, scarcely worth their purchase; consequently the art of snaring is assiduously cultivated; children, from their infancy, are instructed in its rudiments; and, long before they arrive at the wiring of a hare, these embryo heroes ... are able, with horsehair nooses, dexterously to effect the capture of any number of partridges and pheasants. ... During the breeding season ... they industriously gain possession of all the eggs within the range of a Sunday's ramble. ... For these also they obtain a ready sale. Under such circumstances it would be, indeed, something extraordinary, if the diversion of shooting were to be enjoyed as before.'

The organization and methods of the poaching business that

had proved their worth under the Ellenborough Act were maintained and, with improved transport, made more efficient. The way the poachers of this period worked is well described by Charles Kingsley in *Yeast*. 'A large gang of poachers, who had come down from London by rail,' he wrote, 'had been devastating all the covers round, to stock the London markets by the first of October. . . . They didn't care for country justices, not they. Weren't all their fines paid by highly respectable game-dealers at the West End? They owned three dog-carts among them; a parcel by railway would bring them down bail to any amount; they tossed their money away at the public-houses, like gentlemen; thanks to the Game Laws, their profits ran high, and when they had swept the country pretty clean of game, why, they would just finish off the season by a stray highway robbery or two, and vanish into Babylon and their native night.'[1]

Nevertheless the Act was of immense benefit to the community. Any man, and all of his sons provided they took out a certificate, could now shoot game on their own or, by invitation, on anyone else's land, and tenant farmers could be allowed to do so by their landlords. The great advantage of the Act was that by abolishing restrictions which had confined shooting to a privileged few it had removed a grievance which, as Cobbett had said, poisoned country life. In doing so it went a long way towards removing the prejudice against shooting as a sport. Owing to its exclusive nature, organized shooting never won the popular regard which foxhunting enjoyed, but the Game Act of 1832 disposed for ever of the jealousy and bitterness which it too often excited.

To the shooting man an important invention of William's reign, though a foreign one, was the breech-loading gun which, like the percussion gun, was slow in coming into general use owing to the conviction of the older generation of sportsmen that nothing could be an improvement on the gun to which they were accustomed, and in the use of which they were so skilled. It is astonishing to find that doubts about the respective merits of the muzzle-loader and the breech-loader persisted into the second half of the century.

---

[1] As late as 1869 there were no less than 10,345 convictions under the Game Laws in the course of that one year.

'An old country gentleman of the leather gaiter school', wrote William Lennox, 'would as soon think of inserting a cartridge in the breech of his fowling-piece as he would of filling his cellar with African port and sherry. Prejudice then apart, the only way to compare the ordinary percussion, and the breech-loader, is to decide which is the best for killing game, and which for safety.' Quick loading, the outstanding advantage of the breech-loader, meant nothing to him, nor, probably, to a great many other shooting men, and for the same reason. 'We say nothing of quick loading', he wrote, 'because in almost every shooting party two or more guns are allowed, with a man to take the trouble off your hands.' He then recounts the advantages and disadvantages of breech-loaders: 'Among the former may be mentioned the quickness of loading, the satisfaction of being able to do without a ramrod, the pleasure of not having to fumble on a cold frosty morning with half frozen fingers for your pellets and copper-cap, and the comfort of feeling that you have no cap to fly in your eye, and no powder flask to blow up through the incaution of yourself or friend's cigar. The disadvantage, a trifling one, is the weight of the cartridges, and that can easily be remedied by engaging a juvenile to act as ammunition waggon. Whether there is any danger in the construction of the open breech, we leave practical men to decide.'

Shooting men appear to have been more reactionary and conservative than most people, and therefore too ready to condemn as unsporting any departure from established practice. Circumstances, notably the effects of enclosure, were increasingly against shooting over dogs which on all grounds was regrettable, but that was no reason to condemn, as Trollope's contemporary Thomas Jeans did, the alternative methods which the same circumstances imposed. 'In these days', he wrote, 'when the use of dogs is becoming obsolete; when the shooters, each with a pair of guns and a loader, are marshalled in line, a beater between each man, and the marching and counter-marching, and wheeling, and pivoting are performed with the precision of military drill . . . it is rather like waging war against the poor hares and partridges — it may scarcely with propriety be called sport, at least with the old acceptance of the word.'

Meanwhile the Highlands of Scotland were steadily tightening their hold on the hearts of southern sportsmen. 'We have heard it predicted', wrote a *Quarterly* reviewer in 1845, 'that the taste in Scotch sport, which has become a passion in England, would like other passions, be of short endurance. We do not think so. . . . It is not only that Clubland is left desolate as the 12th August approaches; that Parliament is prorogued or deserted; that northern steamers and railways for weeks are crowded with sportsmen and their apparatus of sport; that during the autumn more glimpses of the fashionable world are to be seen in the streets of Inverness than in St. James's Street: there are certain other indications not to be mistaken. Several accidents have of late thrown a number of Highland estates into the market, and these have been for the most part acquired by Englishmen of fortune, men who have grown to love the scene of their youthful sport only less than the green fields of their Southern homes. The new proprietors have established their summer "shealings" in some of the remotest fortresses of the hills, willing to see their sons grow up in the same hardy habits of Highland life which they themselves have acquired; and having no fear lest their daughters should lose in delicacy and grace by setting their feet on the heather and breathing the sweet mountain air.'

The effects of the Reform Bill and the Game Act of 1831 on country life, important though they were, paled before the revolutionary consequences of the invention of railways, 'England's gift to the world'. Few of those whose imaginations were stirred by the opening of the Manchester and Liverpool Railway in 1830 saw how profound was its significance, that the first step had been taken in creating new arteries for the life blood of the nation. So major an operation on the body corporate, from which incalculable benefits were to flow, could not be performed without pain. As the new railroads spread over the country, 2,000 miles of them by 1843, bringing to every class the boon of cheap transportation of goods and persons, they sapped the life out of the old channels of communication. While the road engineers murmured despairingly against 'the calamity of the railways', the turnpike trusts and canal companies wrung their hands at the approach of ruin. Hardly less concerned were the farmers as they saw horse traffic fast becoming merely ancillary to the rail-roads, and the market for corn and forage dwindling. The cares of all those who drew their living from the old transport services clouded the brighter prospect for every class which the railways brought with them. Here we need only take a brief glance at their effect on those aspects of country life which have been the subject of this book.

One of the greatest of the many boons conferred by railways on the rural poor was cheap coal which, as the network of rail spread over the country, gradually became available almost everywhere. In sparsely wooded areas, such as the Shires, lack of fuel was, as we have seen, so grievous an affliction that in winter it mattered even more than the inadequacy of the wretched diet on which labouring families strived to keep themselves alive, and which greatly aggravated the problem of the fireless hearth. Coal now became so cheap that it was within reach of all but the poorest families, and was even sometimes used in preference to wood where this had been readily obtainable. Cheap coal led to the neglect of woodlands, the coppicing of which had been a regular source of income to many a landowner. Thus in *Young Tom Hall* Surtees mentions a big wood where 'the brushwood had ceased to be profitable since the introduction of coal into the country by the Gobblegold Railway'.

The hedgerow pollards and underwood, on which many a farm labourer had depended for fuel, also lost their value. This helped to open the way for the tireless campaign against hedgerows, and particularly hedgerow timber, launched towards the middle of the century by that progressive agriculturist J. J. Mechi, cutler of Leadenhall Street, a mere cockney squire. 'Let us grow corn instead of timber, fences and rubbish', he wrote in 1845, '. . . I am told "We must have timber! What should we do in case of war?" . . . What a gross folly it is to grow our own timber in corn fields . . . when we can import it at one-third the price.' Hedgerow timber being the property of the landlord, Mechi strove to enlist the support of the tenant farmers, many of whom must have thought as he did but dared not say so. 'Above all things', he wrote, 'a tenant must bargain for the removal of all timber trees, pollards, and useless fences . . . and in all cases the tenants should be permitted to burn old pollards into charcoal to be applied to the soil, or used in burning the earth.' Ten years earlier the burning of hedgerow pollards would have been accounted a crime by the whole village.

It was fortunate for the railway promoters that the Reform Bill was passed so soon after the practicability of the railroad had been demonstrated, for it had robbed the county landowners, the railway's worst enemies, of some of their political power. There were few landowners in the country who did not view with horror the mere possibility of a railway passing even near to their estates. A class so wholly devoted to the land could not fail to resent the invasion of the peaceful rural scene by so ugly, noisy, and dirty an invention, but their violent opposition to railways did not spring wholly from social and aesthetic considerations. What they feared was that the cutting up of their farms and the destruction of their game coverts would so reduce the value of their estates as to bring ruin on themselves and their families. To the Duke of Cleveland went the distinction of successfully opposing one railway project on the ground that it would ruin his fox coverts. Many of these squires were to live to learn that a railway could bring great wealth to a landowner, and to regret the success of their obstructive tactics.

Throughout the early decades of the nineteenth century a deep conviction that the future of the country depended primarily upon the entrenched position of the squires and the security of the estates from which they derived their incomes, and which enabled them to serve their country both in Parliament and the provinces, coloured the attitude to reform and innovation. The Duke of Wellington wanted to retain the rotten boroughs as the only means of keeping gentlemen in politics. The old Game Laws had been defended because it was believed that without them game would perish and the gentry leave their estates. The increased speed of the new stage coaches had been condemned because it encouraged the squires and their families to spend money in London rather than on their estates where expenditure best served the national interest. The railways were a double menace; they would destroy foxhunting which anchored squires to their homes, and, by making travel fast and comfortable, encourage extravagant living in London to the neglect of estates and rural interests.

It was soon realized that foxhunting was not doomed, and before many years had passed the most reactionary foxhunters had to admit that the railways had done them much good. 'When railroads were first becoming general in the country',

wrote Trollope, 'there was much fear among many sporting
men that they would destroy hunting. It was clear that they
would cut up and subdivide the country; that they would
carry noise and turmoil into remote spots, thereby banishing
foxes; that they would bring town near to town, thereby
tending to make all the island one city; and that they would be
so fenced as to form insurmountable obstacles to straight riding.
All these arguments have been found to be more or less true;
and yet railroads have done so much towards hunting, that they
may almost be said to have created the sport anew on a wider
and much more thoroughly organized footing than it ever held
before. They have brought men, and with the men their money,
from the towns into the country; and the men and the money
together have overcome all those difficulties which the railroads
themselves have produced.' There was no more bitter opponent
of railways than Surtees, but in the end he was sufficiently converted to make John Jorrocks declare that Euston and the Great
Northern stations were the two best covert hacks in the world.

Another master of hounds, Delmé Radcliffe, had been equally
alarmed when the building of railways began, but he did not
condemn them for wholly selfish reasons. His main concern was
for the effect they would have on the many thousands of people
who derived their livelihood from the conventional transport
services of the country. 'It must be sufficiently obvious to the
most narrow-spirited', he wrote in 1838, 'that . . . these railroads must become the most oppressive monopoly ever inflicted
upon a free country. When all the inns and road-side houses
shall be tenantless, and gone to decay, their present occupants
being lost in the abyss of inevitable ruin which is now opened
for them; when not only posting, and post-horses, but the roads
on which they travelled, shall be, with the Turnpike Acts themselves, matter of history — the means of locomotion will be at
the mercy of the most merciless of all human beings, — a class,
actuated by cupidity, and beyond the reach of that salutary
correction . . . competition. . . . But when we consider the mag-
nitude of the convulsion which this mighty railroad delusion will
effect, the fearful extent of its operation, the thousands of human
beings thrown out of employ, the incalculable diminution in the
number of horses, and the consequent deficiency in demand for
agricultural produce . . . we cannot but wonder at the blind-

ness which has countenanced the growth of a monster, which will rend the vitals of those by whom it has been fostered.'

There was much in this terrible indictment that proved to be true. The posting services, however, were not to become wholly redundant for some years because railway passengers needed local transport just as much as coach passengers. Posting survived until the metalling of the by-roads made it worth everyone's while to keep at least a gig. But the railways killed the more profitable hiring of posters and chaises to long-distance travellers on the trunk roads.

Although it was as plain to most people as it was to Delmé Radcliffe that the coaches could not possibly compete with the much faster and cheaper trains, the coach people were very slow to realize it. This was particularly surprising because the coaching business had already felt the ill effects of the steam engine. The steamboats plying in the Thames estuary and along the east coast had for some years been robbing both the Dover and the North roads of traffic. Trains, the coach people insisted, were so much more dangerous than coaches that there was no need to worry. 'If you get upset in a coach there you are,' they declared, 'but if you get upset in a train where are you?' This silly argument was on the lips of every coachman, guard, and horsekeeper whenever the mails and stages travelled. Even the intelligent Nimrod asked rhetorically, 'Was not the rate of ten miles in the hour *with safety* preferable to twenty, with awful risk to life and limb?' Two of the great men of the road, however, the coachmasters William Chaplin and Benjamin Horne, had no such illusions. They sold their coaches and reinvested their money in the London and Birmingham railway.

The passing of the coaches and the posting business, the lifeblood of the innkeeper's trade, brought ruin to many a country inn. By 1843 the most famous of the great London coach yards, the Bull and Mouth, with only three of its seventy odd coaches surviving, was up for sale. At Hounslow, where 200 coach horses had been stabled, half the head inn had become a shop. At the other end of England, at Barnby Moor, a famous inn, with but one postboy left ('and he can scarcely live'), was all but ruined and paying no rent. The King's Head at Egham was 'just alive and that's all. . . . The good old Duke still sticks to us; we have four horses ordered for him for tomorrow.'

'The large comfortable old posting-houses that existed prior to railways', wrote Surtees, 'have all disappeared . . . or, if any remain, are dragging out miserable existences, with weak worn-out establishments, women waiters, and either antediluvian ostlers or ignorant hobbledehoys, fresh at each quarter, who hardly know how to put on a bridle.' The traditional comfort of the English inn which had been the envy of so many foreigners was almost wholly lost. 'Nothing is now so forlorn', wrote Lennox, 'as a great, rambling, half aired, half appointed country inn; waiter acting boots, boots acting post-boy, or may be, all three, and cook acting chambermaid, barmaid, and all.'

The disappearance within a space of ten years of the great road services which gave regular employment to many thousands of people all over the country caused widespread distress. The railways absorbed most of the booking clerks and guards, but for the 3,000 coachmen there was little alternative employment. 'A coachman,' said one of them, 'if he really be one, is fit for nothing else. . . . His bread is gone when the stable-door is shut.' Some of them, said a man in the Bull and Mouth yard, 'drives busses, some have crept into the country, but, like dead donkies, we sees nothing on 'em'. Thackeray deeply regretted their passing: 'I wonder where they are, those good fellows? Is old Weller alive or dead? . . . Alas! we shall never hear the horn ring at midnight, or see the pike-gates fly open any more.'

None lamented more deeply the passing of the coaches than the ordinary countryman whose life they had done much to brighten. The sound of the horn, the hammering of the hoofs on the highway, the clatter of the wheels and the rattle of the pole chains had been as pleasing to his ears as he toiled in the fields as to his wife and children who daily rushed to the window to see the coach go by. But by the time the railways had driven the last coach off the road, in the early years of Victoria's reign, prosperity had begun to return and a happier era for rural England had already dawned.

BIBLIOGRAPHY

I. ENCLOSURE AND THE LANDSCAPE
(pages 1–12)

Ackers, C. P., *Practical British Forestry*, London, 1949: 44, 64.

Albion, R. G., *Forests and Seapower*, Cambridge, U.S.A., 1926: 46, 95.

Arbuthnot, Mrs., *Journal*, 2 vols., London, 1950: I, 305.

Berry, Miss, *Journals and Correspondence*, 3 vols., London, 1866: II, 355.

Byng, Hon. John, *The Torrington Diaries*, 4 vols., London, 1934–8: I, 80, 180, 213, 373; II, 16, 42, 125; III, 18, 144, 295; IV, 33.

Caird, James, *English Agriculture in 1850–51*, London, 1852: 40–53, 122, 197.

Clapham, J. H., *An Economic History of Modern Britain. The Early Railway Age, 1820–1850*, Cambridge, 1930.

Cobbett, William, *Rural Rides*, 2 vols., London, 1893: I, 35, 44, 98, 107, 118, 129, 202, 207, 237, 283, 399; II, 26, 27, 138, 298, 387.

Curtler, W. H. R., *A Short History of English Agriculture*, Oxford, 1909: 148, 150, 178, 282.

Dixon, Dr., *Essex Review*, XXIV (1915): 7.

Dixon, H. H. (The Druid), *Saddle and Sirloin*, London, 1895: 34.

Fairfax-Lucy, A., *Charlecote and the Lucys*, London, 1958: 253.

Farmer's Magazine, The: I (1800), 371; III (1802), 136.

Fisher, W. R., *The Forest of Essex*, London, 1887: ch. v.

Gaskell, Mrs., *Wives and Daughters*: ch. xviii.

Grant, Elizabeth, *Memoirs of a Highland Lady*, Edinburgh, 1897: 366, 367, 379.

Hammond, J. L. and B., *The Village Labourer, 1760–1832*, London, 1920: 73–81, 318.

Harris, Alan, *The Rural Landscape of the East Riding of Yorkshire, 1700–1850*, London, 1961: 64.

Hawker, Col. Peter, *Diary*, 2 vols., London, 1893: I, 57.

Hennell, T., *Change on the Farm*, Cambridge, 1936: 38, 43, 44.

Howitt, William, *The Rural Life of England*, 2 vols., London, 1838: I, 83; II, 111, 239.

Massingham, H. J., *Country Relics*, Cambridge, 1939: 45.

Mitford, M. R., *Our Village*, 2 vols., London, 1839: I, 7, 27, 47, 130, 132, 139, 303; II, 43.

Prothero, R. E. (Lord Ernle), *English Farming, Past and Present*, London, 1912: 28, 97, 99, 198, 205.

Slater, Gilbert, *The English Peasantry and the Enclosure of Common Fields*, London, 1907: 92–136.
Surtees, R. S., *Hawbuck Grange*: ch. xii.
Trevelyan, G. M., *British History in the Nineteenth Century*, (1782–1901), London, 1922: ch. i, ii, ix.
Wingfield-Stratford, E., *The Squire and His Relations*, London, 1956: 250–339.
Winstone, B., *Epping and Ongar Highway Trust*, London, 1891: 153.

II. COBBETT'S ENGLAND
(pages 13–27)

Berry, Miss: II, 360.
Bewick, Thomas, *A Memoir*, London, 1961: 27.
Byng, J.: I, 369; II, 108.
Chelmsford Gazette, The, 12 Sept. 1823.
Clapham, J. H., ch. iv.
Cobbett, W., *Rides*: I, 18, 35, 73, 321, 380, 382; II, 26, 298, 348, 387.
    Cottage Economy, London, 1823: 11, 12, 29, 32, 77.
Disraeli, Benjamin, *Sybil*: ch. iii.
Donne, W. B., *Old Roads and New Roads*, London, 1852: 71.
Dunlop, O. J., *The Farm Labourer*, London, 1913: 7–54.
Eliot, George, *The Mill on the Floss*, ch. xi.
Fairfax-Lucy, A., 246.
Fisher, W. R., 247.
Hammond, J. L. and B., 73, 77.
Hasbach, W., *A History of the English Agricultural Labourer*, London, 1905: ch. ii, iii.
Howitt, W.: I, 150, 156, 157; II, 112, 128, 130.
Mitford, M. R.: I, 55.
Poor Law Commission, Report, 1834.
Slater, Gilbert, 51.
Trevelyan, G. M., ch. ii.
White, Gilbert, *The Natural History of Selborne*, Letter V.

III. CAPTAIN SWING
(pages 28–45)

Arbuthnot, Mrs.: I, 137; II, 345, 346, 396, 405.
Aspinall, A., *Three Early Nineteenth Century Diaries*, London, 1952: 20.
Bewick, T., 153.
Borrow, George, *The Romany Rye*: ch. x.
Butler, J. E., *Memoir of John Grey of Dilston*, Edinburgh, 1869: 79.

Chelmsford Gazette, The, 4 Oct. 1822.
Cobbett, W., *Rides*: I, 274, 343, 344, 347; II, 335, 336.
Hammond, J. L. and B., ch. ix–xi.
Howitt, W.: I, 155, 233.
Hudson, W. H., *A Shepherd's Life*: ch. xvii.
Mitford, M. R.: II, 287–91, 324.
Prothero, R. E. (Lord Ernle), 316–29.
Smith, Sydney, *Works*, London, 1850: 263.
Stirling, A. M. W., *Coke of Norfolk and His Friends*, 2 vols., London, 1908: I, 269; II, 121.
Turberville, A. S., *A History of Welbeck Abbey*, 2 vols., London, 1939: II, 349.
Young, Arthur, *General Review of Agriculture in Essex*, 2 vols., London, 1807: I, 65.

IV. PIKEMAN AND PACKMAN

(pages 46–60)

Baring-Gould, S., *Old Country Life*: ch. viii.
Byng, J: I, 6, 8, 366; II, 372; III, 88, 91, 126, 255.
Clapham, J. H., 92.
Cobbett, W., *Rides*: I, 173, 200, 360, 379, 380; II, 257.
Curtler, W. H. R., 204.
Defoe, Daniel, *A Tour thro' Great Britain*, 4 vols., London, 1742: I, 83–90.
Dickens, C., *The Old Curiosity Shop*: ch. xlvi.
Donne, W. B., 69, 75, 76.
Eliot, George, *Silas Marner*: ch. xi.
Gunning, Henry, *Reminiscences of Cambridge from the Year 1780*, 2 vols., London, 1854: I, 168.
Jeffreys, Rees, *The King's Highway*, London, 1949: 1–5.
Meteyard, Eliza, *The Life of Josiah Wedgwood*, 2 vols., London, 1865: I, 267.
Mitford, M. R.: II, 5, 58–60.
Prothero, R. E. (Lord Ernle), 203.
Surtees, R. S., *Hillingdon Hall*: chs. xxiv, xxix.
    Mr. Romford's Hounds: ch. xlviii.
    Mr. Sponge's Sporting Tour: ch. xxv.
Webb, Sydney and Beatrice, *English Local Government: The Story of the King's Highway*, London, 1913: 64–7.
Winstone, B., 151, 185, 187.
Young, Arthur, *A Six Weeks Tour*, London, 1769: 88.
    A Six Months Tour, 4 vols., London, 1770: IV, 580.

V. THE SQUIRES
(pages 61–79)

Apperley, C. J. (Nimrod), *My Life and Times*, London, 1927: 125.
  The Life of a Sportsman, London, 1948: 159–61.
Arbuthnot, Mrs.: I, 137, 408.
Berkeley, G. F., *My Life and Recollections*, 2 vols., London, 1865:
  II, 3.
Black Book, The, London, 1835: 24–27, 260–7.
Borrow, George, *Lavengro*: ch. xcvii.
Byng, J: I, 294; II, 238, 324, 325; III, 139, 210.
Clapham, J. H., 54, 312, 313, 349, 541.
Cobbett, W., *Rides*: I, 46, 197; II, 70, 82, 165, 236, 334.
Eardley-Wilmot, J. E., *Reminiscences of Thomas Assheton Smith Esq.*,
  London, 1860: 3.
Fairfax-Lucy, A., 247, 249.
Gaskell, Mrs., *Wives and Daughters*, London, 1949: 52, 83, 192,
  580.
Gentleman's Magazine, The, LVIII (1788).
Goodhart-Rendle, H. G., *English Architecture since the Regency*, London,
  1958: 25–39.
Grant, E., 380.
Greville, C. F., *Memoirs*, 8 vols., London, 1899: V, 16.
Howitt, W.: I, ch. ii–iv, 110, 261.
Kirby, Chester, *The English Country Gentleman*, London, 1937: 57.
Mitford, M. R.: I, 167.
Montalembert, The Comte de, *The Political Future of England*,
  London, 1856: 69, 84, 86, 96, 97.
Neville, Ralph, *English Country House Life*, London, 1925: 31, 47–50,
  152.
Peacock, Thomas Love, *Crotchet Castle*, ch. i.
Prothero, R. E. (Lord Ernle), ch. x, and 207.
Pückler-Muskau, Prince, *A Regency Visitor* (ed. E. M. Butler),
  London, 1957: 186.
Rush, Richard, *The Court of London from 1819 to 1825*, London, 1873:
  98, 322–25, 505.
Smollett, Tobias, *The Adventures of Sir Launcelot Greaves*: ch. xi.
Stirling, A. M. W.: I, 271; II, 75, 102, 104, 338, 399.
Surtees, R. S., *Town and Country Papers*, ed. E. D. Cuming, London,
  1929: 126.
Trevelyan, G. M., ch. i, ii, ix, x.
Webb, S. and B., 344, 347, 383–5.
Wingfield-Stratford, E., 253, 256, 293, 324, 330, 336–9, 352.

VI. THE ENGLAND OF EMILY EDEN
(pages 80–91)

Austen, Jane, *Pride and Prejudice*: ch. xlii.
Barry, F. V., *Maria Edgeworth, Letters*, London, 1931: 200.
Apperley, C. J. (Nimrod), *My Life*: 100.
Cobbett, W., *Rides*: I, 5.
Eden, The Hon. Emily, *The Eden Letters*, 6, 12, 22, 24, 31, 75, 85, 89,
    90, 145, 167, 169, 177, 180, 187, 207, 214, 219, 231, 367.
Farmers' Magazine, The: I (1800), 328–34.
Greville, C.: I, 4, 24, 243; II, 48, 52, 53, 80, 187, 345; III, 47, 48,
    86–8.
Holland, Elizabeth Lady, *Journal*, 2 vols., London, 1908: I, 197.
Howitt, W.: I, 110.
Pückler-Muskau, Prince, 62.
Rush, Richard, 98, 322, 325.
Stirling, A. M. W.: I, 335; II, 7, 247.

VII. BELOW STAIRS
(pages 92–107)

Adams, Samuel and Sarah, *The Complete Servant*, London, 1825.
Apperley, C. J. (Nimrod), *My Life*, 13.
Borrow, George, *Lavengro*: ch. c.
Broughton, T., *Serious Advice and Warning to Servants*, London, 1768.
Byng, J.: I, 48, 53, 230, 248, 256, 323, 362, 364; II, 127, 340, 377;
    III, 221; IV, 133.
Dunster, Charles, *St. James's Street*, London, 1790: 14.
English History from Essex Sources, 2 vols., London, 1952: II, 135.
Eden Letters, 77.
Fairfax-Lucy, A., 259, 260.
Gentleman's Magazine, The, XXXIV (1764): 493.
Grant, Elizabeth, 23.
Heasal, A., *The Servants' Book of Knowledge*, 1733.
Hetch, J. J., *Continental and Colonial Servants in Eighteenth Century
    England*, Smith College Studies in History, Northampton,
    U.S.A., 1954.
    The Domestic Servant Class in Eighteenth Century England, London,
    1956.
Kitchener, William, *The Cook's Oracle*, London, 1822: 17–19, 54.
Lady's Monthly Museum, The, VII (1801): 258.
London Chronicle, The, XXVIII (1770): 472b.
Notes and Queries, 1856: I, 9, 80, 177, 383.

O'Keeffe, John, *Dramatic Works*, 4 vols., London, 1798: I, 228.
  Recollections of the Life of John O'Keeffe, 2 vols., London, 1826: I, 120.
Peel, Mrs. C. S., *A Hundred Wonderful Years*, London, 1929: ch. x, xi.
Sackville-West, V., *Knole and the Sackvilles*, London, 1922: 191, 192.
Servant's Guide, The, London, 1830.
Silliman, Benjamin, *A Journal of Travels in England, Holland and Scotland*, 2 vols., New Haven, U.S.A., 1820: I, 219, 272.
Stuart, D. M., *The English Abigail*, London, 1926: 147.
Thackeray, W. M., *Vanity Fair*: ch. xix, xxxvii.
Townley, J., *High Life Below Stairs*, London, 1759.
Turberville, S.: II, 59, 60.
Walpole, Horace, *Letters*, 16 vols., Oxford, 1905: XIII, 39; XIV, 95.
Whatman, Susanna, *Housekeeping Book*, ed. T. Balston, London 1956.
Woodforde, James, *The Diary of a Country Parson*, 5 vols., London, 1931: V, 231, 355.
Woodruff, Douglas, *The Tichborne Claimant*, London, 1957: 5.

VIII. THE SLOW MARCH OF PROGRESS
(pages 108–126)

Apperley, C. J. (Nimrod), *The Life of a Sportsman*, 119, 196.
  My Life, 56, 125, 178, 225.
  Memoir of the Life of the late John Mytton, London, 1899: 3.
Arbuthnot, Mrs.: I, 304.
Bedfordshire, V.C.H., III (1912): 363.
Berkeley, G. F., I, 297, 313.
Berry, Miss: II, 347, 349, 382, 404; III, 349, 355, 451.
Byng, J.: I, 359, 371; II, 222, 363.
Cecil, Mrs. E. (A. Amherst), *A History of Gardening in England*, London, 1910: ch. xii, xiii.
Cobbett, W., *Rides*: I, 172; II, 63.
Creevey Papers, The, ed. H. Maxwell, 2 vols., London, 1933: I, 50.
Dixon, Dr., *The Essex Review*, XXIV (1915): 7–8.
Dunno, *The Antiquities of Dunstable*, 2 vols., Dunstable, 1821: I, 19.
Eardley-Wilmot, J. E., 11.
Eden Letters, 135, 203, 216, 217, 235.
Fairfax-Lucy, A., 271.
Goodhart-Rendell, H. G., 27.
Grant, E., 48–52, 106, 257.
Greville, C.: I, 197.
Gronow, Captain, *Reminiscences and Recollections*, 2 vols., London, 1900: I, 55.

Hadfield, M., *Gardening in Britain*, London, 1860: ch. v, vi.
Hare, Augustus, *The Story of My Life*, 3 vols., London, 1833: III, 46.
Howitt, W.: I, 25–7, 104; II, 271.
Osbaldeston, G., *Squire Osbaldeston*, ed. E. D. Cuming, London, 1926: VI, x, 48, 198, 244.
Peel, Mrs., 33.
Pückler-Muskau, 108.
Rush, Richard, 323, 506.
Surtees, R. S., *Town and Country Papers*: 61, 68.
Thackeray, W. M.: ch. xxxviii, xli.

IX. THE FAMILY TRAVELS POST
(pages 127–139)

Adams, S. and S., 372, 397, 407.
Apperley, C. J. (Nimrod), *The Horse and the Hound*, Edinburgh, 1843: 143, 152–4.
Ball, R. F., and Gilbey, T., *The Essex Foxhounds*, London, 1896: 35.
Bindley, Charles (Harry Hieover), *Stable Talk and Table Talk*, 2 vols., London, 1846: 91.
Blake, B. P., *Essex Archaeological Society Transactions*: XXV (1960), 341.
Bovill, E. W., *The England of Nimrod and Surtees*, London, 1959: 165–9.
Byng, J.: I, 53, 84, 85, 117, 319; II, 70, 116, 151; III, 58, 96, 106, 114, 116, 117, 127, 158, 235, 314.
Creevey Papers: II, 129.
Dixon, H. H. (The Druid), *Saddle and Sirloin*, 45.
Donne, W. B., 82.
Eden, E., 118, 119, 278.
Grant, E., 12, 32, 38, 68, 112, 155, 360.
Greville, C.: I, 8; II, 48.
Hare, Augustus, *The Gurneys of Earlham*, 2 vols., London, 1895: I, 233; II, 3.
Houblon, Lady Alice Archer, *The Houblon Family*, 2 vols., London, 1907: I, 149.
Howitt, W.: I, 110.
Lennox, Lord William, *Coaching*, London, 1876: 110.
  Pictures of Sporting Life, 2 vols., London, 1860: I, 133.
Pückler-Muskau, 204.
Stirling, A. M. W., *Annals of a Yorkshire House*, 2 vols., London, 1911: II, 224.
  Coke: II, 482.
Surtees, R. S., and Cuming, E. D., *Robert Smith Surtees*, Edinburgh, 1924: 180.

X. SWELL DRAGSMEN
(pages 140–157)

Apperley, C. J. (Nimrod), *The Chace, the Turf, and the Road*, London, 1837: 67–134.
The Horse and the Hound: 141–8.
My Life: 15, 97, 118, 241, 242, 251, 278, 300.
The Life of a Sportsman: 83, 183, 289.
Bindley, Charles (Harry Hieover), *Stable Talk*: I, 27–9, 75–92.
Birch Reynardson, C. T. S., *Down the Road*, London, 1875.
Borrow, G., *Lavengro*: ch. lix.
The Romany Rye: ch. xxvi.
Bovill, E. W., 127–169.
Byng, J.: I, 330.
Corbett, Edward, *An Old Coachman's Chatter*, London, 1891.
Cross, T., *The Autobiography of a Stage Coachman*, 2 vols., London, 1861.
De Quincey, Thomas, *Miscellanies*, London, 1854: 292.
Dickens, Charles, *Martin Chuzzlewit*: ch. xiii, xxxvi.
Nicholas Nickleby: ch. v.
The Old Curiosity Shop: ch. xlvii.
The Pickwick Papers: ch. xxiii, xxxiii, xxxv, xliii, lii, lv.
Dixon, H. H. (The Druid), *Saddle and Sirloin*, 49–55.
Harper, C. G., *Stage Coach and Mail in Days of Yore*, 2 vols., London, 1903.
Harris, S., *Old Coaching Days*, London, 1882.
The Coaching Age, London, 1885.
Hawker, P., *Diary*: I, 22.
Hughes, Thomas, *Tom Brown's Schooldays*: ch. iv.
Hunt, Leigh, *Essays and Sketches*: 'Coaches'.
Irving, Washington, *The Sketch Book*, London, 1859: 135.
Jeans, Thomas, *The Tommiebeg Shootings*, London, 1860: 183.
Lennox, W., *Coaching*.
McCausland, H., *The English Carriage*, London, 1948.
Malet, Capt. H. E., *Annals of the Road*, London, 1876.
Pecchio, Count, *Observations of an Italian Exile*, London, 1833: 201.
Pückler-Muskau, 40.
Raumer, F. von, *England in 1835*, 3 vols., London, 1836: III, 135.
Servant's Guide, The, 222.
Surtees, R. S., *Tours*, 132, 133.
Jorrock's Jaunts and Jollities: The Road.
Ask Mamma: ch. i.
Vale, Edmund, *The Mail-Coach Men*, London, 1960: ch. ii.

XI. JOE MANTON AND PETER HAWKER
(pages 158–173)

Airlie, Mabell, Countess of, *Lady Palmerston and Her Times*, 2 vols., London, 1922: I, 106, 146.

Annals of Sporting, The, XIII (1828): 109.

Apperley, C. J. (Nimrod), *The Life of John Mytton*, 61.
My Life, 83.

Arbuthnot, Mrs.: I, 371, 432.

Berkeley, G. F., *My Life*: I, 223, 225, 228, 229.

Book of Sports, The, 2 vols., London, 1843: II, 39, 75, 76, 81.

Byng, J., I, 325.

Cook, Col. John, *Observations on Fox-Hunting*, London, 1826: 43.

Daniel, W. B., *Rural Sports*, 3 vols., London, 1802–1813: II, 394, 395, 484, 509–520; III, 400.

Davies, E. W. L., *Memoir of the Rev. John Russell*, London, 1883: 239.

Eden Letters, 104, 121.

Grant, E., 36, 73, 271, 399.

Greener, W. W., *Modern Shot Guns*, London, 1888: 1–5.
The Gun and Its Development, London, 1910: ch. iv, v.

Greville, C.: I, 24.

Hawker, Lt.-Col. Peter, *Instructions to Young Sportsmen*, London, 1825: 74, 79, 98, 102, 106–8, 141, 156.
Diary: I, 54, 105, 159, 173, 174, 210; II, 248, 280, 284, 356, 363.

Howitt, W.: I, 112.

Idle, Christopher, *Hints on Shooting and Fishing*, London, 1855: 2, 8, 10, 14, 73.

Jeans, Thomas, 266, 282.

Johnson, T. B., *The Shooter's Preceptor*, London, 1838: 31–49.

Lennox, W., *Sporting Life*: I, 47, 48, 66–71, 332, 347, 355; II, 194, 195.
Fifty Years' Biographical Reminiscences, 2 vols., London, 1863: II, 141, 143.

Mayer, John, *The Sportsman's Directory*, London, 1828: 28, 30, 177.

Neville, Ralph, 150, 151.

Osbaldeston, G., 67, 68.

Payne-Gallwey, Sir Ralph, *Letters to Young Shooters*, 3 vols., London, 1899: II, Letter 1.

Quarterly Review, The: LXIII (1839): 76.

Sporting Magazine, The: II (1793), 301; LII (1818), 20.

Stirling, A. M. W., *Coke*: I, 331, 437; II, 165, 297, 364, 368.

Surtees, R. S., *The Analysis of the Hunting Field*: ch. xvi.
Plain or Ringlets?: ch. lii.

Thackeray, W. M.: ch. xli.
Thornton, Col. T., *A Sporting Tour*, London, 1896: 114, 115, 220.
Trevelyan, G. M., 168.
Trollope, Anthony, *British Sports and Pastimes*, London, N.D.: 131, 136, 151, 152.

XII. THE POACHING WAR
(pages 174–196)

Annals of Sporting, The: I (1822), 95, 197; XIII (1828), 110.
Annual Register, The: XXXVII (1795), 29, 183, 184; LXIX (1828), 375, 377.
Berkeley, G. F., *My Life*: I, 158, 208, 233.
Black Book, The, ed. 1831: 209–11; ed. 1835: 268–71.
Book of Sports, The: I, 34.
Brougham, Lord Henry, *Speeches*, 4 vols., London, 1838: II, 373.
Byng, J.: I, 334; III, 298.
Caird, J., 40, 41.
Chitty, Joseph, *Essays on the Game Laws*, London, 1770: 5, 6.
Cobbett, W., *Rides*: I, 152–4, 223, 247, 248, 279, 280, 362–4; II, 84, 119, 201–7, 222, 229, 240n., 334, 335.
Daniel, W. B.: II, 427, 428; III, 412.
Eden, The Hon. Eleanor, *The Autobiography of a Working Man*, London, 1862: 29–34.
Essex Standard, The, 29 Nov., 1839.
Farmer's Magazine, The: I (1800), 25, 26, 266.
Gentleman's Magazine, The, LI (1781): 591.
Hammond, J. L. and B., 162–75.
Hansard, *Parliamentary Debates*, XXXVI (1817): 921–4.
Hawker, P., *Diary*: I, 22, 47–9, 137; II, 31.
 Instructions, 148, 254–62, 382–416.
Howitt, W.: II, 95, 296.
Hudson, W. H., *The Shepherd's Life*, ch. vii.
Idle, C., 76–9.
Kirby, Chester, 'The Attack on the English Game Laws', in *The Journal of Modern History*, IV (1932): 18.
 'The English Game Law System', in *The American Historical Review*, XXXVIII (1932–3): 240–60.
Lennox, W., *Sporting Life*: I, 353–5.
MacQueen, T. Potter, *England in 1830*, London, 1831: 2.
Mayer, J., 6, 106, 107.
Mechi, J. J., *A Series of Letters on Agricultural Improvement*, London, 1845: 10.
Smith, S., 244–52, 263, 313–21, 331–7, 379–87.

Sporting Magazine, The: II (1793), 363; XXV (1805), 228, 339; LIX (1822), 9–14.

Sportsman's Cabinet, The, 2 vols., London, 1803: 107.

Taplin, William, *Observations on the Present State of the Game Laws*, London, 1772: 1–39.

Walker, D., *Hertfordshire*, London, 1794: 53.

Webb, S. and B., 597.

XIII. THE DEBT TO HUGO MEYNELL
(pages 197–213)

Apperley, C. J. (Nimrod), *The Chace*, 10, 44.

   The Horse and the Hound, 70, 77, 197, 207.

   Remarks on the Condition of Hunters, London, 1837: 31–44, 48, 198, 256.

Beckford, Peter, *Thoughts upon Hunting*, Letters: XVI, XXIII.

Bindley, Charles (Harry Hieover), 216.

Bovill, E. W., 31–124.

Brockman, H. A. N., *The Caliph of Fonthill*, London, 1956: 56, 96.

Byng, J.: I, 7, 36, 264; II, 314.

Cobbett, W., *Rides*: I, 380.

Cook, J., 55, 56, 98, 105, 151, 173.

Delmé Radcliffe, F. P., *The Noble Science*, London, 1839: 13, 111, 155.

Dixon, H. H. (The Druid), *Scott and Sebright*, London, 1912: 263, 310, 366.

Eardley-Wilmot, J. E., 41, 63, 218, 219.

Hampshire, V.C.H.: I (1900), 356.

Horlock, K. W. (Scrutator), *Horses and Hounds*, London, 1855: 72.

Mayer, J., 135.

Osbaldeston, G., 92, 128, 131, 190, 191, 202.

Smith, Thomas, *Extracts from the Diary of a Huntsman*, London, 1838: 94, 99, 163.

Surtees, R. S., *Analysis*, 121, 292.

   Handley Cross: ch. i.

   Hawbuck Grange: ch. ii.

   Mr. Romford's Hounds: ch. xxxiii.

   Plain or Ringlets?: ch. xliv, lxv.

   Tours, 64, 68, 69, 108, 253.

   Town and Country, 117, 135, 192, 194.

Trollope, A., 72, 80, 83, 100.

Vyner, R. T., *Notitia Venatica*, London, 1892: 5, 8, 10, 15, 46, 49, 56, 66, 203, 205, 285.

Whyte-Melville, G. J., *Riding Recollections*, London, 1878: 135.

XIV. ESSEX *v.* CAPEL
(pages 214–232)

Apperley, C. J. (Nimrod), *Nimrod's Hunting Tours*, London, 1926: 86.
Arbuthnot, Mrs.: II, 353.
Ball, R. F., and Gilbey, T., 101.
Beckford, Peter, Letter XXIII.
Book of Sports, The: I, 4.
Borrow, George, *The Romany Rye*: ch. vi.
Brockman, H. A. N., 56, 96.
Byng, J.: I, 264; II, 314.
Cobbett, W., *Rides*: I, 364, 369.
Cook, J., 65, 126.
Cumming, E. D., *British Sport Past and Present*, London, 1908: 6.
Daniel, W. B.: III, 4, 12.
Davies, E. W. L., 104, 108, 134.
Dixon, H. H. (The Druid), *The Law of the Farm*, London, 1878: 365.
    Scott and Sebright, 323, 388.
Fairfax-Lucy, A., 311.
Farmer's Magazine, The: I (1800), 25.
Hertfordshire, V.C.H.: I (1902), 356.
Horlock, K. W. (Scrutator), 72.
Howitt, W.: I, 45.
King's Bench, Court of, *Term Reports*, I, (4 ed.), London, 1794:
    334–8.
Lever, Tresham, *The Letters of Lady Palmerston*, London, 1857: 14.
Osbaldeston, G., 100.
Smith, S., 319.
Smith, T., 163.
Sporting Magazine, The: I (1792–93), 319.
Surtees, R. S., *Analysis*, 172, 173, 99–114.
    Handley Cross: ch. xxxix.
    Tours, 95.
Times, The, 26 July 1809.
    11 July 1816.
Trial Between George Earl of Essex and the Hon & Rev. Wm. Capel, The,
    London, 1810.
Trollope, A., 75–77.
Vyner, R. T., 68, 86, 221, 232, 239, 241, 312.

XV. REFORM AND RAIL
(pages 233–243)

Apperley, C. J. (Nimrod), *The New Sporting Almanack*, London, 1843: 26–29.

Byng, J.: III, 85.

Chapman, J. H.: ch. ix, xi.

Cobbett, W., *Rides*: I, 280n.

Curtler, W. H. R.: ch. xix.

Davies, E. W. L., 74.

Delmé Radcliffe, F. P., 128–30, 277–80.

Dixon, H. H. (The Druid), *Silk and Scarlet*, 263.
  Saddle and Sirloin, 34.

Donne, W. B., 79.

Early Victorian England, 2 vols., London, 1934: I, ch. i, v.

English History from Essex Sources, 45.

Greener, W. W., *The Gun*, 122.

Hasbach, W.: ch. iii.

Jeans, T., 266.

Kingsley, C., *Yeast*: ch. ix.

Lennox, W., *Coaching*, 219.
  Sporting Life: I, 342–4.

Mechi, J. J., 10, 92–112.

Prothero, M. R. (Lord Ernle): ch. xv.

Quarterly Review, The: LXXVII (1846), 69; LXIII (1839), 73.

Surtees, R. S., *Plain or Ringlets?*: ch. lxii.
  Town and Country Papers, 197.
  Young Tom Hall: ch. xlix.

Thackeray, W. M.: ch. vii.

Trevelyan, G. M., *British History*: ch. xiii, xiv, xv.
  English Social History, London, 1942: 531–3.
  Lord Grey of the Reform Bill, London, 1920: 311–49.

Trollope, A., 77, 78, 153.

INDEX

PRINTED IN GREAT BRITAIN
BY ROBERT MACLEHOSE AND CO. LTD
THE UNIVERSITY PRESS, GLASGOW